David Hume

Treatise of Morals

And Selections from the Treatise of the Passions

David Hume

Treatise of Morals
And Selections from the Treatise of the Passions

ISBN/EAN: 9783744664400

Printed in Europe, USA, Canada, Australia, Japan

Cover: Foto ©Thomas Meinert / pixelio.de

More available books at **www.hansebooks.com**

David Hume

Treatise of Morals
And Selections from the Treatise of the Passions

ISBN/EAN: 9783744664400

Printed in Europe, USA, Canada, Australia, Japan

Cover: Foto ©Thomas Meinert / pixelio.de

More available books at **www.hansebooks.com**

HUME'S

TREATISE OF MORALS:

AND SELECTIONS FROM THE

TREATISE OF THE PASSIONS.

WITH AN INTRODUCTION BY

JAMES H. HYSLOP, Ph.D.,

INSTRUCTOR IN LOGIC, ETHICS, AND PSYCHOLOGY, COLUMBIA COLLEGE,
NEW YORK.

———▸•◂———

BOSTON, U.S.A.:

PUBLISHED BY GINN & COMPANY.

1893.

Ginn & Company
The Athenæum Press
Boston

EDITOR'S PROSPECTUS.

THE Ethical Series, of which this book on Hume's Ethics, by Dr. J. H. Hyslop, is the initial number, will consist of a number of small volumes, each of which will be devoted to the presentation of a leading system in the History of Modern Ethics, in selections or extracts from the original works. These selections will be accompanied by explanatory and critical notes. They will also be introduced by a bibliography, a brief biographical sketch of the author of the system, a statement of the relation of the system to preceding ethical thought, and a brief explanation of the main features of the system and its influence on subsequent ethical thought. The volumes will be prepared by experienced teachers in the department of Ethics and with special reference to *undergraduate instruction and study* in colleges.

The series at present will include six volumes as follows :

HOBBES, Professor G. M. Duncan, Yale University ;
CLARKE, President F. L. Patton, Princeton University ;
LOCKE, the Editor of the Series ;
HUME, Dr. J. H. Hyslop, Columbia College ;
KANT, Professor John Watson, Queen's University, Canada.
HEGEL, Professor J. Macbride Sterrett, Columbian University.

The increasing interest in the study of Ethics and the consequent enlargement of the courses in college curricula, suggest to every teacher the need of better methods of teaching the subject than those which have quite generally prevailed in the past. Instruction in the History of Ethics, like instruction in the History of Philosophy, has largely been based on text-books or lectures giving expositions of, and information about, the various systems. Such methods, although serviceable, are not as stimulating and helpful as those which put the student in direct contact with the text of the author, enabling him to study the system itself rather than to study about the system. Undoubtedly the best plan would be to have the student read the entire work of the author, but all teachers will probably concede the impracticability of this in *undergraduate* work, if a number of systems is to be studied, which is usually desirable. Only inferior, in my judgment, to the best, but impracticable plan, is the plan of the " Ethical Series," — to study selections or extracts from the original works, embodying the substance of the system. The " Series " makes provision for such work in a convenient and comparatively inexpensive manner. That the plan of instruction on which the " Series " is based is in the interest of better scholarship, I am assured by my own experience, and by that of many other teachers in the leading colleges of the country, with whom I have communicated. It is with the earnest hope of facilitating instruction and study in the History of Ethics that this series is issued.

E. HERSHEY SNEATH.

YALE UNIVERSITY,
January 25, '93.

TABLE OF CONTENTS.

———•———

PREFACE.

THE student will observe that the whole of Hume's original treatise on Morals has been included in the present volume and that the selections are taken only from his work on the "Passions." Portions of the latter have been included because of their importance to a correct understanding of Hume's ethical principles. The main portion of them consists in his discussion of "free will." The whole of the treatise on Morals has been included in order to prevent the volume from being fragmentary, or at least to prevent it from being more so than is necessary for an adequate conception of his system.

I have chosen the original work rather than the revised form of 1751, because the later contains no essential changes of view. Hume himself, in a letter to Gilbert Elliott, says: "The philosophical principles are the same in both." Even if this confession had not been made, the judgment of T. H. Green would have sufficed to justify the course taken, since he pronounced the difference between them to be too small to create any obligations of a serious kind on the part of one performing the task here undertaken.

JAMES H. HYSLOP.

COLUMBIA COLLEGE.

BIBLIOGRAPHY.

HUME'S WORKS.

A Treatise of Human Nature. Being an attempt to introduce the experimental Method of Reasoning into Moral Subjects. 3 vols. London, 1739.

Essays, Moral and Political. Vol. I., 1741; Vol. II., 1742.

Philosophical Essays, 1748.

Political Discourses, 1751.

Inquiry concerning the Principles of Morals, 1751.

History of England. (The reigns of James I. and Charles I.), 1754; (Charles II. and James II.) 1756; (Early period of English History and down to James I.) 1762.

Four Dissertations: The Natural History of Religion; of the Passions; of Tragedy; of the Standard of Taste, 1757.

Two Essays: (On Suicide and the Immortality of the Soul), 1777.

Dialogues concerning Natural Religion, 1779.

BIOGRAPHICAL REFERENCES.

My own Life. David Hume. (Preface to Editions of his works). Life and Correspondence of David Hume. By J. H. Burton. 2 vols. 1846.
An Account of the Life and Writings of David Hume. By Thomas Edward Ritchie, 1807.
Hume. By Thomas H. Huxley, 1879.
Letters of David Hume to William Strahan. By G. Birbeck Hill, 1888.
Hume. By William Knight. Blackwood's Philosophic Classics, 1886.

CRITICAL AND OTHER REFERENCES.

Hume's Treatise of Human Nature, with an Introduction. By Thomas H. Green, 1882.
Introduction to Hume's Philosophical Works. By Thomas H. Green. Philosophical Works, Vol. I.
Hume's Treatise of Human Nature. By Selby–Bigge, 1888.
Die Ethik David Hume's in ihrer geschichtlichen Stellung. By Georg von Gizycki, 1878.
Hume-Studien. A. Meinong, 1877.
Leben und Philosophie David Hume's. Jodl, 1872.
Hume. Thomas H. Huxley, 1879.
Outlines of the History of Ethics, Sidgwick, 1886.
Geschichte der Ethik. Jodl, Band I, 1882.
English Thought in the Eighteenth Century. Leslie Stephen, 1876.
Hume. William Knight, Blackwood's Philosophic Classics, 1886.
Grundprobleme in Hume. J. H. W. Stuckenberg, 1887.
Eine Untersuchung über die Principien der Moral. Dr. G. Garrique Masaryk, 1883.

BIOGRAPHICAL SKETCH.

DAVID HUME was born at Edinburgh on the 26th of April (O. S.) 1711. His family claimed aristocratic connections on both sides, and the fact of this connection was .regarded very naturally with some pride by Hume himself. His father died when Hume was an infant, and hence the education of the son was left to the mother. Of his early life and education little is known. We might say almost nothing is known except what he himself stated in a very brief autobiography which was written shortly before his death and published in the next edition of his History of England. He appears to have entered the Greek class at the University of Edinburgh in 1723, but did not graduate. He very early acquired a passion for literature, which finally, after some vicissitudes of fortune, determined his choice of a career. It was probably this taste with the want of positive and aggressive elements in his character which led his mother to remark of him: "Our Davie's a fine, good-natured crater, but uncommon wake-minded." The former part of this judgment proved to be just and accurate, but Hume's subsequent fame and influence rather belied the second part of it. This trait was the opposite of the general characteristic in his race which is intellectually pugnacious and active, and it very probably explains his sceptical tendencies by referring them to a constitutional disposition to cautious and deliberate habits.

In 1727, after leaving Edinburgh, Hume came to Nine-wells, the name of his father's estate, and here he was occupied with general reading and private study in his favorite way. The next year he began the study of the law, but soon abandoned it for work more congenial to his tastes. He spent the hours on Cicero and Vergil which others supposed were spent on Voet and Vinnius. After giving up the law he remained six years at Ninewells before attempting to fix upon a definite career. In 1834 he decided to enter upon a commercial life and went to Bristol for this purpose. But this undertaking proved as distasteful as the law and was in its turn abandoned. His fortune being too small to guarantee his independence in England, Hume resolved after the failure at Bristol to reside in France where he could prosecute his literary studies with the small income at his command. He first settled at Rheims and afterward at La Fleche in Anjou. Here he spent three years, carrying out the plan which he had formed while at the university, and returned to London in 1737 with a perfect knowledge of the French language and the first two volumes of the *Treatise on Human Nature*, which he published the following year. The third volume appeared in 1740. The work, however, much to Hume's chagrin and disappointment, met with no favor. Of its reception, he himself says in his autobiography: " It fell dead born from the press, without reaching such distinction, as even to excite a murmur among the zealots." This latter part of the remark shows that he was quite conscious of the sceptical character of his work. But his sanguine temperament soon overcame his disappointment, which at first seems to have been very keen, and we find him again at Ninewells carrying on his studies, mainly in the direction of politics and political economy. As a result of this, in 1741 he published the first volume of his Essays, which met with some success and reanimated his hopes. A copy of the volume was sent to Bishop Butler, the famous author of the *Analogy*, and his high praise of the work made him a

friend of Hume who entertained a very high respect for the
Bishop in spite of the wide differences between them on
matters of religious belief.   In 1742 the second volume of
the Essays was published and met with considerable success.   By this time, both the man and his works were sufficiently known and respected to have him brought forward
in 1744 as a candidate for the chair of Moral Philosophy in
the University of Edinburgh.   But "the zealots" seem
now to have been apprised of the nature of his philosophy,
and brought against him the charge of infidelity.   The
influence of his friends could avail nothing, and he was
defeated by Mr. James Balfour, the man who had severely
criticised Hume's Treatise on Human Nature.   Perhaps
Hume's revenge is found in the superior estimation which
history has assigned him over his competitor.   The grounds
upon which he was rejected created a life-long bitterness in
Hume against the Scottish clergy.   But he ought to have
had the sagacity to know either that the general tenor of
his writings was out of sympathy with the religious spirit
of his countrymen, or that the fanaticism of that time would
not tolerate in an orthodox chair a voice so uncertain as
his upon the theological questions then agitating the
church.   Huxley humorously reproaches him for failing to
see the natural impropriety of his becoming "a Presbyterian
teacher of Presbyterian youth."

In 1745 he became guardian to the Marquis of Annan-
dale, but this appointment proved unsatisfactory and the
next year found him acting as secretary to General St. Clair
who was commissioned upon an expedition to Canada and
afterward in 1748 as ambassador to the court of Turin,
whither Hume followed him in the same capacity as before.
It was in this latter year that he published the "Philosophic
Essays," or "Inquiry Concerning Human Understanding."
He returned to London in 1749 and, soon after, his mother
died.   Between this time and 1751 he resided with his

brother and sister at Ninewells and occupied himself with the composition of his "Dialogues on Natural Religion," which were not published until after his death, the "Inquiry Concerning the Principles of Morals," and the "Political Discourses." The last two were published in 1751, the Principles of Morals being a recast of the volume on that subject in the "Treatise." In the same year he again failed of election to a professor's chair, the chair of Logic at the University of Glasgow.

At the end of the period of which we have just spoken, Hume returned to Edinburgh and took up his residence in the Townmarket, having acquired a sufficient fortune to give him a modest competence. A year afterward the Faculty of Advocates in that city elected him their librarian, but not without considerable opposition from religious zealots. Hume writes with some humor of this and other episodes of the incident, and expresses much satisfaction at the result. The salary was only forty pounds a year, but the resources of a large library compensated him in part for this meagre remuneration and he was delighted with the opportunities which the position offered him for continuing his literary pursuits. The duties of his office allowed him leisure to write the History of England, the first volume of which appeared in 1754, the second in 1756, and the last two in 1759. Hume seems to have entertained rather extravagant expectations of its success, and if we are to accept his disappointment as a measure of the results, we should have to record the work as a failure. But its reception was much better than Hume's wounded vanity would seem to imply. For the sales were much larger than he would have us believe.

About this time an incident took place which is of interest in estimating the influences affecting Hume's attitude towards religion. In 1754 the presentment by the grand jury of Middlesex against the philosophic works of Lord

Bolinbroke led in the following year to the prosecution of Hume for heresy before the courts of the General Assembly of Scotland. After considerable discussion upon the questions whether Hume was amenable to this court, whether he was a Christian, and whether there was any propriety in proceeding against him, the matter was dropped and came to nothing. The Presbytery dismissed the process and Hume thus fortunately escaped the dangerous consequences of a clerical inquisition.

While the History was in process of publication Hume was active in other lines of literature. In 1757 appeared four dissertations, one on "The Natural History of Religion," one on "Tragedy," one on "The Standard of Taste," and one on "The Passions," the last being a revision and modification of the second book of the "Treatise." In the meanwhile the bitterness which he had felt on account of the imagined failure of his History, assumed a violent form of animosity against the English whom he supposed to be in a conspiracy to hold the Scotch in contempt. As a consequence of these rancorous feelings toward the English, the second portion of his History became a mere party pamphlet in favor of the Tories and against the Whigs, and he even went so far as to purge the first volumes of all statements which might seem to savor of Whig sympathies. The fact is interesting as showing an underlying vein of dogmatism and bias in a man who has generally passed as the Coryphaeus of scepticism, and may explain certain features of his style in his philosophic works when first published.

In 1763 Hume accepted the post of secretary to Lord Hertford who went as ambassador to France. Here he became acquainted with that brilliant coterie of French philosophers and literati of that time, including Montesquieu, Helvetius, Diderot, Rousseau, and Turgot, with some of whom he had before exchanged correspondence. On his return from Paris in 1766 he was accompanied by Rousseau whose suspicious and ungrateful temper soon provoked a quarrel which separated them, although only after Hume had acquitted himself of all blame in the matter. For two years after his return he remained in London as under-secretary to General Conway, and finally settled in 1769 at Edinburgh with an income increased to £1000 a year and with the determination of spending the remainder of his days in ease. His home in St. David's Street, which was so named because of a humorous and ironical allusion to Hume's religious beliefs by some one who chalked the name upon the wall, "was the centre of the accomplished and refined society which then distinguished Edinburgh." In the spring of 1775 he fell ill with the malady that had carried off his mother, and died on August 26th, 1776. He was buried on the eastern slope of Calton Hill.

Hume very early showed traces of a predisposition to philosophy. A remarkable letter written at sixteen years of age shows unusual precocity of philosophic taste and expression, although it indicates no more than his brooding over a vague and indistinct ideal which was an aspiration to realize the attainments he admired in the classic models of Greece and Rome. When he was eighteen he passed through an intellectual crisis which Mr. Huxley compares with a similar event in the life of John Stuart Mill. The comparison seems a little strained, but the incident is of interest because it turns upon the question of virtue and moral discipline, qualities which came in to divert Hume's attention from his philosophic dreaming, and to suggest another form of culture than that which at first attracted his imagination. For a while Hume gave himself up to serious reflections after the manner of ancient moralists. He lost during this period some of his native intellectual balance, but soon afterward he regained his natural robust health and with it recovered his former equability of temperament.

He had all his life a cheerful and complacent disposition and this characteristic fitted him for a literary life and for the sceptical pursuits which he chose to follow. He was equally disqualified by temperament, by circumstances, and by the company with which he associated, for the defence or advocacy of positive convictions upon the more abstruse subjects of philosophic speculation. This may or may not have been a merit. Which of the two it is not necessary to decide. The fact is referred to as indicating a constitutional quality which more or less determined the negative nature of his convictions on the more abstract questions of philosophy. To all who have gotten beyond the need of defending the peculiar philosophic and theological theories of that time, this mental poise and sceptical self-control over misdirected enthusiasm has much to admire in it. It must be confessed, however, that Hume did not sustain this attitude in an equal measure toward all subjects. His experience with the clergy and religious problems generally sufficed to make him a sceptic always in this direction, but politics and disappointed vanity soured his temperament only to make him quite positive in his political beliefs after the doubts of his earlier years had been dispelled by maturer reflection and a larger experience. But in his first works we feel the force and example of a very cool and subtle judgment, and the irony of its passionless reflections very naturally annoys those who have a disposition for enthusiasm, and who must accept the first theory at hand, for the peculiar purposes of advocates. This characteristic he retained to the last in spite of his positive views in politics and economics.

INTRODUCTION.

PRELIMINARY OBSERVATIONS ON HUME'S SCEPTICISM.

THE task of correctly estimating the philosophy of Hume is incumbered with unusual difficulties. We have first to determine whether he really had a system or not; whether, in order to expose their contradictions, he was merely developing views for which he himself claimed no personal responsibility, or whether he meant to present positive doctrines in the place of the systems of Locke and Berkeley. We generally assume to know that a man is either a realist, an idealist, a sensationalist, a rationalist, a materialist, an empiricist, a transcendentalist, a sceptic, or what not. With this knowledge we have an opportunity to discuss his point of view accordingly, to estimate its agreement or disagreement with facts. We may defend it, or we may criticise it. But in all cases our method of treating a man will be determined solely by the consideration whether we are dealing with his doctrine, or with his reasoning, or with both. If he is supposed to occupy a given position in philosophy we may defend or attack it in its relation to facts, or in its relation merely to logical reasoning. But if a man cannot be said to have any positive opinions of his own we are limited to the consideration of his reasoning. For instance, an idealist or a realist may be exposited, defended, or criticised. We may test his doctrine by its conformity or nonconformity with admitted truths. We may take him seriously to mean what his language implies. But if a man be a sceptic we have nothing to do with his private opinions, but only with his reasoning. A sceptic is a man who presumably has no opinions of his own upon the subject at hand, but assumes certain premises which others furnish him, and then merely deduces conclusions that flow from them. He claims no responsibility for the truth of the premises, nor for the conclusion, but only for the legitimacy of the process by which that conclusion is reached. Were processes of reasoning infallible there would be no escape from his clutches. The strength of his position, however, lies in the superior security of logical processes as compared with the psychological which are in the first instance, the originators of knowledge. Hence, inasmuch as he is not responsible for the data of his argument, he can be judged only at the bar of logic. He applies his method only in order to develop contradictions, or such disagreeable results as those who admit the premises are not disposed to accept. He is careful not to embarass himself with the duties of an advocate. A man of this kind is not subject to criticism for his opinions, but only for the character of his reasoning. It is probable also that he is chargeable with no other fallacy than an equivocation or a *non sequitur.* He is never exposed to the charge of a *petitio principii* which is the fallacy of a man who has opinions. But the possibility of an equivocation or a *non sequitur* is great enough to offer good opportunities for impeachment. Yet fallacies of this kind may be less frequent than errors of assumption, and hence the sceptic, not making any assumptions of his own, is exempt from so many liabilities which affect others that he is less vulnerable to attack, and not at all by the usual weapons of controversy.

The ideal sceptic may not often be realized. He may alternate between dogmatism and scepticism as convenience requires, or he may be an imperfect master of his method. Again he may merely simulate scepticism on emergency for the sake of the immunity which it affords against criticism, or he may push the method to such extremities that it breaks down under its own weight. Such were the ancient sceptics among the Greeks. Their scepticism was so naive and extravagant that it was very ineffective against the convictions of common sense. This was mainly because it was directed against perception and not against reasoning. But modern sceptics have been much more secure against ridicule. They have enjoyed the immunity of impeaching doctrines and accepting facts while they appeared to be discrediting both of them. They have been shrewd enough to accept the facts of knowledge, and only to dispute the theories of it and to suggest its limitations. Consequently, wherever they appear they are the signal either for general assault, or for a more profound investigation of philosophical problems.

Hume has always been regarded as a sceptic, and he himself would probably not have cared to dispute this verdict. So general has this view of him been that it would be taken as presumption to qualify or to deny it, and it would open new possibilities to most students if they could be made to believe that Hume's reputation in this respect was a mistaken one. For it would expose him to new methods of attack. It is not my purpose, however, to dispute the general correctness of the prevalent judgment, because it is not to be denied that Hume was a master of sceptical methods. But nevertheless I am disposed to qualify this opinion in order to explain certain characteristics in his writings and certain inconsistencies in those who regard him as a sceptic and yet speak of his philosophic system.

Before doing so, however, it is well to remark the radical difference between two states of mind which go under the name of scepticism. They are religious scepticism and philosophic scepticism. They are both alike in· the respect that they represent a state of doubt. But the former is a doubt of certain facts and beliefs, and the other is a doubt of the grounds of them, or the theories explaining them. It is true that there are cases where the two forms of doubt coincide, and these are those in which theology and philosophy interpenetrate. But usually religious scepticism is a doubt of the validity and certitude of asserted facts which are assumed to attest the truth and authority of something else, while philosophic scepticism does not necessarily impeach the value of any facts, but only the grounds on which they are assumed to rest; that is, the proof of them. The disbelief of a fact or an assumed truth may be felt without reference to any of its supposed grounds, and merely on the principle that it is opposed to experience, but the disbelief of a philosophic theory is not incompatible with the acceptance of all that the theory endeavored to support, while it often has the effect of implying a distrust of facts on the frequently accepted but false assumption that unproved truths are inadmissible. Were it not for this advantage dogmatism might more easily triumph over its opponent.

In regard to Hume there can be no doubt that he was a religious sceptic. His life and works leave this fact indubitable. It is quite as certain that he must be considered a philosophic sceptic, but with a qualification. His reputation for being a sceptic comes from two considerations. The first is his emphatic repudiation of the main doctrines which characterized the religious mind of the time, and the second is his cautiousness about admitting anything for which he may be made responsible. The latter means that he had assumed his premises from predecessors and had drawn conclusions from these premises which were not agreeable to the defenders of the reigning philosophy. But there is a characteristic in the style of Hume which suggests a criticism of the loose habit of calling him a sceptic, because, although he is a sceptic quite frequently, he is not always one. This characteristic has two features in it. The first is the discussion of his subject in a manner to make most readers believe that he is enunciating his own doctrines. Not only the air of seriousness, but the mode of expression would induce most persons to interpret him in this light. The second feature is the modification of the fundamental conceptions of Locke and Berkeley in such a way that, instead of seeming to argue from premises which he assumes neither to affirm nor deny, he appears to be stating views of his own. This character-istic is so strong that most readers would have to be told not to take him too seriously in order to realize that he is a sceptic. Undoubtedly we can suppose him assuming the premises of Locke and Berkeley, but the dogmatic style of his statements and his persistent silence about these two philosophers would generally prevent the suspicion of a purely sceptical motive. One writer tells us that there is no reason to suppose that Hume did not accept as true the principles from which he argued, and the same writer im-plies in his remarks that the hesitancy and doubt which gave rise to Hume's reputation for scepticism came from a real perplexity about the problems he was trying to solve, and not from any desire to evade responsibility for his premises. However this may be it is certain that his style is much more that of a dogmatist than of a sceptic.

When Hume wrote the Treatise of Human Nature he was decidedly more sceptical than he was in his latter days. The age at which he wrote precluded the probability that he would be so assured in his convictions as to be wholly dogmatic and self-dependent, and it also rendered it unlikely that his mastery of philosophic method would be so complete as to prevent the betrayal of a style against which a trained sceptic would be secure. But there was an element in Hume's temperament and mental constitution which conflicted with perfectly sceptical deportment. He was not wholly indifferent about philosophic principles. He had too keen an insight into truth to be wholly the victim of that intellectual paralysis which is the mark of certain kinds of scepticism. A true philosophic sceptic is a man who either has no power to perceive truth and always doubts it for that reason, or effectively conceals his perception in order to discredit the arguments by which it is sought to be established. In other words he is a man who only sees, or only affects to see, a weakness in constructive theories about things. Hume undoubtedly had many qualities of a genius for this task of breaking down theories. He had a well balanced judgment, and above all that freedom from bias which a healthy man always has, who does not allow himself to be frightened by ignorant fears about unlikely consequences, and who knows that truth is too often associated with ideas that have no necessary connection with it. His sceptical tendencies were supplemented by a native insight into the possibility or probability of what could not be demonstrated, and this gave him the consciousness of knowledge while he saw as clearly the weakness of the constructive theories which endeavored to import extrinsic and often irrelevant evidence into the support of truth. His intuitive insight was as good as his ratiocinative powers, and often led him to betray in his style the existence of opinions which an astute sceptic would effectually conceal. It is only a false emphasis upon the value of theoretical and ratiocinative knowledge that ever leads to scepticism, and it does this by disparaging a natural trust in one's insight for the less exempted power of reason. Hume's scepticism thus came from a desire to see both capacities in harmony. He had no intellectual difficulties in seeing the truth, but he desired to enjoy the traditional security of seeing it put beyond question by a process of proof, and as he perceived the fallacies in existing arguments directed to that end he could appear only as a man questioning the validity of general beliefs. Others did not see the distinction which he drew or implied, and which Kant made emphatic, between

the world of experience and the world of dialectic conceptions, and hence they mistook the nature and scope of his
scepticism, and failed as well to notice the element of dogmatism in his intuitive acceptance of empirical truths.
Had Hume not longed too much to give these truths a
ratiocinative basis he would have been more constructive in
his methods, and would have escaped the imputation of
scepticism along with Locke and Berkeley. But failing to
distinguish between empirical and "transcendental" knowledge, he brought the former under the impeachment which
his scepticism produced against the latter. And yet his
native insight into truth is so clear and his sympathy with
empirical and scientific knowledge is so strong, that he cannot evade the manners of a dogmatist in various emergen-
cies of his speculations. He cannot always maintain the
scoffing indifference of an ideal sceptic and hence it is
almost impossible to avoid thinking that he has simulated
this attitude merely to purchase the immunities which such
a position confers.

There are some interesting facts which confirm the view
here taken of Hume. In the first place the third volume of
the Treatise does not draw so distinctly from the philosophy
of Locke and Berkely as does the first book. The same
might be said of the second book which treats of the passions, except that portion which treats of the freedom of the
will. Unlike these two books also the third did not run
counter to the generally accepted theory of ethics, except,
perhaps, in the matter of the relation of "reason" to moral
distinctions; and even this was in conflict only with a small
school of thinkers, whom Mr. Martineau describes as "intellectualists," and who did not represent the prevalent theory
of the day. Hume drew from other systems for his ethics
what Locke and Berkeley did not directly supply for him.
The consequence was that there were no reasons for sus-
pecting scepticism in this part of his speculations, because

they were in accord with the prevailing doctrines of the time. His evident sympathy with the position that moral conceptions were the product of a "moral sense," or a "sentiment," advocated by Hutcheson and Shaftesbury, allied him very closely with the schools who opposed the explanations of moral ideas by association, because this view eviscerated those ideas of their moral content. This is the more remarkable because, having made havoc in the first book of speculations about causal connection by means of the doctrine of association, it was open to him as a sceptic to dissolve the moral systems of the day in the same manner, instead of accepting with them the appeal to a form of intuitive ideas. But his scepticism seems to extend no farther than metaphysics, while his ethics escapes its analysis. The conflict between theology and utilitarianism had not yet begun, and hence Hume could accept the position of Hutcheson and Shaftesbury without fear of controversy.

A still more striking proof of the claim here made is the dogmatic tone of the "Principles of Morals," published in 1752. There is nothing in that edition to suggest a sceptic. Its style is thoroughly dogmatic,—dogmatic in the sense that it represents positive convictions, and a well defined explanation of the nature and origin of moral distinctions. Scepticism does not propose theories, but disputes them; it is occupied with the *reductio ad contradictionem* and the *reductio ad absurdum* of prevailing opinions upon any given subject. But there is not a trace of this method in the later work. Hume here proposes as definite and positive a system of ethics as any predecessor or successor ever conceived, and he does so without finding it necessary to set aside more than a few special doctrines. His work, too, is in the interest of a view which neither the school of Reid nor that of Benthan has any reason to dispute. The earlier work is less positive and assured in its tone, but it advocates the same doctrine.

Hume's political bias as shown in his history and in his treatment of political doctrines is an indication of the dogmatic instinct in his mental constitution. We can readily admit that it may not have existed to the same extent in the earlier period of his literary activity, but it was there nevertheless, as might be inferred from his attempt to explain the idea of causal connection by association. As a sceptic he was under no obligation to explain this idea. He would have done all that a sceptic is called to do if he had thrown sufficient doubt upon the idea to discredit its validity. But so far from stopping with an exposure of the difficulties and contradictions involved in the Lockian and existing theories of that idea, he went out of his way to propose an explanation of the origin of it, which implied the existence of the very thing he had previously discredited. This is not the wisdom of a sceptic, but is the characteristic of a man who has too good an insight to be the victim of merely formal reasoning. The only difference between the dogmatism of this procedure and that displayed in his attitude toward political matters was in the amount of unreasoning prejudice which he showed in the latter and not in the philosophic method employed.

It is not to be denied, however, that Hume had his thoroughly sceptical moods, nor that the general influence of his philosophy has been sceptical. Only we must insist that this tendency is not exhibited in his system of morals, and hence the system must be treated as his express doctrine, for the statements and consistency of which he may be held responsible. The sceptical nature of his general influence can be best represented by a comparison with Bishop Butler.

Butler had a strong and judicious intellect. He was quite as dispassionate as Hume, and probably had a greater confidence than he in the ability and right of reason to solve the problems agitating the age in which he lived. It

was this, no doubt, that prevented him from being a sceptic. He was a man whom Hume himself respected however
much he chose to differ from him. But he was firmly
attached to the side of theology and yet he represented that
cool, logical temperament which, while it assumes the need
of a philosophy, is keenly sensible of the strength of scepticism. The nature of the philosophic and theological controversies of the time appears very clearly in the problems
of Butler's Analogy. Those problems were the existence of
God, miracles, immortality, and revelation. Butler's argument was designed to show that the objections urged
against the Christian system, which now passes under the
name of Theism, applied with equal force against the doctrine of natural religion or Deism, as then accepted by the
rationalists. This was only to say that objections which
overthrew the Christian scheme overthrew Deism and
necessitated the acceptance of Atheism which the deist
opposed as heartily as the Christian. Or put in another
way, it placed the deist between the alternatives of Atheism
and Christianity. Such a statement of the case had its
sceptical implications, because it did not prove the alternative which men were to choose. It left every one free to
accept the validity of the objections to Christianity or
revealed religion and thus to force upon himself the conclusion of dogmatic scepticism. This consequence was of
course counteracted in Butler by his known belief that the
Christian system was adequately supported, and he undoubtedly relied upon the general religious consciousness
of the time to adopt his side of the question. The deistic
school also would have accepted the same conclusion if it
had felt itself reduced to admit the disjunction implied by
Butler, and there is no doubt that Butler made out a sufficiently strong case for the deists to feel compelled to modify
their position, as subsequent developments have shown.
Hume, however, had no interests to bind him to the theistic

point of view, and having started with a doubt of the philosophic positions, upon which Theism was founded, he chose the sceptical alternative, which was only to say to Butler that he had been given the liberty of choosing Atheism, if he admitted the force of the argument against revealed religion, and that he did not find the evidence for this alternative to it so overwhelming as Butler had assumed. Butler was hardly prepared for this position. He had assumed the case against Atheism to be so plain that no rational mind would incline in that direction, and would have been at an entire loss to meet a man who admitted the argument against Deism. Hume therefore appears as endeavoring to prove that the sceptical attitude is quite as rational as the one advocated by Butler. He had a twofold *ad hominem* argument in his support. First, he had only to admit what the deist was not expected to admit ; namely, the cogency of the objections asserted by Butler to apply equally against natural and revealed religion. Second, he could assert that miracles, the existence of God, revelation, personal identity, causality, etc., were ideas not found in experience, according to the system of Locke, and hence were fictions, as all "complex ideas" were in that philosophy. This reasoning afforded a splendid destructive weapon at the time, at least so far as metaphysical and theological theories were concerned.

But there was no ground for applying the method to ethics. Neither Locke nor Berkeley had said enough on this subject to involve them in sceptical controversies, nor was the subject connected with the problems of the time in a way to tempt a sceptic with a *reductio ad absurdum* of it. The same ethical principles were admitted by nearly all schools. Had Hume lived to see the doctrine of Evolution, or had he appreciated and sympathized with the principles of Hobbes, he might have turned scepticism upon moral principles with as much ingenuity and effect as upon the problems of metaphysics. But in addition to not being as cynical and pessimistic as Hobbes, there was no influence to lead him into a destructive policy regarding ethics. And more than this, the moral systems of contemporaries and predecessors were so in accord with the philosophy of Locke that the one point which Hume might have been disposed to attack was not present to tempt his antagonism. This was the opposition between the doctrine of an innate moral sense and the doctrine of utilitarianism. Until the time of Hartley, Bentham, and Mill these doctrines remained in perfect harmony. The systems of Hutcheson and Shaftesbury, while advocating the theory of a "moral sense," did not pretend to advance this view with the object of opposing the theory of happiness or utilitarianism. On the contrary, they distinctly made this end the object of their "moral sense." Cudworth, Clarke, and Wollaston had advocated an intuitive and intellectual morality, but not in a way to oppose the doctrine of happiness. They were opposed only to the doctrines of conventionalism and of sensuous pleasure, or hedonism. Hume criticised the general position of these men when he denied that reason had any function in originating moral distinctions. But the position of the intellectualists was never generally accepted, while the prevailing systems, such as they were then, were not more affiliated with theological doctrines than with scientific and political views. Indeed, as Mill astutely observes, in one of his essays, utilitarian principles were staunchly defended by theologians until they discovered that utilitarianism was the favorite theory of sceptics and atheists, when they suddenly changed their attitude. Hence Hume had no motive to apply scepticism to morals, for it was his dislike of theological doctrines that was the motive to all his scepticism. He could agree with his contemporaries on ethical matters in the main without compromising his free-thinking and without prejudicing his philosophy, or he could disagree with them without espousing the cause of the orthodox in any important respect. The consequence was that he accepted the prevailing tendencies to utilitarianism and adapted his theory to the psychology which had been borrowed with modifications from the philosophy of Locke. On this account, therefore, we feel bound to qualify the charge of strict scepticism against his system at large and to treat his ethics as we should that of any other writer belonging to that age. With this understanding of his position we can enter into an exposition and criticism of his doctrine.

EXPOSITION AND CRITICISM.

Hume's conception of the field of moral philosophy was the same as that of his age. It was supposed to comprise the whole area of the sciences occupied with the life and action of men, history, political economy, psychology, æsthetics, metaphysics, and theology. To these were opposed physics, chemistry, astronomy, etc., which were known as the natural sciences. This looser conception of moral science affected the treatment of the problems now passing under the notice of ethical theories, in that it prevented the present and current radical distinction between psychology and ethics. This fact will be apparent to all who examine the contents of the three parts of the Treatise. The first part, after the example of Locke, was on the Understanding, which concerned perception and reasoning, and the problems of knowledge. The second was on the Passions, or as we should now denominate them, the Emotions,— a division which might be regarded as an anticipation on Hume's part of the threefold division of mental phenomena into intellect, feeling, and will, which is so often accredited to Kant. It of course only implies such a division by separating the treatment of the " passions " from that of moral principles generally. But the interesting feature of the system is that a problem which is quite universally regarded as an ethical problem, namely, the freedom of the will, is examined and discussed under the head of the passions instead of under the head of morals. The third part discusses the origin and nature of moral distinctions, both in general and in particular. But why Hume does not consider the freedom of the will in this part of his work is inexplicable, unless we suppose either that he regarded it as a psychological question, or that he very shrewdly excluded it from morals on the ground that a system of ethics could be constructed without reference to it. The latter can hardly be the true supposition, because he himself, although affirming the doctrine of determinism, asserts the existence of free will in one sense of the term, in the only sense in which, he says, it can be maintained to have a meaning at all, and because he also asserts that this freedom is a necessary condition of moral principles. He therefore probably regarded the question as psychological, and this supposition accords with his treatment of the matter under the passions. It is possible to maintain that he considered the problem of ethics to be exclusively occupied with a theory of the nature and origin of moral ideas, and as not concerned with any psychological conditions of their validity, and that the nature and functions of the will were assumed in all problems of theoretical ethics. But in spite of this real or apparent separation of the two parts of the Treatise, the discussion of the passions is very closely connected with the principles of morals, because it deals with the elements which have to be regarded as the motives of conduct, and with the doctrine of freedom which must be regarded as the condition of ethical speculation. On this account the passions must be subject to examination and criticism wherever Hume's theory of morals is a matter of consideration.

Everywhere throughout the system of Hume one fundamental distinction appears at its basis. It is Locke's distinction between "simple" and "complex ideas," although somewhat modified in the adoption. In Locke there were "simple ideas," both of sensation and reflection, while reflection was also the source of "complex ideas." Reflection thus does duty for perceptional, conceptional, and ratiocinative functions. But with Hume it seems that sensation was the proper source of "simple ideas" or "impressions," and reflection of "complex ideas." Still Hume is not clear or uniform in this matter, and we shall have to examine his usage a little more fully in order to make it clear.

Locke uses the term "idea" to denote the objects of both perception and thought. Hume, however, remarking this perversion of its usage, chooses, in one passage at least, to limit it to the conceptions of the understanding, which, in his view, differ only in vivacity or degree from the impressions of sense. In consequence of this limitation of the term Hume uses the term "perception" to denote all mental states of the understanding, whether "simple" or "complex," and divides these perceptions into *impressions* and *ideas*. By "impressions" he means "all our sensations, passions, and emotions, as they make their first appearance in the soul." By "ideas" he means "the faint images of these (impressions) in thinking and reasoning." When he comes to treat of the passions he divides "impressions" into the "*original*" and the "*secondary*." The former include all the sensations and the feelings of pleasure and pain ; the latter are the feelings or emotions which " proceed from these original ones, either immediately or by the interposition of its idea," namely, of pleasure or pain. That is, the secondary passions arise from experiences of pleasure and pain.

It is to be remarked in this analysis that Hume does not regard pleasure and pain as passions : only those states which exercise a prompting influence upon the will are to be regarded as passions. Hume's division places pleasure and pain among the "impressions" of the understanding and not as impulsive feelings, which he considers the passions to be. In other words, in Hume, the passions are equated with the desires and aversions, and so express what later writers have meant by the term when considering them as impulsive emotions, or as the class of feelings which are on the one hand contrasted with the reflex feelings of pleasure and pain, these being the effects and concomitants of action, and which on the other hand constitute the motives to volition, being in this case the causes of action. In this scheme it is apparent that Hume cannot regard pleasure and pain as motives to action, but only as reactions upon stimulus, or as concomitants of sensations which are such reactions. He would be obliged to distinguish between pleasure and pain and the ideas of them. The consequences of his doctrine will be evident when we come to consider his treatment of freedom and the theory of utilitarianism.

The divisions of the passions into the "calm" and the "violent," and again into the "direct" and the "indirect," have only a psychological interest. The classification of them under the first division is not carried out or completed. The meaning of the second division is made more clear. But since both divisions represent motives to action the distinction into "calm" and "violent," and "direct" and "indirect" is of no special importance in a theory of moral principles. The direct passions are "desire, aversion, grief, joy, hope, fear, despair, and security;" the indirect are "pride, humility, ambition, vanity, love, hatred, envy, pity, malice, generosity, with their dependents." Both the direct and indirect passions are said to arise from pleasure and pain, only that the indirect are found "in conjunction with other qualities." "In conjunction with other qualities," means in Hume's parlance "concurrence with certain dormant principles of the human mind." But the nature and differences between the two classes are not further discussed by him and in fact have no special bearing upon his problem, although it probably became him to explain his mysterious allusion to "certain dormant principles of the human mind."

It is in connection with the sections on the direct passions that Hume discusses the freedom of the will. On this subject he is a pronounced determinist, although with qualifications. He admits that we are free agents in one sense of the term ; namely, in the sense that we can do as we desire, or that we can act according to our pleasure. But he denies that we can act without a motive. This position is asserted most distinctly in the revised account of the passions, published in the Essays in 1752, when Hume became convinced that some form of liberty must be assumed in order to have the first conditions of any moral principles at all. The doctrine is stated, however, in the first edition of the Treatise, where he draws the distinction between the "liberty of spontaneity" and the "liberty of indifference." He admits the former, but denies the latter.

It is important always to remember this characteristic of Hume's doctrine before opposing it, because it must not be adjudged out of its relation to the ideas of the time. In fact, no theory of this question, or of any other, should be criticised until we ascertain the contemporary and antecedent views in relation to which the particular doctrine under consideration was conceived. Time generally introduces a change of relations and conceptions which very greatly modifies the import of a doctrine. In this way, to use an apt phrase of John Stuart Mill, what is true in one age may not be true in another, merely because a change of content may accompany a retention of the same language. It will be apparent to those who do not approach the theory of Hume from a purely abstract conception of it, as a doctrine of determinism, that it was conceived solely as a refutation of the so-called liberty of indifference, a position which has not been held by any respectable freedomist since that time. The speculation preceding Hume, and to some extent contemporaneous with him, was predominantly in sympathy with this doctrine. This conception implied motiveless volition, and this absence of determining motives was assumed to represent the proper condition of freedom. It was Hume's task to show that no such a state of things ever existed, and there is no reason to dispute his claim on this matter. Unless the freedom of the will can be sustained without assuming that conception of it which is illustrated by the story of the ass between the two bundles of hay, it must be frankly abandoned, and determinism adopted in its place. This Hume asserted in a very positive way by show-ing that there was nothing capricious, casual, or motiveless about human conduct ; that we act according to law ; that we are orderly and rational, and that expectations can be entertained regarding what we are likely to do with much the same certainty as we predict events in the physical world. His arguments on the matter, it should be remarked, were nothing more nor less than those with which disputants were familiar in his own time, and can be found fully stated in such writers as Hobbes and Collins. He was, therefore, not alone in the view he defended. But Hume, it must be remembered, had the advantage, first, of presenting his arguments sceptically, and, second, of defining the terms connected with the question in a way to involve his desired conclusion, while these terms represented by supposition the current notions of them. His own concessions to the freedomists were concealed by the want of emphasis upon them in order that they might not avail themselves of an ambiguity to parade in an apparent triumph over the determinist. Hume was shrewd enough to see and perhaps to appreciate, but not to advocate at length any other conception of the terms in the dispute than such as were necessary to refute the prevailing doctrine. He remarked that he would not pretend to argue with any one who assumed different conceptions of freedom to start with. This was his warning that he would confine himself in the argument to current conceptions of the problem and that he would relieve himself, as far as possible, of responsibility for his premises, or, at least, that he would put himself in a position to escape responsibility when necessary. He seems, however, to be accepting in good faith the data from which he argues, and it is this fact which gives his argument so much force. But whether he was serious in accepting his data may be a question, and upon the settlement of this depends the matter of his scepticism, and the method of criticising him. It is to be noticed that the form in which he presented the case for determinism is unusually clear and forcible ; the more so from the fact that Hume evidently does not propose to shrink from the consequences of his doctrine. He faces a paradox or a supposed absurdity with unblanched courage, and makes his reader feel that there is no way to evade the conclusion but to question the premises. That uncritical period was very slow to perceive this resource. Reid, however, did discover a way of escape, and set about a reconstruction of the problem all along the line, in the theory of morals as well as in the theory of knowledge ; and if we are to accept the judgment of Prof. Seth in the matter Reid was not far removed from Kant in his treatment of these questions.

We have, therefore, an instance, as already intimated, where the treatment of Hume must be determined entirely by the manner in which we regard his position. If we assume that he is a sceptic, we cannot treat his arguments seriously as his own. We should be at liberty only to consider the character of his reasoning and to throw the responsibility for unacceptable conclusions upon those of his predecessors who had unwarily furnished him with such dangerous premises. If we regarded him as a dogmatist, we should be able to consider his problem on its merits and to dispute his assumptions, as well as his reasoning, on the ground that he seriously accepted the data from which he argued. But in regard to the question of freedom we cannot regard him as wholly one or the other. He is sufficiently both to put himself in a position of limited liability. He reserves to himself, on the one hand, the right to throw his premises upon others' shoulders in order to escape an impeachment for a *petitio principii;* and on the other, he retains enough of positive conceptions in the liberty of spontaneity to protect his theory of morals. Hence his arguments may be considered as sceptical and negative against the liberty of indifference, but as irrelevant to any other conception of the problem. This circumstance makes it unfair to Hume to treat his views as opposed to the doctrine of freedom in general, and so we have to attack him always with a proviso. Again, if he could not take shelter in the privileges of a sceptic, and if he did not admit one form of free agency, we might accuse him of mis-conceiving the nature of the problem. But the perpetual immunity from criticism against his data, which his astute manner gives him, compels the student to throw the responsibility for error mainly upon his predecessors, while his one concession of free spontaneity secured moral science against the consequences of unconditional determinism. Hence the only resource left to those who do not like Hume's conclusions, and yet wish to hold him to account while they grant him the privileges of a sceptic, is to reproach the consistency of his reasoning.

There are two points, therefore, which can be brought against him, which are of considerable force and which do not make him responsible for his premises. The first is the contradiction involved in his treatment of the idea of necessity or necessary connection. The second is his ignorance of the manner in which previous philosophy had employed the term "reason" in connection with the doctrine of the will and the motivation of conduct. The latter exposes Hume to the charge of a misconception which leads to an inconsistency in his entire system of morals.

In regard to the first of these considerations it is to be noted that Hume had disputed the existence of necessary or causal connection, when discussing the doctrine of Locke in the first part of the Treatise. There is a contradiction between this denial of necessity or causation, and the use of such a connection between phenomena to refute the doctrine of freedom. If motives and volitions, according to the empirical and associational theory, are connected only by co-existence or sequence, the former is not a cause of the latter, according to Hume's own conception of the case, because he disputes the very existence of causation. It is impossible to distinguish between uncaused and free volition. Indeed if Hume were to suppose that volition is thus uncaused, on the ground that all connection between phenomena is associative, he would be admittting the freedom of indifference in a far worse sense than the advocates of that doctrine have ever maintained. He would actually be assuming a beginning of something without a cause, the very contradiction of natural science and of all the principles upon which scepticism is usually dependent. The defenders of the freedom of indifference never went so far as to maintain that a volition could originate without a cause. They assumed or affirmed that the cause was the intelligent ego, and that it was not the motive which caused or causes the volition. They merely claimed that in so far as the motive was related to volition the latter could exist without it, and hence the proper refutation of this position was to show that it could not so exist and that the act could not properly be a volition unless it had a motive. But to reduce all events to co-existences and sequences of phenomena and then, while excluding, in this way, all causal connection between them, to suppose that these events have an origin, each one having its beginning in the series, is to assume or assert a *creatio ex nihilo*. A volition thus originating would be not only motiveless, but causeless. Every event which comes into existence must do so of its own accord, or on account of some cause. If it be the former it is uncaused and spontaneous ; if it be caused, the argument would stand presumptively in favor of the determinists' claim, so far as the general law of causation can be said to do it at all, but it would be against the sceptical doctrine of Hume, discrediting, as it did, the existence of causal connection. Hume is reduced to the alternative of choosing between freedom and the existence of causality. There can be no doubt about the dilemma in which he is placed. On the one hand, the denial of necessary connection implies that events, and among them volitions, have no cause, are free spontaneous creations. On the other hand, to regard such events as caused is to grant the existence of more than mere co-existences and sequences and thus to surrender the sceptical conclusion to which his argument in the first book of the Treatise led. The whole force of his argument against freedom depends upon the validity of the idea of causation. This is not to say that freedom is denied, if causation is believed or proved to be true, but that the first condition of disproving freedom exists in the assumption of causal connection. But when that idea is impeached there is nothing left to prevent the supposition that volitions among other events are causeless, whether they be motiveless or not. The contradiction then in Hume is clear.

The reply to this criticism, however, is evident, and it would be that the contradiction is not Hume's own ; that he is merely employing the methods of scepticism, and that he is responsible only for the *ad hominem* character of the argument. His defenders can say that in one place he is merely disproving Locke's right to the idea of necessary connections from the premises, and in the other he is showing that the same school cannot hold to the doctrine of liberty if they admit the causality of all events and yet include volitions among them. In this manner the apparent inconsistency of Hume is only his statement of the double inconsisteney of the philosophy, of which he is giving a *reductio ad absurdum;* namely, the inconsistency, on the one hand between its doctrine of experience and the conception of causality, and on the other between the motiveless and uncaused character of volition, and the causation of all events.

There is no doubt that to thus regard Hume's position as purely sceptical acquits him of responsibility for the contradiction we have indicated. But we have two rejoinders to this supposition of its sceptical nature. The first is that, granting Hume's scepticism, our argument applies with full force to all who dispute the existence of necessary connection, and these include all who have taken Hume seriously upon the subject, among them the Positivists. They must choose between causality and freedom. They cannot deny both of them. The second rejoinder is that Hume cannot be properly regarded as wholly a sceptic in this matter. Had he been content merely to point out the inconsistencies of the philosophy of Locke, he might have been exempt from the charge of contradiction. But he did not stop with this criticism of Locke. He went on to propose a theory of his own, a procedure which took him wholly without the pale of scepticism and places him among the dogmatists. As a sceptic he should express no opinions about the idea of causality. He should merely have shown that Locke had no right to it in his system, and should have left the reader ignorant in regard to his own views. But instead of this he produces an argument of his own to deny the existence of causality. He admitted that we have, as a fact, the *idea* of necessary connection other than mere co-existence and sequence, but in order to show its illusory character he undertakes to explain its origin by the doctrine of association. He starts with the view of Locke that experience gives us co-existences and sequences, mere facts of connected occurrences, and concedes that causal connection is superadded to these. But in order to show that this superadded idea is only a mistaken co-existence or sequence, he shows the influence of long and frequent association in producing an idea of connection which we mistake for a necessary one. This is simply a reduction of the idea of necessary connection to association, and no one ever supposed that association contains the causal nexus, which is something in addition to it. Hume's own doctrine, therefore, is a denial of causation and thus contradicts his attempt to set aside freedom on the ground of the law of cause and effect. To secure himself against this accusation, Hume must give up his theory of the origin of our idea regarding necessary connection. If he had been content to show that the Lockians had no right to the idea of causality, as being excluded from the primary data of knowledge, and that with this idea they have no right to the doctrine of freedom, as long as freedom means indifference to motives, he would not have been disturbed in his argument. But the moment he endeavors to prove that the idea of a causal nexus other than association is an illusion, he assumes a position which makes any other doctrine than freedom a most rank absurdity.

Throwing aside Hume's inconsistency as a sceptic and admitting the law of causation, the defence to which his argument is entitled is that we must admit the causation of volitions and the invariable concomitancy of motives with them. This indisputably refutes the doctrine of indifference, and unless we can reconcile the theory of freedom with the caused character of volitions it must be abandoned. Hume's argument undoubtedly forces this conclusion upon us, because the only alternative to it is the assumption that volitions are not events or have no origin. But it may not be wholly and only to Hume's credit that the case is thus made out ; for the determinists who preceded him make the same conclusion quite as inevitable, although probably not quite so clear. It must also be said for the advocates of freedom that they were not all even apologists for that abused conception of it represented by the liberty of indifference. They were many of them careful to repudiate such a doctrine, and Hume may be suspected of insincerity or misrepresentation for not stating this fact instead of appearing to make us believe that the doctrine he attacked was the only one existing at the time. He can escape the suspicion only by pleading ignorance in regard to the history of philosophy. It is true that many persons have conceived the doctrine of freedom after the manner imputed to them by Hume, but they have not been so numerous as to justify a disregard of those who held a different view. Besides, Hume could not have had in mind a sceptical reduction of Locke's theory of freedom, because when we have eliminated the paradoxes of Locke's discussion of the problem we have a view precisely identical with that which Hume admits to be true ; namely the freedom of spontaneity. Hume could have been thinking only of the dogmatic philosophers and theologians for whom he felt a strong antagonism. He was ever ready to torment these adversaries with the conclusions from their own premises and delighted to see them writhe under the hopeless confusion in which their contradictions left them. It would be too charitable to Hume as well as false in fact to suppose that he was morally in earnest about either the truth or the value of his conclusions so eagerly demonstrated. He was bent on weakening the convictions of those who were willing to toy with philosophy as long as it did not undermine their faith or threaten the integrity of their traditional dogmas. There was a disposition to mischief in Hume's nature which greatly qualifies his claim to sincerity and it is attested by his own moods of complete indifference, both moral and intellectual, in regard to the results of his speculations. In spite of some dogmatic feeling there was the malice of a sceptic in him and it was this trait which created distrust in the seriousness of his argument, and forfeited the respect that attached to the more radical but more earnest philosophy of contemporary Frenchmen. Diderot, Helvetius, and Condillac were quite as sceptical as Hume, so far as theology was concerned, but they were terribly in earnest about the doctrines which they wished would supplant those of tradition, and modern humanitarianism may be said to have received its second birth at their hands. No such movement can trace its lineage to Hume's influence. Yet this fact should not be used too much to his discredit, nor should we because of certain moral defects in his temperament either unduly depreciate the merits of his philosophy or unfairly burden scepticism with the responsibility for the world's intellectual errors and practical ills. For the claim can be very justly made that quite as much good comes to the world from scepticism as from dogmatic and impulsive moral earnestness, because the latter is always in danger of becoming intolerant and overbearing. Both mental attitudes have their place. Scepticism is the antidote of intolerance. It is the mother of deliberative habits and deliberation is essential to all rational life and conduct. It is the only instrument which can enable us to get an adequate conception of the various conditions with which we have to deal in the intellectual and moral problems of the world. Without it we are disposed to assume a greater uniformity in the nature of men and of life than actually exists. What we require is a knowledge of the diversities of nature and circumstance under which men think and act, and we can expect to attain it only under the impulse of a certain amount of change in the ideas of our earlier periods of belief. On the other hand, moral earnestness is the condition of all noble action. Yet it must be wisely cultivated and applied. But it is necessary to counteract the paralyzing influence of doubt and hesitation, which if left to themselves result in inaction. The two functions require to be judiciously combined, the one to prevent unadjusted life, and the other to prevent inertia. In purely speculative philosophy, however, they may often be separated to a great advantage. Here we are concerned only with the naked truth of things apart from the personal interests with which our feelings, even those of the loftiest nature, may become associated, and in order to assure the judicial calmness necessary to estimate abstract truth rightly, we require often to divest ourselves of every impulse attaching us to preconceived opinions and purposes. Hume possessed this characteristic of intellectual self-control and poise to a very marked degree and it was a source of great strength to his philosophy. He undoubtedly had an eye to mischief when any theological doctrines were concerned. But this fact, while it might justify some suspicion of his disinterestedness, must not weigh in estimating the nature and value of his reasoning. Bad motives will not nullify the force of good logic ; and hence we are compelled to test his philosophy by other than moral criteria.

The second peculiarity of Hume's treatment of the will is his denial that "reason" alone can influence it as a motive power, or that "men are only so far virtuous as they conform themselves to its dictates." The first temptation of most students of philosophy would be to oppose Hume's position, and yet a little examination might show that after all the doctrine is not so far removed from that of Kant and common sense as might be imagined. For both agree that the "good will" is an indispensable factor in virtue, and it may be claimed that Hume's is only a negative statement of this view.

In the discussion of this question the student must be careful not to misunderstand or to misrepresent the real position of Hume. He is often said, or thought, to have denied all influence of "reason" upon the will, and his argument lends much color to this view, because of his incomplete exposition of the functions of reason, and because of the vast amount of negative argument on his part to show the inability of "reason" to furnish motive power. It is true that the impression left by his general language is that "reason" is excluded from all relation and influence upon volition, and it appears that the occasional use of the term "alone" or its equivalent is the only resource for defence which his apologists can produce. This is important and conclusive, but it would have conduced more to clearness had so important a qualification been more conspicuous in the general discussion. Hume's position is saved by his distinct assertion that "reason *alone** can never be a motive to any action of the will," and this is his real point of view in spite of apparent argument to the contrary. The general drift of his discussion undoubtedly favors the separation of "reason" and will, or volition, and justifies a measure of criticism in order to counteract its influence or to correct the very natural misunderstanding occasioned by it. Were he defending the entire independence of volition from the influence of reason there is an *ad hominem* argument which would be absolutely conclusive against him. It is the fact that he distinctly places pleasure and pain among the "impressions," which are not "passions," but data of the under-

* Italics are our own.

standing or reason, although the passions may arise from or upon the occasion of impressions. The passions are the only motives to action which Hume recognizes, and as pleasure and pain, according to his view, are not passions, they cannot be motives. And yet Hume founds his utilitarianism upon the supposition that pleasure and happiness are the motives of conduct. But since pleasures and pains are "impressions," or data of the understanding, and are not passions, and since the passions are the only motives to volition, Hume must either have given up his utilitarianism and with it the assumed motivation of pleasure and pain, or he must have admitted the motivation of the understanding or reason, as pleasure and pain, in his view, are among its functions. Again, inasmuch as it is not pleasure and pain, considered as present states, that are assumed to be motives, but the *ideas* of them that are the real motives, it might be said that "reason" is thus necessarily implicated in volition, as a motive power to it, for ideas have no other source than reason. This fact is conclusive in the case. But it does not militate against the real position of Hume as qualified by his inconspicuous admission. It in fact illustrates the positive view which it was his duty to have constructed after having implied that reason was in some way related to volition. The criticism, however, has been necessary for several reasons. First, it was necessary to make clear the inconsistency of any system which virtually denied the motive nature of pleasure and pain, and affirmed the theory of utilitarianism while regarding them as products of the understanding, and not as passions. Second, the case offered a good opportunity for explaining the real relation between volition and pleasure and pain, and between reason and volition, which is that *ideas* are as much motives as passions,—a position, which, although not made clear by Hume, is distinctly anticipated by him in the admission, on the one hand, that reason has some relation to conduct, and in the assertion, on the other, that conduct is not virtuous solely on the ground of its conformity to reason. And again it was necessary to exhibit the proper proportions of apology and criticism belonging to his view. These considerations, even if they do not take the shape of a refutation, justify our animadversions, on the ground that every student should be put on guard against misrepresentation of Hume, and against deductions from his doctrine which have ignored the important concessions already mentioned.

There is a farther consideration of Hume's view, which partakes of the nature of both a criticism and an apology. We may first remark that he is disposed to beg the question of the relation between reason and volition by using the term "reason" in its ratiocinative sense. It is indisputably true that ratiocinative reason can never produce a motive to volition. Logical processes are not motives, and no philosopher was ever careless enough to suppose that they were. The ambiguities of language in the Platonic system and its traditions might have lent some color to such a misunderstanding, but responsible thinkers have not given any ground to suppose that they would defend such a view. Hence it creates some surprise to see Hume insinuating by his treatment of the question that they had taught such a doctrine. In fact there is reason to charge Hume either with ignorance or with disingenuousness in the matter. He either did not know adequately the history of philosophy, or he wished to avail himself of a manifest but ambiguous truth in order to impeach the intellectualists of the day. If he was resorting consciously to an equivocation to support his cause he forfeits all respect for his argument. This view of him, however, is, we are convinced, not the true one. It is an accusation which it would be hard to prove, and can be nothing more than a presumption taken from his known sympathy with the cause of scepticism. Besides his sympathy with the doctrine .of a moral sense acquits him of disingenuousness, as it indicates a desire on his part not so much to play the sceptic with the school of Cudworth and Clarke as to prepare a way for his doctrine of moral sentiment. But we have a right to assert that Hume does not seem sufficiently acquainted with the history of the term to understand what the intellectualists meant by the motivation of reason in volition. We shall have occasion to refer to this question again when considering his moral theory in its more special character. It is referred to here for two purposes ; first in order to understand the peculiar nature of his doctrine of the will, and second in order to illustrate the difficulties in dealing with him merely as a sceptic, or as one who had not recognized in any form a relation between reason and volition.

Were we to assume that he denied all relations between the two, we could better understand the feeling which the freedomists of that day would entertain toward him. Accustomed as they were to connect freedom with rational as opposed to instinctive or passionate action, they would very naturally resent in strong language any attempt to widen the distance between reason and will by disregarding the established language and distinctions of philosophy, or to diminish the influence of reason upon conduct by giving morals over to the sentiments ; because turning the will over exclusively to the passions and instincts was, in the well defined conceptions of the day, as in Plato and his school, to make all conduct non-moral by regarding it as the result of mechanical motives or unconscious and irrational impulses. It may be that motive force has other elements than mere perceptive and ratiocinative ideas, but volition can never be truly moral until it is qualified by the rational element ; that is, until ideas of the intellect inform the motives to action. These ideas need not be those of the reflective stage of life. It is sufficient that they represent the consciousness of an end, although the reflective type may be the higher of the two. But in the general thought of his own and previous ages "reason" represented a motive opposed to blind instinct, and one which was opposed to the pure emotions. The term was taken in its broad sense of *mind*, and not of logical processes. It was this fact which Hume seems to have wholly ignored and he is reproachable for some lack of insight in not apprehending the true meaning of his contemporaries and predecessors. It was a strange oversight on his part. For no kind of freedom, not even that of spontaneity, which Hume admits, could be possible under the supposition that reason had no relation to volition, taking that term to denote the general power of consciousness. What he did, without being conscious of it, was to place conduct entirely under the agency of instinct or passion, in so far as his system separated reason and the will. This was effected by his failure to distinguish between "motives" as merely efficient causes of volition, and as final causes of it, or final and efficient causes together. In much of the traditional philosophy instinct and instinctive impulses were considered as efficient causes of conduct in which the agent was not supposed to be intelligent ; and where only efficient causes operated, they being always regarded as external. Because the instinct was an impulse or influence outside of consciousness, the action could in no way be taken as the agent's own voluntary effort, and hence was not considered spontaneous or free. Such "motives" are mechanical in their nature, or are analogous to mechanical forces, so far as their relation to volition is concerned. But a true "motive" to action must be a state of consciousness, an idea of an end, in order to make the action moral at all. It also requires impulsive force, and it is true that this motive efficiency does not come from it as an idea, but from the desire that is coupled with it. But, nevertheless, it will not be a true "motive" unless it contains the element of consciousness, or the consciousness of an end, because the act cannot be a volition without this accompaniment. Hence Hume's general tendencies are toward a determinism which contradicts his admission of spontaneity. He interprets "motive" to mean causal efficiency and denies this power to reason, so that volition, not coming from reason, but from the passions, can in no sense be intelligent, or coincide with his conception of free spontaneity. His error is, therefore, either in his misconception of the term "motive," which leads to the contradiction just mentioned, or in his denial of reason as a motive power while making pleasure and pain, its products, the motives to conduct. In either case there is a contradiction involved, both of them involving his theory of determinism, because as long as the *assumptions* of his own system include at least the concomitant motivation of reason in every volition, this fact and the freedom of spontaneity appear to offset the conclusions based upon a purely mechanical conception of the term "motive."

There are passages also which show that Hume does not, and cannot escape the influence of traditional usage in his employment of the term "reason." This appears in some of his references where it denotes perceptive as well as ratiocinative processes, and as he could not question its function to supply ideas of ends involved in every volition this usage, perhaps an unwitting concession on his part, either implicates him in the very doctrine which the whole spirit of his discussion has the effect of denying, as usually interpreted by the general reader, or it furnishes data for reproaching him with a surprising failure to apprehend correctly the teaching of the history of philosophy. A man of his insight and knowledge, in order to evade the accusation either of ignorance or of equivocation, should have seen that "reason" was, in general parlance, a term for all the intellectual energies, whether intuitive or ratiocinative. The possession of the first of these qualifications was sufficient to connect it with the will much more closely than the general spirit of his argument would indicate.

The next subject for consideration is Hume's theory of moral principles. We have already alluded to the separation which he makes between the doctrine of freedom and the theory of morals, and to the fact that he probably regarded that doctrine as a psychological question. We must remark farther that he was probably wiser than he knew at the time. His discussion of the will in connection with the passions made it necessary to abandon all psychological matters when he came to the problem of morals. This was a great gain, and students will hardly fail to perceive how it was, consciously or unconsciously, an anticipation of Kant's method, which aimed to present the *deduction* not the historical *genesis* of moral ideas and principles. Hume begins an entirely new system and method with his third book, although in one important respect he is still linked to the past. It is in regard to his doctrine of a "moral sense."

With Locke and the contemporaries of Hume the problem was mainly genetic. This is to say that it was concerned with the origin of moral distinctions. But there are two kinds of "origin," quite distinct in their nature, and yet usually complicated with each other in the same questions. They are the psychological and the historical origin of ideas. Both are quite different from the logical deduction of principles, and all three constitute as many distinct problems for philosophy. The psychological "origin" of ideas properly concerns their mental source and the mental elements constituting them. Their historical "origin" is a question of the time they come into existence and of the circumstances which elicit them into consciousness. Their deduction is occupied with a determination of the general principles upon which particular moral ideas rest for their meaning and authority, and this investigation can be carried on without any reference to the "origin," *a priori* or empirical, of moral ideas. Now Locke's polemic against "innate ideas" committed him to the view that moral conceptions were not a part of the original constitution of the mind, or of a simple faculty, but were the product of experience. He treated them as "complex ideas," which, although their elements might have a natural source in the mind, were themselves derived, as subsequent thinkers expressed it, by association. Hence he did not raise or discuss the question in regard to the special mental source of these ideas. He was occupied mainly with their historical genesis. But his system assumed, with the general belief of the age; that moral distinctions were purely intellectual, if it did not directly assert the fact. Scepticism is in a peculiar situation here. It can hardly attack Locke's empiricism without strengthening the doctrine of "innate ideas," which would make scepticism appear rather unnatural, to say the least. Hence it must appeal to another resource in order to attain its object. Hume's sceptical tendency, therefore, on the one hand, and his sympathy with the doctrine of a "moral sense," on the other, permit him only one resort. He departs from Locke and the intellectualists so far as to consider whether moral distinctions are intellectual or "sentimental" in their source. This mode of discussion enables him to avoid implicating his scepticism in an indirect defence of "innate ideas," while he can support the naturalness or nativity of moral principles and avail himself of the difference between reason and passion to refute intellectualism, on the one hand, and to prepare the way for emphasizing the motive element of morality, on the other. Hence Hume's first step is to deny that "reason" is the source of moral distinctions, and to affirm that it is "sentiment." His grounds for this position are the same as those by which he limited the influence of reason upon the will. Morals, he asserts, have to do with the distribution of praise and blame, and as these cannot apply to ideas, which are the products of reason, he thinks that reason cannot be the source of the distinction we make between vice and virtue.

It is difficult to criticise Hume's position on this question. There is so much truth in his point of view when correctly understood, and so much that is worthy in the object at which he aims, that criticism against him may appear to be dictated by a general dislike of his philosophy. It is easy to make his reputation among the orthodox a text for a homily against scepticism. But such a policy directed against his morals would be a grave mistake. Hume is not so sceptical in this part of his work as in the book on the understanding. He is not aiming to destroy certain views out of sheer mischief, nor to merely expose the difficulties of existing beliefs. All this we have previously explained. On the contrary, the only negative criticism he indulges is done in order to prepare the way for a constructive theory of morals on the lines of Hutcheson, Shaftesbury and Reid. We should never lose sight of this fact in estimating his doctrine. He attacks the intellectualists of the day, not in behalf of scepticism, but in the interest of a doctrine of "moral sense," which, although it was founded in the sentiments rather than in the understanding, preserved all that was valuable in the theory of "innate ideas" and suggested an element in moral principles and conduct not properly recognized by that view.

Students of the history of ethics will easily remark that Hume, when opposing intellectualism, has in mind the rather erratic doctrines of Clarke and Wollaston, and there is much in their views to justify his criticism of them. In fact it is an apology for Hume to know what the views of the extreme intellectualists were. And yet he did not fully appreciate the basis and the spirit of their doctrine, and in some cases misrepresented it, though perhaps unconsciously.

The reason for this is his misunderstanding of the term " reason " in the history of morals. He still seems to think that it denotes only a ratiocinative power and that previous writers regarded " morality, like truth, to be discerned merely by ideas and by their juxtaposition and comparison." But this supposition represents an entire misunderstanding of the case. Previous writers had no intention of affirming that moral principles had a ratiocinative origin. What they intended was to assert a derivation independent of blind instincts, in order both to vindicate the freedom of the will and to contrast what we call rational with impulsive conduct.

At the risk of some repetition we must refer again to the history of this term. The original antithesis which Plato wished to establish was that between conscious and unconscious conduct ; or perhaps better, between intentional and unintentional conduct. He did this by distinguishing between " reason " ($\nu o\hat{\upsilon}\varsigma$) and impulse or passion ($\epsilon\pi\iota\theta\upsilon\mu\iota\alpha$ and $\theta\upsilon\mu\acute{o}\varsigma$). His system assumed that passion acted without reference to a conscious purpose, or idea of an end to be intentionally realized. Although psychology in the course of its development has changed its conception of the passions in this respect, gradually coming to regard them as conscious, but non-deliberative, it still retained the old antithesis between reason and impulse or passion, while the term " reason " was also doing service for both the perceptive ($\nu o\hat{\upsilon}\varsigma$) and the ratiocinative ($\lambda\acute{o}\gamma o\varsigma$) function of the mind. There were tendencies at the time of Hume to limit reason to its ratiocinative import, as is evinced by the threefold division of the mind into " sense," " understanding," and " reason." The understanding was the faculty of conceptions and judgments, and reason the logical faculty. In this view the more comprehensive conception of the term was forgotten. This whole tendency is quite as apparent in Kant as in Hume and others ; and it created a very natural resource for those who felt the difference between "speculative" and "practical" thought.

Now when in the later psychology the passions came to be regarded as conscious influences upon the will, they absorbed all that Plato had meant by reason, and hence nothing was left of his antithesis except such as clings by tradition to the forms of language, and the irremovable difference between ratiocinative and impulsive functions. It was clear that the purely contemplative and perceptive exercise of reason could not be a "motive" to volition in the same manner as the passions, and hence upon this transparent fact, while unconscious of the equivocal addition made to the functions of the passions, and assuming the traditional import of the term that they were the motive efficients of the will, an easy argument was constructed both for determinism and against the motivation of reason. But here it was that Hume forgot or ignored the synthetic, that is to say, complex character of "motives." They must consist of ideas of ends *and* motive impulses, the former derived from reason, in the comprehensive sense, and the latter from desire, as has already been remarked. In this way he might have seen what current usage meant by the term and have qualified his criticism. By such a course he would have discovered that the motivation of reason was not opposed, but really at the basis of his own doctrine of a "moral sense."

This, we think, can be made out from a statement that represents the doctrine of Hume in a nutshell. "Actions," he says, "may be laudable or blamable, but they cannot be reasonable or unreasonable : laudable or blamable, therefore, are not the same with reasonable or unreasonable." Nothing can be truer than this if we mean that volitions cannot be like logical or perceptive processes ; and if historical writers had intended that they should be so considered, Hume's position could not be contested. But his limitation of the terms "reasonable" and "unreasonable" is a distortion of both their original and their traditional import, and it is amazing to find Hume either unaware of the fact, or resorting to a transparent equivocation for the sake of a temporary logical triumph. His own position gets its cogency only by making the most of an obliquity which is entirely of his own producing. He cannot find it as a concession of the intellectualists. The only excuse he might be entitled to use would be an inference from the logical distinction between understanding and reason. But what he would gain by this expedient would be lost by accepting "sense" instead of understanding as the source of moral principles, because the elimination of intellectual elements with the understanding would result only in either the absurdity of making all moral ideas sensuous and more definite and uniform in conception than their actual relativity and Hume's appeal to this fact would justify, or in using the term "sense" as a real equivalent of understanding and reason, internal perception, which was evidently the import intended by Hutcheson and Shaftesbury. Looked at in this light his contention seems no better than a logomachy. "Reasonable" and "unreasonable" as applied to morals in Hume's own time were intended to express conformity and non-conformity to the laws determined by consciousness as opposed to blind instinct, and not to denote merely ratiocinative processes. There was nothing, therefore, out of the way in the common view, unless some stickler for logical usage chose to misinterpret or misrepresent accepted language.

In spite of this, however, there is a very important truth in Hume's position, which ought, perhaps, to exempt him from unqualified censure. His distinction between the functions of reason and passion in relation to morality calls attention anew to the fact that there is no necessary connection between knowledge and virtue ; that morality is not the perception of right, but the willing of it. Only, Hume should not have used language which implied that moral distinctions arose outside of reason. That which he really emphasized, in spite of his misrepresentation of the matter, was what may be called the moral as compared with the intellectual side of conduct. The distinction he had in mind was the same as that of Aristotle between the "natural" and the "acquired virtues." To urge this was only to say that the distinctive characteristic of morality is a quality of will, and to recognize this fact was to anticipate the analysis which Kant worked out without involving himself in the paradox of excluding "reason" from a prominent influence upon morality. Moral action, said Kant, consists first in the "good will," which was not a "speculative," but a "practical" function of "reason." Knowledge conditioned, but did not constitute moral conduct, according to him. Hume's real view is not far enough removed from this to criticise it unqualifiedly. As a practical moralist he saw that in dealing with men the problem was to move their wills less than it was to convince their intellects, and hence their characters were to be estimated and their wills moved by other elements than mere knowledge.

There is a just criticism, nevertheless, which can be produced against Hume at this point. He puts forward as his problem the origin and foundation of moral principles, and in discussing it he confuses two distinct questions. Instead of discussing only the way in which moral distinctions originated he enters into the question of what it is that makes an action moral. In this way he fails to distinguish between the *psycho-gonic* question and what may be called the *deductive* or *psycho-derivative* question. The former has to do with the genesis of moral distinctions, ideas, or principles, and the other with the coefficients of moral action. Had Hume recognized the difference between the

INTRODUCTION.   53

two problems he would not have entered the controversy
about the relation of reason to the will, and could have
sustained his intended position with better success and less
difficulty.   Moral principles originate in ideas, but they are
realized by motive agencies superadded to them and having
their efficiency in the passions or emotions.   The emphasis
of the latter factor was the merit of Hume's position, but
unfortunately he made it in language which put the matter
at the expense of the relation between reason and the will.
    In the first edition of his *Morals* Hume does not define
his relation to utilitarianism so distinctly as in the edition of
1752.   After stating the case in favor of a "moral sense"
and the import of the terms "natural" and "artificial," by
which he expects to describe moral principles in general, he
proceeds to discuss the origin of the ideas of justice and
injustice.   Justice he seems to regard as the fundamental
conception out of which all other moral principles arise.
Hence he does not begin, as Plato and moralists generally
would have done, with an investigation of the *summum
bonum*.   This is simply assumed to be pleasure.   In the
later edition he uses the term utility to define this good, and
thereby indicates more clearly the point of view from which
his principles of morals are to be judged.
    It is not necessary here to enter into a general discussion
of utilitarianism in order to determine either the merits or
demerits of Hume's special doctrine.   We are interested only
in the extent to which Hume could support his doctrine
from the premises assumed.   In general, we regard the
doctrine of utilitarians as possessing sufficient merits to
secure it against unqualified criticism.   It requires only to
be modified, although this modification may be radical, in
order to be commended to general acceptance.   Like most
other one-sided theories it is liable to misapplication and
abuse.   But in so far as Hume is concerned this liability is
not so great, for the simple reason that he did not develop

the doctrine after the manner of Bentham and Mill. He was too much bound by the genetic conception of the moral problem, after Locke's example, to devote himself wholly to the deductive question as it appeared to them. Yet his position on the matter is open to a unique criticism which weakens his utilitarianism, although we may find in his psychological analysis a very interesting conception of the matter which may modify the force of the criticism, or suggest to the utilitarian a very effective defence of his theory; a defence also which will not antagonize the opposing doctrine.

We know that utilitarianism requires pleasure to be the ultimate end of conduct. The defenders of the theory assert that pleasure and pain are the motives of all action. It would be unfair to them to say that this expresses exactly what they mean. They intend to say that it is either the idea or the desire of pleasure and aversion to pain, perhaps both the idea and the desire, that form the motive to conduct. Certainly this is the only defensible meaning that can be advanced. A double difficulty is, therefore, suggested by Hume's position on the matter. In the first place, assuming as he does that all action is for pleasure or to avoid pain, he cannot allow them to be motives to volition, because he excludes them from the passions and places them among the impressions of sense and reflection. Even if pleasure and pain as present states could be regarded as motives in the ordinary theory of utilitarianism they could not be so considered in Hume's conception of the problem, because of the above mentioned psychological analysis. He would, therefore, be compelled either to abandon his utilitarianism or to modify his view of the relation between pleasure and pain, and the will. But these alternatives are forced upon him only because he had denied or greatly disparaged the common view about the motivation of reason in volition. In the second place, having maintained that ideas and impressions could not be motives to volition, and having classed pleasure and pain among them, Hume virtually excluded the latter from a place among the ends of conduct. But utilitarianism has no right to existence unless it can claim pleasure to be the ultimate end of action, and in so far as Hume makes it impossible so to regard pleasure he cuts away the foundations of his theory. He may be right about the fact that pleasure is such an end, but his classification of it among the impressions and ideas nullifies his claim to that assertion.

Hume's psychological position, however, suggests a very interesting analysis of the ethical problem. In his discussion on the origin of the idea of justice he shows very clearly his peculiar conception of the term "motive," to denote merely an impulse to volition, and an impulse that cannot properly be regarded as representing a preconceived idea. It is merely the *efficient* cause of volition without the *final.* For instance, he asserts in italics, the summary of a long discussion, "that no action can be virtuous, or morally good, unless there be in human nature some motive to produce it, distinct from the sense of its morality." We do not care at this point of the discussion to dispute this view. But we wish only to call attention to the conception of the term "motive," which, as in his illustration of benevolence being moral without the conscious recognition of its goodness, must denote a blind instinct, and this conclusion is enforced by his exclusion of "reason" from a determination of morality. The "motive" of action is thus not only a mere efficient cause, but it is also different from the end of conduct, and from the idea of that end. Accepting for the moment this conception of the case we have three distinct elements recognized, at least by implication, in Hume's position. They are the motive, the end, and the "sense of morality." Two interesting facts can be deduced from this view. First, Hume clearly distinguishes between the morality of conduct and the sense of its morality. This distinction can be reduced to that between instinctive or unreflective, and conscious or reflective morality, which is quite an important one to make in discussing the theory of ethics. Instinctive morality is conduct which we can call good on the ground that the end sought is approvable and the agent has the disposition to seek it without a temptation to do otherwise. In this form, morality has not reached its rational stage. Conscious or reflective morality is the conduct of a man who knows that what he is doing is right, and so has a sense of its worth and binding character. Here morality is rational. But Hume was shut out of developing his doctrine up to this point by his exclusion of reason from a part in it, and yet his analysis requires that the doctrine be developed in this very way. In the second place, if the development of the theory of ethics goes so far beyond Hume's restriction of the term "motive" to mere desire, independent of "ideas" or consciousness, as to admit the accompaniment of the "sense of morality," there will be the basis for an interesting reconciliation between utilitarianism and Kantianism, in which the categorical imperative is the only spring of true morality. For by combining the "motive" and the "sense of morality," as modern moralists do in regarding the "motive" as a synthesis of an idea and an impulse, we have only to distinguish between the motive and the consequent in order to see that the good sought may be one thing and the motive to it represent an entirely distinct element of consciousness. That is, utility or pleasure might be the *summum bonum*, while the pursuit of it would get its moral character, not from the fact that man had an impulse in that direction blindly considered, but from the fact that he sought it rationally or under the sense of duty. In this way we might hold that "the sense of morality" was the *formal*, and utility the *material* element of virtue, a position which after all is not only that of Kant as reflected in his recognition of "universal happiness' as the end of moral action, but is also quite in keeping with Hume, who makes the virtue of conduct to consist wholly in the motive.

The strangest thing in the case is, that Hume should have admitted, as he did, that "the sense of morality" should motivate volition and yet not give it moral character. This was no better than making morality a matter of pure, blind instinct. It might be consistent with the denial of the motivation of the will by reason, but this consistency was purchased at the expense of everything which elevated man's conduct above that of the animal. Hence, the moment that " the sense of morality" was recognized by philosophers as both a motive to volition and a determinant of high merit in it, Hume's doctrine that the "motive" only could moralize conduct, was transformed into Kant's theory of the "good will."

There are some very paradoxical remarks by Hume in his treatment of justice, and since he is here dealing with the fundamental principles of morals, they require some consideration. The first most interesting fact to be noticed is his conception of justice. He does not define it clearly, but only indicates the class of phenomena to which it belongs and whose essential nature it shares. In the first part of the book he had discussed the relation of moral principles to "nature," and after recognizing three different meanings for the term decides that moral principles are "artificial." In this latter class he places justice. "There are some virtues," he says, "that produce pleasure and approbation by means of an artifice or contrivance, which arises from the circumstances and necessity of mankind. Of this kind I assert *justice* to be."

The first criticism which this observation would instigate, would be, especially if Cudworth had an opportunity to attack it, that it is the old conventionalism of the sophists and sceptics rejuvenated. The language unmistakably suggests this view, but the criticism nevertheless misrepresents the real and true position of Hume. For he is careful to say that although justice is conventional in its origin it is not arbitrary, and he enforces this remark by the farther assertion that the framers of moral rules always had to rely upon some ultimate principles in the constitution of man. "The utmost politicians can perform," he says, "is to extend the natural sentiments beyond their original bounds ; but still nature must furnish the materials, and give us some notion of moral distinctions." This effectually sets aside the old doctrine of relativity and of conventionalism, although it may not make his own view so intelligible as is desired. But previous to his investigation into the nature of this "artifice" by which ideas of justice came into existence, Hume ventures upon a short, and, he thinks, convincing proof of his position. It consists of an analysis of moral action, to some features of which we have already alluded.

"The external performance," says Hume, "has no merit. We must look within to find the moral quality." He then affirms that this quality is found in the motive, but as this cannot be directly ascertained in others the actions have to be regarded as the signs of the motives. In this way, he concludes that "all virtuous actions derive their merit only from virtuous motives," and adds farther that "the first virtuous motive, which bestows a merit on any action, can never be a regard to the virtue of that action, but must be some other natural motive or principle." But Hume has to face the question whether "the sense of morality or duty" may not motivate volition without the existence of any other "natural motive or principle," and he answers it by saying : "Though, on some occasions, a person may perform an action merely out of regard to its moral obligation, yet still this supposes in human nature some distinct principles, which are capable of producing the action and whose moral beauty renders the action meritorious."

Hume's doctrine of morality may possibly be tested by this last remark. He admits that sometimes volition may be motivated by the sense of duty, and we may ask how he can reconcile with this admission the assertion that it " supposes in human nature some distinct principles which are capable of producing the action." It may be a fact that there are such " principles," but Hume mistakes a connection of fact for a connection of implication. The existence of other motives to action is not implied by the existence of the sense of duty, although in fact we may find them invariably associated. Again, if " the sense of morality or duty " *alone* may produce an action, how can it consist with this to suppose other motives as necessarily operative and implied? But not to urge this contradiction, which may be due to mere carelessness, we may still ask how it is possible for the action to be a sign of the motive if both " the sense of morality " and some " natural motive or principle " may either separately or together motivate volition? According to Hume the " natural motive " determines the merits of conduct, and if so, to which motive does the act as a sign testify? If it attests only the " natural motive," there is no circumstance in which the existence of " the sense of morality " can be proved. But if it attests "the sense of morality " in any case, according to Hume, the act could not be moral for the lack of the accompanying "natural motive." If it attests the existence of both motives there is no reason for distinguishing their sanctifying power. In fact, Hume has not provided for those cases in which there is a struggle between duty and interest, although the difference which he assumes between " the sense of morality " and " natural motives " requires him to do so. Where that struggle exists and the motive of duty is obeyed, we have evidence of the *sole* motivation of " the sense of morality," so that the establishment of this fact would bring upon Hume's position all the criticisms we have advanced.

Again, to make virtue consist in action from a motive other than a regard to its morality is to affiliate his doctrine with that which makes virtue purely a matter of instinct, in the narrower sense of the term. This is consistent enough in Hume after depreciating the influence of reason upon conduct, and although we may not be able to reproach him with an inconsistency here, probably so bold a statement of his position or of what it implies will expose its inherent weakness. But we have this object much less in view than to call attention to an omission on his part which led him into his paradoxical assertions and exposed him to the *reductio ad absurdum* just mentioned. It was his failure to distinguish between naive or unreflective, and conscious or reflective morality. His view that the virtue of an act consisted solely in the character of the motive did not permit him to distinguish between internal and external morality. To him all morality had to be internal ; that is, representative of character, not of a physical order in the world. But he could have distinguished between instinctive or natural and conscious or rational morality. We may say that the differences between them are in kind or in degree, just as we are pleased to state the case, but they are not opposed to each other. Hume's failure, however, to recognize this double character of conduct, which we approve as "moral," involved him in two difficulties : first, in making virtue dependent on impulses which have generally been regarded as *non-moral*, on the ground that they were purely instinctive, while affirming that the motive was the sole source of virtue, and second, in assuming that "the sense of morality" gave no merit to conduct, while he could hardly have denied that the consciousness of obligation greatly increased the individual's responsibility. The trouble is that Hume had no means of solving the problem in the comparison between those who have no temptations and those who resist them. Only those without temptations could be moral or immoral in his system.

What Hume was seeking to show, however, in the paradoxical position, that all virtuous conduct must be derived from motives "distinct from the sense of morality," was the fact that "the sense of morality" is an "artificial" product of man's necessity and circumstances. Here we have the true motive to his doctrine, and in it we may trace very clearly the lineage of the theories of Bentham, Mill, Spencer, and evolutionists generally. We know how it has been developed by these writers and do not require more than to recognize its historical relations. Hume takes the matter up in the section on "the Origin of Justice and Property." What the position amounts to, on general principles, is, that all the ideas passing current among traditional moralists as representative of *rational* morality are conventional in their origin, but not arbitrary, as Hume would say. This is to say that the sense of duty, or the categorical imperative, is not among the natural endowments of man.

We shall enter neither into the statement of his doctrine nor into a criticism of his argument on this particular point. To treat the matter with due exhaustiveness we should be obliged to go into the complicated theories of the associationists and evolutionists. It must suffice for the present merely to indicate this general direction of his speculation. To say that morality is conventional is to reanimate the old controversy of the sophists, except that Hume saves himself from the imputation of their shallowness, by admitting a natural element at the same time as the basis of the convention. But in asserting a place and influence for convention at all, he merely stated in more traditional language Bentham's doctrine of "political sanctions," and Herbert Spencer's theory of "political restraint" or "control," and these views are the true descendants of Hume's.

The error in all of them lies less in the assertion that political influences and conventions affect our current moral ideas than in the implication usually understood, perhaps wrongly, that these agencies create morality instead of merely making it effective or eliciting it into consciousness. It may be said that Hume's admission of a natural element at the foundation of convention involves this view of the case, and we grant that it does. Only Hume had not distinguished between the *ratio fiendi* of moral *ideas* and the *ratio fiendi* of *morality*, a mistake, however, which was very general in that age. What he ought to have remarked was the fact that convention and law can only give motive efficiency to moral conceptions already existent, instead of using language which implies that the quality of conduct was a matter of creation by government. In spite of this criticism, however, it is always possible for a defender of Hume to say that his admission of "natural" principles at the basis of convention was a recognition of this view, and even if we do not accord him the credit of consciously proposing this distinction it is there as a greater or less tribute to his understanding and as a concession to the opponents of pure empiricism. And yet in making this concession Hume may have been a victim of the equivocations which he himself had exposed in the use of the term "natural." But if this be so, it is hardly possible to make anything intelligible out of his system. Besides, we cannot so easily explain the inconsistency between affirming that "moral distinctions are derived from a moral sense," which must be natural if anything, and affirming that they are the creations of convention or "artifice." Hume's only escape from this criticism would be to maintain that the "moral sense" and "the sense of morality or duty" were the same and that both were products of experience. But he seems nowhere to make this claim, while the only rational implications of his statements are that the "moral sense" is a natural endowment and that "the sense of morality or duty" is an empirical product, a conclusion which either establishes a contradiction in Hume's system or indicates that the controversy between the apriorist and empiricist represents an entirely false conception of the true ethical problem.

It is also a pertinent question to ask a sceptic whó, like Hume, cherishes considerable animosity toward theology, whether the view that conscience or "the sense of morality" is not a natural endowment of man, does not leave the whole field of ethics open to the theologian? Certainly a purely negative conclusion like this would do so. But Hume's escape from such an imputation lies in his positive view that "the sense of morality" is a conventional product of social life and its necessities. This asserts a human as opposed to a divine origin of the moral law. But it is not apparent in this doctrine that human convention and "artifice" are any better sources of morality than the arbitrary enactments of the divine will. Indeed it would puzzle any mind to tell the difference. Hume here lost his opportunity to show that the theologian was the real empiricist and that his doctrine defining morality as a creation of the divine will was in conflict with its *a priori* origin in reason. Hume might, in this contingency, have made a strong *ad hominem* argument in favor of his theory of a moral sense, by using the theologian's prejudice against empiricism to refute the created character of moral distinctions. As it is, however, the assertion that convention can originate morality is a tacit admission of the theologian's point of view ; namely, the created nature of morality.

Again, it may be a question whether Hume would have a right to appeal to the conception of a conventional origin of moral distinctions as a refutation of theological and intuitive views, because, after his radical distinction between "natural motives" to volition and "the sense of morality," asserting that the latter is an "artificial" product and that it cannot confer any merit upon conduct, he is left without a shred of ground upon which to base a theory of empiricism. If "the sense of morality" were, in Hume's view, a modification of "natural" impulses, it could confer merit upon conduct ; but since it cannot confer this merit, according to his statements, it cannot have the moral characteristics of "natural motives," and it is the motive, in Hume's view, that determines the character of the act. Hence it is apparent that the origin of "the sense of morality" by convention is in no way the origin of a moral impulse, so that Hume's empiricism can in no respect legitimately antagonize the theories of apriorism in so far as they maintain the naturalness of moral principles. A rather conclusive confirmation of this, also, is Hume's own statement near the close of Section II., where he is discussing the origin of justice and property. "Any artifice of politicians," he says, "may assist nature in the producing of those sentiments which she suggests to us, and may even, on some occasions, produce alone an approbation or esteem for any particular action ; but 'tis impossible it should be the sole cause of the distinction we make betwixt vice and virtue. For if nature did not aid us in this particular, 't would be in vain for politicians to talk of *honorable* or *dishonorable*, *praiseworthy* or *blameable.* These words would be perfectly unintelligible, and would no more have any idea annexed to them, than if they were a tongue perfectly unknown to us. The utmost politicians can perform, is, to extend the natural sentiments beyond their original bounds ; but still nature must furnish the materials, and give us some notion of moral distinctions."

This remarkable concession very greatly limits the area of "artificial" moral conceptions, and it would have been well for the empirical successors of Hume if they could have granted as much. It is not a little interesting to note that, while claiming him as the father of modern empiricism, barring the claim of Locke, they systematically ignore the ineradicable limitations he puts upon that doctrine. Hume himself also seems unaware of the fact that his position in this passage practically admits the unique and original nature of "the sense of morality," since the passage limits the function of convention merely to extending moral principles and conceptions already in existence. But in spite of the inconsistency which, in one conception of the terms, can be charged upon Hume for these and other statements, there is so much truth in his position, when we distinguish, as he did not, between the origin of the *intension* and the origin of the *extension* of moral ideas, that it is an ungrateful task to criticise him severely. We should rather quote him to show that modern empiricists have departed from their much vaunted master in their efforts to make morality wholly conventional. The proper criticism against Hume is that, in common with the moralists of his age, he treated the subject as if the problem was the *origin* and not rather the *ground* and *validity* of morality. The empiricists of to-day have not fully learned this fact, owing, no doubt, to their failure to appreciate the work of Kant. They simply adopted one half of Hume's principles and shunned Kant as they would Augustine or Aquinas, and as a consequence treat the whole problem of Ethics as if it were natural history. Hume saw better than this, and had he extricated himself from the confusion of treating the question as a controversy between natural and conventional morality; that is, as a problem of the *ratio fiendi* rather than the *ratio essendi* of moral principles, he might have contested with Kant the palm of philosophic honors. As it is he simply comes short of that result and leaves the student in perpetual fear of doing him injustice, if the system is criticised without qualification, and of ignoring one half his theory if he is represented as a pure empiricist. In fact, Hume simply marks a transition, and his Ethics show all the instability and incompleteness of analysis which character-izes a transitional period. It remained for subsequent schools to cut a better path into the wilderness. Their success is still *sub judice.* But they represent two distinct tendencies, the empirical or evolutionistic and the transcen-dental or Kanto-Hegelian, both properly tracing their lineage to Hume.

JAMES H. HYSLOP.

COLUMBIA COLLEGE.

BOOK II.

OF THE PASSIONS.

PART I.

OF PRIDE AND HUMILITY.

SECTION I.

Division of the Subject.

As all the perceptions of the mind may be divided into *impressions* and *ideas*, so the impressions admit of another division into *original* and *secondary*. This division of the impressions is the same with that which[1] I formerly made use of when I distinguish'd them into impressions of *sensation* and *reflection*. Original impressions or impressions of sensation are such as without any antecedent perception arise in the soul, from the constitution of the body, from the animal spirits, or from the application of objects to the external organs. Secondary, or reflective impressions are such as proceed from some of these original ones, either immediately or by the interposition of its idea. Of the first kind are all the impressions of the senses, and all bodily pains and pleasures : Of the second are the passions, and other emotions resembling them.

'Tis certain, that the mind, in its perceptions, must begin somewhere ; and that since the impressions precede their correspondent ideas, there must be some impressions, which without any introduction make their appearance in the soul. As these depend upon natural and physical causes, the examination of them wou'd lead me too far from my present subject, into the sciences of anatomy and natural philosophy.

[1] Book I. Part I. sect. 2.

For this reason I shall here confine myself to those other impressions, which I have call'd secondary and reflective, as arising either from the original impressions, or from their ideas. Bodily pains and pleasures are the source of many passions, both when felt and consider'd by the mind; but arise originally in the soul, or in the body, whichever you please to call it, without any preceding thought or perception. A fit of the gout produces a long train of passions, as grief, hope, fear; but is not deriv'd immediately from any affection or idea.

The reflective impressions may be divided into two kinds, *viz.*, the *calm* and the *violent*. Of the first kind is the sense of beauty and deformity in action, composition, and external objects. Of the second are the passions of love and hatred, grief and joy, pride and humility. This division is far from being exact. The raptures of poetry and music frequently rise to the greatest height; while those other impressions, properly called *passions*, may decay into so soft an emotion, as to become, in a manner, imperceptible. But as in general the passions are more violent than the emotions arising from beauty and deformity, these impressions have been commonly distinguish'd from each other. The subject of the human mind being so copious and various, I shall here take advantage of this vulgar and specious division, that I may proceed with the greater order; and having said all I thought necessary concerning our ideas, shall now explain those violent emotions or passions, their nature, origin, causes, and effects.

When we take a survey of the passions, there occurs a division of them into *direct* and *indirect*. By direct passions I understand such as arise immediately from good or evil, from pain or pleasure. By indirect such as proceed from the same principles, but by the conjunction of other qualities. This distinction I cannot at present justify or explain any farther. I can only observe in general, that under the indirect passions I comprehend pride, humility, ambition, vanity, love, hatred, envy, pity, malice, generosity, with their dependants. And under the direct passions, desire, aversion, grief, joy, hope, fear, despair and security. I shall begin with the former.

[Hume then proceeds to give the "objects" and "causes" of pride and humility, both of which conceptions he takes in a very broad sense. "The object," he says, "is self, or that succession of related ideas and impressions, of which we have an intimate memory and consciousness." He does not think it possible, however, that the cause can be the same as their object. Hence he says : "Pride and humility, being once rais'd, immediately turn our attention to ourself, and regard that as their ultimate and final object ; but there is something farther requisite in order to raise them : something which is peculiar to one of the passions, and produces not both in the very same degree. The first idea, that is presented to the mind, is that of the cause or productive principles. This excites the passion connected with it ; and that passion, when excited, turns our view to another idea, which is that of self. Here then is a passion plac'd betwixt two ideas, of which the one produces it, and the other is produced by it. The first idea, therefore, represents the *cause*, the second the *object* of the passion." The causes of pride and humility are then enumerated and are made to consist of a great variety of "subjects," as Hume chooses to call them, as distinguished from the "objects" of the passion. They are "every quality of mind, whether of the imagination, judgment, memory, or disposition ; wit, good sense, learning, courage, justice, integrity; all these are the causes of pride ; and their opposites, of humility." Further causes, to go beyond merely mental qualities are, "beauty strength, agility, good mien, address in dancing, riding, fencing, and of his dexterity in any manual business or manufacture." But these are not all. "Country. family. children, relations, riches. houses, gardens, horses, dogs, clothes : any of these may become a cause of either pride or of humility." In regard to the causes Hume farther distinguishes between the "*quality*" which operates and the subject on which it is plac'd." In the case of a beautiful house considered as the cause of a passion, the beauty is the quality, and the house is the subject.

The next section takes up the derivation of the causes and objects of the two passions. Hume's purpose is to find what it is that connects them with the passions. He maintains that their influence "proceeds from an *original* quality or primary impulse " of the individual who has the passions. and that it is the distinguishing characteristic of these passions to be natural. But in order to explain how it is that such a variety of causes and objects is connected with the same effect : that is, how such different "causes" as a house and wit may be sources of pride. Hume proceeds to show "that 'tis from natural principles this variety of causes excite pride and humility. and that 'tis not by a different principle each different cause is adapted to its passion." and this is accomplished by referring to the law of association of ideas. as enabling different "subjects" to affect the individual in the same way. It is the manner in which they concur to produce pleasure and pain that links them with the same end. and as "all agreeable objects. related to ourselves. by an association of ideas and of impressions. produce pride. and disagreeable ones humility." we may find in this concurrence the unity of the principle affecting the passions concerned. Hume admits five limitations to his principle. but they do not affect the main distinctions in question according to his view. His next task is then to show how the various "causes" including "vice and virtue." "beauty and deformity." "external advantages and disadvantages." "property and riches." and "the love of fame " affect pride and humility.

Part II. on the Passions gives the same treatment of "love and hatred" as is given to pride and humility. Hume distinguishes in the same manner as before between the "causes" and the "objects" of them. As in pride and humility the "object" is self, so in love and hatred the "object" is others. The "causes" are diversified as before, but are related to a thinking being, and are such qualities as "virtue, knowledge, wit, good sense, good humour." Physical objects do not awaken them. The remainder of this section is occupied with special cases of influence upon the two passions.

A separate and peculiar treatment is given to "benevolence and anger." They are not regarded as forms, but only as accompaniments, of love and hatred. The last two passions, therefore, entail desire and aversion. "Pride and humility are pure emotions in the soul unattended with any desire, and not immediately exciting us to action. But love and hatred are not completed within themselves, nor rest in that emotion which they produce, but carry the mind to something further." Love and hatred have not only a cause and object, but also an *end*, which they reach through desire and aversion. Benevolence and anger are the accompanying agents or means to this end. The discussion of compassion, of malice and envy, and of mixed emotions is only a consideration of modified forms and circumstances of the second general class of emotions and passions which Hume regards as preliminary to his examination of the desires and the will. In them he means to define the mental excitements expressing the various manifestations of pleasure and pain, and so to indicate the causes and objects of the states of mind affecting self and others as the conditions of all the movements of the will. It is interesting to remark that his analysis and classification excludes from them all impulsive characteristics. They have "objects," but not *ends* unless they become complicated with the desires and aversions.

The matter, however, has mainly a psychological interest, and requires notice only in order to understand Hume's discussion in this connection of the freedom of the will, which, although more properly appearing as a part of the required ethical postulates, is examined as a part of the psychology of the emotions.   This is part third of his chapters on the passions.]

PART III.

OF THE WILL AND DIRECT PASSIONS.

SECTION I.

Of liberty and necessity.

WE come now to explain the *direct* passions, or the impressions, which arise immediately from good or evil, from pain or pleasure.   Of this kind are, *desire and aversion, grief and joy, hope and fear.*

Of all the immediate effects of pain and pleasure, there is none more remarkable than the WILL ; and tho', properly speaking, it be not comprehended among the passions, yet as the full understanding of its nature and properties, is necessary to the explanation of them, we shall here make it the subject of our enquiry.   I desire it may be observ'd, that by the *will*, I mean nothing but *the internal impression we feel and are conscious of, when we knowingly give rise to any new motion of our body, or new perception of our mind.* This impression, like the preceding ones of pride and humility, love and hatred, 'tis impossible to define, and needless to describe any farther ; for which reason we shall cut off all those definitions and distinctions, with which philosophers are wont to perplex rather than clear up this question ; and entering at first upon the subject, shall examine that long disputed question concerning *liberty and necessity;* which occurs so naturally in treating of the will.

'Tis universally acknowledg'd, that the operations of external bodies are necessary, and that in the communication of their motion, in their attraction, and mutual cohesion, there are not the least traces of indifference or liberty. Every object is determin'd by an absolute fate to a certain degree and direction of its motion, and can no more depart from that precise line, in which it moves, than it can convert itself into an angel, or spirit, or any superior substance. The actions, therefore, of matter are to be regarded as instances of necessary actions ; and whatever is in this respect on the same footing with matter, must be acknowledg'd to be necessary. That we may know whether this be the case with the actions of the mind, we shall begin with examining matter, and considering on what the idea of a necessity in its operations are founded, and why we conclude one body or action to be the infallible cause of another.

It has been observ'd already, that in no single instance the ultimate connexion of any objects is discoverable, either by our senses or reason, and that we can never penetrate so far into the essence and construction of bodies, as to perceive the principle, on which their mutual influence depends. 'Tis their constant union alone, with which we are acquainted ; and 'tis from the constant union the necessity arises. If objects had not an uniform and regular conjunction with each other, we shou'd never arrive at any idea of cause and effect ; and even after all, the necessity, which enters into that idea, is nothing but a determination of the mind to pass from one object to its usual attendant, and infer the existence of one from that of the other. Here then are two particulars, which we are to consider as essential to necessity, *viz.* the constant *union* and the *inference* of the mind ; and wherever we discover these we must acknowledge a necessity. As the actions of matter have no necessity, but what is deriv'd from these circumstances, and it is not by any insight into the essence of bodies we discover their connexion, the absence of this insight, while the union and inference remain, will never in any case, remove the necessity. 'Tis the observation of the union, which produces the inference ; for which reason it might be thought sufficient, if we prove a constant union in the actions of the mind, in order to establish the inference, along with the necessity of these actions. But that I may bestow a greater force on my reasoning, I shall examine these particulars apart, and shall first prove from experience, that our actions have a constant union with our motives, tempers, and circumstances, before I consider the inferences we draw from it.

To this end a very slight and general view of the common course of human affairs will be sufficient. There is no light, in which we can take them, that does not confirm this principle. Whether we consider mankind according to the difference of sexes, ages, governments, conditions, or methods of education; the same uniformity and regular operation of natural principles are discernible. Like causes still produce like effects; in the same manner as in the mutual action of the elements and powers of nature.

There are different trees, which regularly produce fruit, whose relish is different from each other; and this regularity will be admitted as an instance of necessity and causes in external bodies. But are the products of *Guienne* and of *Champagne* more regularly different than the sentiments, actions, and passions of the two sexes, of which the one are distinguish'd by their force and maturity, the other by their delicacy and softness ?

Are the changes of our body from infancy to old age more regular and certain than those of our mind and conduct ? And wou'd a man be more ridiculous, who wou'd expect that an infant of four years old will raise a weight of three hundred pound, than one, who from a person of the same age, wou'd look for a philosophical reasoning, or a prudent and well-concerted action ?

We must certainly allow, that the cohesion of the parts of matter arises from natural and necessary principles, whatever difficulty we may find in explaining them: And for a like reason we must allow, that human society is founded on like principles; and our reason in the latter case, is better than even that in the former; because we not only observe, that men *always* seek society, but can also explain the principles, on which this universal propensity is founded. For is it more certain, that two flat pieces of marble will unite together, than that two young savages of different sexes will copulate? Do the children arise from this copulation more uniformly, than does the parents care for their safety and perservation? And after they have arriv'd at years of discretion by the care of their parents, are the inconveniencies attending their separation more certain than their foresight of these inconveniencies, and their care of avoiding them by a close union and confederacy?

The skin, pores, muscles, and nerves of a day-labourer are different from those of a man of quality: So are his sentiments, actions and manners. The different stations of life influence the whole fabric, external and internal; and these different stations arise necessarily, because uniformly, from the necessary and uniform principles of human nature. Men cannot live without society, and cannot be associated without government. Government makes a distinction of property, and establishes the different ranks of men. This produces industry, traffic, manufactures, law-suits, war, leagues, alliances, voyages, travels, cities, fleets, ports, and all those other actions and objects, which cause such a diversity, and at the same time maintain such an uniformity in human life.

Shou'd a traveller, returning from a far country, tell us, that he had seen a climate in the fiftieth degree of northern latitude, where all the fruits ripen and come to perfection in the winter, and decay in the summer, after the same manner as in *England* they are produc'd and decay in the contrary seasons, he wou'd find few so credulous as to believe him. I am apt to think a traveller wou'd meet with as little credit, who shou'd inform us of people exactly of the same character with those in *Plato's* republic on the one hand, or those in *Hobbes's Leviathan* on the other. There is a general course of nature in human actions, as well as in the operations of the sun and the climate. There are also characters peculiar to different nations and particular persons, as well as common to mankind. The knowledge of these characters is founded on the observation of an uniformity in the actions, that flow from them ; and this uniformity forms the very essence of necessity.

I can imagine only one way of eluding this argument, which is by denying that uniformity of human actions, on which it is founded. As long as actions have a constant union and connexion with the situation and temper of the agent, however we may in words refuse to acknowledge the necessity, we really allow the thing. Now some may, perhaps, find a pretext to deny this regular union and connexion. For what is more capricious than human actions ? What more inconstant than the desires of man ? And what creature departs more widely, not only from right reason, but from his own character and disposition ? An hour, a moment is sufficient to make him change from one extreme to another, and overturn what cost the greatest pain and labour to establish. Necessity is regular and certain. Human conduct is irregular and uncertain. The one, therefore, proceeds not from the other.

To this I reply, that in judging of the actions of men we must proceed upon the same maxims, as when we reason concerning external objects. When any phænomena are constantly and invariably conjoin'd together, they acquire such a connexion in the imagination, that it passes from one to the other, without any doubt or hesitation. But below

this there are many inferior degrees of evidence and probability, nor does one single contrariety of experiment
entirely destroy all our reasoning. The mind ballances the
contrary experiments, and deducting the inferior from the
superior, proceeds with that degree of assurance or evidence,
which remains. Even when these contrary experiments are
entirely equal, we remove not the notion of causes and
necessity ; but supposing that the usual contrariety proceeds
from the operation of contrary and conceal'd causes, we
conclude, that the chance or indifference lies only in our
judgment on account of our imperfect knowledge, not in the
things themselves, which are in every case equally necessary,
tho' to appearance not equally constant or certain. No
union can be more constant and certain, than that of some
actions with some motives and characters ; and if in other
cases the union is uncertain, 'tis no more than what happens
in the operations of body, nor can we conclude any thing
from the one irregularity, which will not follow equally from
the other.

'Tis commonly allow'd that mad-men have no liberty.
But were we to judge by their actions, these have less regularity and constancy than the actions of wise-men, and
consequently are farther remov'd from necessity. Our way
of thinking in this particular is, therefore, absolutely inconsistent ; but is a natural consequence of these confus'd
ideas and undefin'd terms, which we so commonly make use
of in our reasonings, especially on the present subject.

We must now shew, that as the *union* betwixt motives and
actions has the same constancy, as that in any natural
operations, so its influence on the understanding is also the
same, in *determining* us to infer the existence of one from
that of another. If this shall appear, there is no known
circumstance, that enters into the connexion and production
of the actions of matter, that is not to be found in all the
operations of the mind ; and consequently we cannot,

without a manifest absurdity, attribute necessity to the one and refuse it to the other.

There is no philosopher, whose judgment is so riveted to this fantastical system of liberty, as not to acknowledge the force of *moral evidence*, and both in speculation and practice proceed upon it, as upon a reasonable foundation. Now moral evidence is nothing but a conclusion concerning the actions of men, deriv'd from the consideration of their motives, temper and situation. Thus when we see certain characters or figures describ'd upon paper, we infer that the person, who produc'd them, would affirm such facts, the death of *Cæsar*, the success of *Augustus*, the cruelty of *Nero;* and remembring many other concurrent testimonies we conclude, that those facts were once really existent, and that so many men, without any interest, wou'd never conspire to deceive us ; especially since they must, in the attempt, expose themselves to the derision of all their contemporaries, when these facts were asserted to be recent and universally known. The same kind of reasoning runs thro' politics, war, commerce, œconomy, and indeed mixes itself so entirely in human life, that 'tis impossible to act or subsist a moment without having recourse to it. A prince, who imposes a tax upon his subjects, expects their compliance. A general, who conducts an army, makes account of a certain degree of courage. A merchant looks for fidelity and skill in his factor or super-cargo. A man, who gives orders for his dinner, doubts not of the obedience of his servants. In short, as nothing more nearly interests us than our own actions and those of others, the greatest part of our reasonings is employ'd in judgments concerning them. Now I assert, that whoever reasons after this manner, does *ipso facto* believe the actions of the will to arise from necessity, and that he knows not what he means, when he denies it.

All those objects, of which we call the one *cause* and the other *effect*, consider'd in themselves, are as distinct and separate from each other, as any two things in nature, nor can we ever, by the most accurate survey of them, infer the existence of the one from that of the other. 'Tis only from experience and the observation of their constant union, that we are able to form this inference ; and even after all, the inference is nothing but the effects of custom on the imagination. We must not here be content with saying, that the idea of cause and effect arises from objects constantly united ; but must affirm, that 'tis the very same with the idea of these objects, and that the *necessary connexion* is not discover'd by a conclusion of the understanding, but is merely a perception of the mind. Wherever, therefore, we observe the same union, and wherever the union operates in the same manner upon the belief and opinion, we have the idea of causes and necessity, tho' perhaps we may avoid those expressions. Motion in one body in all past instances, that have fallen under our observation, is follow'd upon impulse by motion in another. 'Tis impossible for the mind to penetrate farther. From this constant union it *forms* the idea of cause and effect, and by its influence *feels* the necessity. As there is the same constancy, and the same influence in what we call moral evidence, I ask no more. What remains can only be a dispute of words.

And indeed, when we consider how aptly *natural* and *moral* evidence cement together, and form only one chain of argument betwixt them, we shall make no scruple to allow, that they are of the same nature, and deriv'd from the same principles. A prisoner, who has neither money nor interest discovers the impossibility of his escape, as well from the obstinacy of the gaoler, as from the walls and bars with which he is surrounded ; and in all attempts for his freedom chuses rather to work upon the stone and iron of the one, than upon the inflexible nature of the other. The same prisoner, when conducted to the scaffold, forsees his death as certainly from the constancy and fidelity of his guards as from the operation of the ax or wheel. His mind runs along a certain train of ideas : The refusal of the soldiers to consent to his escape, the action of the excutioner ; the separation of the head and body; bleeding, convulsive motions, and death. Here is a connected chain of natural causes and voluntary actions ; but the mind feels no difference betwixt them in passing from one link to another ; nor is less certain of the future event than if it were connected with the present impressions of the memory and senses by a train of causes cemented together by what we are pleas'd to call a *physical necessity*. The same experienc'd union has the same effect on the mind, whether the united objects be motives, volitions and actions ; or figure and motion. We may change the names of things ; but their nature and their operation on the understanding never change.

I dare be positive no one will ever endeavour to refute these reasonings otherwise than by altering my definitions, and assigning a different meaning to the terms of *cause, and effect, and necessity, and liberty, and chance*. According to my definitions, necessity makes an essential part of causation ; and consequently liberty, by removing necessity, removes also causes, and is the very same thing with chance. As chance is commonly thought to imply a contradiction, and is at least directly contrary to experience, there are always the same arguments against liberty or free-will. If any one alters the definitions, I cannot pretend to argue with him, 'till I know the meaning he assigns to these terms.

SECTION II.

The same subject continu'd.

I BELIEVE we may assign the three following reasons for the prevalence of the doctrine of liberty, however absurd it may be in one sense, and unintelligible in any other. First, After we have perform'd any action ; tho' we confess we were influenc'd by particular views and motives; 'tis difficult for us to perswade ourselves we were govern'd by necessity, and that 'twas utterly impossible for us to have acted otherwise ; the idea of necessity seeming to imply something of force, and violence, and constraint, of which we are not sensible. Few are capable of distinguishing betwixt the liberty of *spontaniety*, as it is call'd in the schools, and the liberty of *indifference;* betwixt that which is oppos'd to violence, and that which means a negation of necessity and causes. The first is even the most common sense of the word ; and as 'tis only that species of liberty, which it concerns us to preserve, our thoughts have been principally turn'd towards it, and have almost universally confounded it with the other.

Secondly, there is a *false sensation or experience* even of the liberty of indifference ; which is regarded as an argument for its real existence. The necessity of any action, whether of matter or of the mind, is not properly a quality in the agent, but in any thinking or intelligent being, who may consider the action, and consists in the determination of his thought to infer its existence from some preceding objects : As liberty or chance, on the other hand, is nothing but the want of that determination, and a certain looseness, which we feel in passing or not passing from the idea of one to that of the other. Now we may observe, that tho' in reflecting on human actions we seldom feel such a looseness or indifference, yet it very commonly happens, that in performing the actions themselves we are sensible of something like it : And as all related or resembling objects are readily taken for each other, this has been employ'd as a demonstrative or even an intuitive proof of human liberty. We feel that our actions are subject to our will on most occasions, and imagine we feel that the will itself is subject to nothing ; because when by a denial of it we are provok'd to try, we feel that it moves easily every way, and produces an image of itself even on that side, on which it did not settle. This image or faint motion, we perswade ourselves, cou'd have been compleated into the thing itself ; because, shou'd that be deny'd, we find, upon a second trial, that it can. But these efforts are all in vain ; and whatever capricious and irregular actions we may perform ; as the desire of showing our liberty is the sole motive of our actions ; we can never free ourselves from the bonds of necessity. We may imagine we feel a liberty within ourselves ; but a spectator can commonly infer our actions from our motives and character ; and even where he cannot, he concludes in general, that he might, were he perfectly acquainted with every circumstance of our situation and temper, and the most secret springs of our complexion and disposition. Now this is the very essence of necessity, according to the foregoing doctrine.

A third reason why the doctrine of liberty has generally been better receiv'd in the world, than its antagonist, proceeds from *religion*, which has been very unnecessarily interested in this question. There is no method of reasoning more common, and yet none more blameable, than in philosophical debates to endeavour to refute any hypothesis by a pretext of its dangerous consequences to religion and morality. When any opinion leads us into absurdities, 'tis certainly false ; but 'tis not certain an opinion is false, because 'tis of dangerous consequence. Such topics, therefore, ought entirely to be foreborn, as serving nothing to the discovery of truth, but only to make the person of an antagonist odious. This I observe in general, without pretending to draw any advantage from it. I submit myself frankly to an examination of this kind, and dare venture to affirm, that the doctrine of necessity, according to my explication of it, is not only innocent, but even advantageous to religion and morality.

I define necessity two ways, conformable to the two definitions of *cause*, of which it makes an essential part. I place it either in the constant union and conjunction of like objects, or in the inference of the mind from the one to the other. Now necessity, in both these senses, has universally, tho' tacitely, in the schools, in the pulpit, and in common life, been allow'd to belong to the will of man, and no one has ever pretended to deny, that we can draw inferences concerning human actions, and that those inferences are founded on the experienc'd union of like actions with like motives and circumstances. The only particular in which any one can differ from me, is either, that perhaps he will refuse to call this necessity. But as long as the meaning is understood, I hope the word can do no harm. Or that he will maintain there is something else in the operations of the matter. Now whether it be so or not is of no consequence to religion, whatever it may be to natural philosophy. I may be mistaken in asserting, that we have no idea of any other connexion in the actions of body, and shall be glad to be farther instructed on that head : But sure I am, I ascribe nothing to the actions of the mind, but what must readily be allow'd of. Let no one, therefore, put an invidious construction on my words, by saying simply, that I assert the necessity of human actions, and place them on the same footing with the operations of senseless matter. I do not ascribe to the will that unintelligible necessity, which is suppos'd to lie in matter. But I ascribe to matter, that intelligible quality, call it necessity or not, which the most rigorous orthodoxy does or must allow to belong to the will. I change, therefore, nothing in the receiv'd systems, with regard to the will, but only with regard to material objects.

Nay I shall go farther, and assert, that this kind of necessity is so essential to religion and morality, that without it there must ensue an absolute subversion of both, and that every other supposition is entirely destructive to all laws both *divine* and *human*. 'Tis indeed certain, that as all human laws are founded on rewards and punishments, 'tis suppos'd as a fundamental principle, that these motives have an influence on the mind, and both produce the good and prevent the evil actions. We may give to this influence what name we please ; but as 'tis usually conjoin'd with the action, common sense requires it shou'd be esteem'd a cause, and be look'd upon as an instance of that necessity, which I wou'd establish.

This reasoning is equally solid, when apply'd to *divine* laws, so far as the deity is consider'd as a legislator, and is suppos'd to inflict punishment and bestow rewards with a design to produce obedience. But I also maintain, that even where he acts not in his magisterial capacity, but is regarded as the avenger of crimes merely on account of their odiousness and deformity, not only 'tis impossible, without the necessary connexion of cause and effect in human actions, that punishments cou'd be inflicted compatible with justice and moral equity ; but also that it cou'd ever enter into the thoughts of any reasonable being to inflict them. The constant and universal object of hatred or anger is a person or creature endow'd with thought and consciousness ; and when any criminal or injurious actions excite that passion, 'tis only by their relation to the person or connexion with him. But according to the doctrine of liberty or chance, this connexion is reduc'd to nothing, nor are men more accountable for those actions, which are design'd and premeditated, than for such as are the most casual and accidental. Actions are by their very nature temporary and perishing ; and where they proceed not from some cause in the characters and disposition of the person, who perform'd them, they infix not themselves upon him, and can neither redound to his honour, if good, nor infamy, if evil. The action itself may be blameable ; it may be contrary to all the rules of morality and religion : But the person is not responsible for it ; and as it proceeded from nothing in him, that is durable or constant, and leaves nothing of that nature behind it, 'tis impossible he can, upon its account, become the object of punishment or vengeance. According to the hypothesis of liberty, therefore, a man is as pure and untainted, after having committed the most horrid crimes, as at the first moment of his birth, nor is his character any way concern'd in his actions ; since they are not deriv'd from it, and the wickedness of the one can never be us'd as a proof of the depravity of the other. 'Tis only upon the principles of necessity, that a person acquires any merit or demerit from his actions, however the common opinion may incline to the contrary.

But so inconsistent are men with themselves, that tho' they often assert, that necessity utterly destroys all merit and demerit either towards mankind or superior powers, yet they continue still to reason upon these very principles of necessity in all their judgments concerning this matter. Men are not blam'd for such evil actions as they perform ignorantly and casually, whatever may be their consequences. Why? but because the causes of these actions are only momentary, and terminate in them alone. Men are less blam'd for such evil actions, as they perform hastily and unpremeditately, than for such as proceed from thought and deliberation. For what reason? but because a hasty temper, tho' a constant cause in the mind, operates only by intervals, and infects not the whole character. Again, repentance wipes off every crime, especially if attended with an evident reformation of life and manners. How is this to be accounted for? But by asserting that actions render a person criminal, merely as they are proofs of criminal passions or principles in the mind; and when by any alteration of these principles they cease to be just proofs, they likewise cease to be criminal. But according to the doctrine of *liberty* or *chance* they never were just proofs, and consequently never were criminal.

Here then I turn to my adversary, and desire him to free his own system from these odious consequences before he charge them upon others. Or if he rather chuses, that this question shou'd be decided by fair arguments before philosophers, than by declamations before the people, let him return to what I have advanc'd to prove that liberty and chance are synonimous; and concerning the nature of moral evidence and the regularity of human actions. Upon a review of these reasonings, I cannot doubt of an entire victory; and therefore having prov'd, that all actions of the will have particular causes, I proceed to explain what these causes are, and how they operate.

SECTION III.

Of the influencing motives of the will.

NOTHING is more usual in philosophy, and even in common life, than to talk of the combat of passion and reason, to give the preference to reason, and to assert that men are only so far virtuous as they conform themselves to its dictates. Every rational creature, 'tis said, is oblig'd to regulate his actions by reason; and if any other motive or principle challenge the direction of his conduct, he ought to oppose it, 'till it be entirely subdu'd, or at least brought to a conformity with that superior principle. On this method of thinking the greatest part of moral philosophy, ancient and modern, seems to be founded; nor is there an ampler field, as well for metaphysical arguments, as popular declamations, than this suppos'd pre-eminence of reason above passion. The eternity, invariableness, and divine origin of the former have been display'd to the best advantage : The blindness, unconstancy, and deceitfulness of the latter have been as strongly insisted on. In order to shew the fallacy of all this philosophy, I shall endeavour to prove *first*, that reason alone can never be a motive to any action of the will ; and *secondly*, that it can never oppose passion in the direction of the will.

The understanding exerts itself after two different ways, as it judges from demonstration or probability ; as it regards the abstract relations of our ideas, or those relations of objects, of which experience only gives us information. I believe it scarce will be asserted, that the first species of reasoning alone is ever the cause of any action. As it's proper province is the world of ideas, and as the will always places us in that of realities, demonstration and volition seem, upon that account, to be totally remov'd, from each other. Mathematics, indeed, are useful in all mechanical operations, and arithmetic in almost every art and profession : But 'tis not of themselves they have any influence. Mechanics are the art of regulating the motions of bodies *to some design'd end or purpose;* and the reason why we employ arithmetic in fixing the proportions of numbers, is only that we may discover the proportions of their influence and operation. A merchant is desirous of knowing the sum total of his accounts with any person : Why? but that he may learn what sum will have the same *effects* in paying his debt, and going to market, as all the particular articles taken together. Abstract or demonstrative reasoning, therefore, never influences any of our actions, but only as it directs our judgment concerning causes and effects ; which leads us to the second operation of the understanding.

'Tis obvious, that when we have the prospect of pain or pleasure from any object, we feel a consequent emotion of aversion or propensity, and are carry'd to avoid or embrace what will give us this uneasiness or satisfaction. 'Tis also obvious, that this emotion rests not here, but making us cast our view on every side, comprehends whatever objects are connected with its original one by the relation of cause and effect. Here then reasoning takes place to discover this relation ; and according as our reasoning varies, our actions receive a subsequent variation. But 'tis evident in this case, that the impulse arises not from reason, but is only directed by it. 'Tis from the prospect of pain or pleasure that the aversion or propensity arises towards any object : And these emotions extend themselves to the causes and effects of that object, as they are pointed out to us by reason and experience. It can never in the least concern us to know, that such objects are causes, and such others effects, if both the causes and effects be indifferent to us. Where the objects themselves do not affect us, their connexion can never give them any influence ; and 'tis plain, that as reason is nothing but the discovery of this connexion, it cannot be by its means that the objects are able to affect us.

Since reason alone can never produce any action, or give rise to volition, I infer, that the same faculty is as incapable of preventing volition, or of disputing the preference with any passion or emotion. This consequence is necessary. 'Tis impossible reason cou'd have the latter effect of preventing volition, but by giving an impulse in a contrary direction to our passion ; and that impulse, had it operated alone, wou'd have been able to produce volition. Nothing can oppose or retard the impulse of passion, but a contrary impulse ; and if this contrary impulse ever arises from reason, that latter faculty must have an original influence on the will, and must be able to cause, as well as hinder any act of volition. But if reason has no original influence, 'tis impossible it can withstand any principle, which has such an efficacy, or ever keep the mind in suspense a moment. Thus it appears, that the principle, which opposes our passion, cannot be the same with reason, and is only call'd so in an improper sense. We speak not strictly and philosophically when we talk of the combat of passion and of reason. Reason is, and ought only to be the slave of the passions, and can never pretend to any other office than to serve and obey them. As this opinion may appear somewhat extraordinary, it may not be improper to confirm it by some other considerations.

A passion is an original existence, or if you will, modi-fication of existence, and contains not any representative quality, which renders it a copy of any other existence or modification. When I am angry, I am actually possest with the passion, and in that emotion have no more a reference to any other object, than when I am thirsty, or sick, or more than five foot high. 'Tis impossible, therefore, that this passion can be oppos'd by, or be contradictory to truth and reason ; since this contradiction consists in the disagreement of ideas, consider'd as copies, with those objects, which they represent.

What may at first occur on this head, is, that as nothing can be contrary to truth or reason, except what has a reference to it, and as the judgments of our understanding only have this reference, it must follow, that passions can be contrary to reason only so far as they are *accompany'd* with some judgment or opinion. According to this principle, which is so obvious and natural, 'tis only in two senses, that any affection can be call'd unreasonable. First, When a passion, such as hope or fear, grief or joy, despair or security, is founded on the supposition of the existence of objects, which really do not exist. Secondly, When in exerting any passion in action, we chuse means insufficient for the design'd end, and deceive ourselves in our judgment of causes and effects. Where a passion is neither founded on false suppositions, nor chuses means insufficient for the end, the understanding can neither justify nor condemn it. 'Tis not contrary to reason to prefer the destruction of the whole world to the scratching of my finger. 'Tis not contrary to reason for me to chuse my total ruin, to prevent the least uneasiness of an *Indian* or person wholly unknown to me. 'Tis as little contrary to reason to prefer even my own acknowledg'd lesser good to my greater, and have a more ardent affection for the former than the latter. A trivial good may, from certain circumstances, produce a desire superior to what arises from the greatest and most valuable enjoyment ; nor is there anything more extraordinary in this, than in mechanics to see one pound weight raise up a hundred by the advantage of its situation. In short, a passion must be accompany'd with some false judgment, in order to its being unreasonable ; and even then 'tis not the passion, properly speaking, which is unreasonable, but the judgment.

The consequences are evident. Since a passion can never, in any sense, be call'd unreasonable, but when founded on a false supposition, or when it chuses means insufficient for the design'd end, 'tis impossible, that reason and passion can ever oppose each other, or dispute for the government of the will and actions. The moment we perceive the falshood of any supposition, or the insufficiency of any means our passions yield to our reason without any opposition. I may desire any fruit of an excellent relish ; but whenever you convince me of my mistake, my longing ceases. I may will the performance of certain actions as means of obtaining any desir'd good ; but as my willing of these actions is only secondary, and founded on the supposition, that they are causes of the propos'd effect ; as soon as I discover the falshood of that supposition, they must become indifferent to me.

'Tis natural for one, that does not examine objects with a strict philosophic eye, to imagine, that those actions of the mind are entirely the same, which produce not a different sensation, and are not immediately distinguishable to the feeling and perception. Reason, for instance, exerts itself without producing any sensible emotion ; and **except in the** more sublime disquisitions of philosophy, or in the frivolous subtilties of the schools, scarce ever conveys any pleasure or uneasiness. Hence it proceeds, that every action of the mind, which operates with the same calmness and tranquillity, is confounded with reason by all those, who judge of things from the first view and appearance. Now 'tis certain, there are certain calm desires and tendencies, which, tho' they be real passions, produce little emotion in the mind, and are more known by their effects than by the immediate feeling or sensation. These desires are of two kinds ; either certain instincts originally implanted in our natures, such as benevolence and resentment, the love of life, and kindness to children ; or the general appetite to good, and aversion to evil, consider'd merely as such. When any of these passions are calm, and cause no disorder in the soul, they are very readily taken for the determinations of reason, and are suppos'd to proceed from the same faculty, with that, which judges of truth and falshood. Their nature and principles have been supposed the same, because their sensations are not evidently different.

Beside these calm passions, which often determine the will, there are certain violent emotions of the same kind, which have likewise a great influence on that faculty. When I receive any injury from another, I often feel a violent passion of resentment, which makes me desire his evil and punishment, independent of all considerations of pleasure and advantage to myself. When I am immediately threaten'd with any grievous ill, my fears, apprehensions, and aversions rise to a great height, and produce a sensible emotion.

The common error of metaphysicians has lain in ascribing the direction of the will entirely to one of these principles, and supposing the other to have no influence. Men often act knowingly against their interest : For which reason the view of the greatest possible good does not always influence them.   Men often counter-act a violent passion in prosecution of their interests and designs: 'Tis not therefore the present uneasiness alone, which determines them.   In general we may observe, that both these principles operate on the will ; and where they are contrary, that either of them prevails, according to the *general* character or *present* disposition of the person.   What we call strength of mind, implies the prevalence of the calm passions above the violent ; tho' we may easily observe, there is no man so constantly possess'd of this virtue, as never on any occasion to yield to the solicitations of passion and desire.   From these variations of temper proceeds the great difficulty of deciding concerning the actions and resolutions of men, where there is any contrariety of motives and passions.

SECTION IV.

Of the causes of the violent passions.

THERE is not in philosophy a subject of more nice speculation than this of the different *causes* and *effects* of the calm and violent passions.   'Tis evident passions influence not the will in proportion to their violence, or the disorder they occasion in the temper ; but on the contrary, that when a passion has once become a settled principle of action, and is the predominant inclination of the soul, it commonly produces no longer any sensible agitation.   As repeated custom and its own force have made every thing yield to it, it directs the actions and conduct without that opposition and emotion, which so naturally attend every momentary gust of passion.   We must, therefore, distinguish betwixt a calm and a weak passion ; betwixt a violent and a strong one.   But notwithstanding this, 'tis certain, that when we wou'd govern a man, and push him to any action, 'twill commonly be better policy to work upon the violent than the calm passions, and rather take him by his inclination, than what is vulgarly call'd his *reason.* We ought to place the object in such particular situations as are proper to encrease the violence of the passion. For we may observe, that all depends upon the situation of the object, and that a variation in this particular will be able to change the calm and the violent passions into each other. Both these kinds of passions pursue good, and avoid evil; and both of them are encreas'd or diminish'd by the encrease or diminution of the good or evil. But herein lies the difference betwixt them : The same good, when near, will cause a violent passion, which, when remote, produces only a calm one. As this subject belongs very properly to the present question concerning the will, we shall here examine it to the bottom, and shall consider some of those circumstances and situations of objects, which render a passion either calm or violent.

'Tis a remarkable property of human nature, that any emotion, which attends a passion, is easily converted into it, tho' in their natures they be originally different from, and even contrary to each other. 'Tis true ; in order to make a perfect union among passions, there is always requir'd a double relation of impressions and ideas ; nor is one relation sufficient for that purpose. But tho' this be confirm'd by undoubted experience, we must understand it with its proper limitations, and must regard the double relation, as requisite only to make one passion produce another. When two passions are already produc'd by their separate causes, and are both present in the mind, they readily mingle and unite, tho' they have but one relation, and sometimes without any. The predominant passion swallows up the inferior, and converts it into itself. The spirits, when once excited, easily receive a change in their direction ; and 'tis natural to imagine this change will come from the prevailing affection. The connextion is in many respects closer betwixt any two passions, than betwixt any passion and indifference.

When a person is once heartily in love, the little faults and caprice of his mistress, the jealousies and quarrels, to which that commerce is so subject ; however unpleasant and related to anger and hatred ; are yet found to give additional force to the prevailing passion. 'Tis a common artifice of politicians, when they wou'd affect any person very much by a matter of fact, of which they intend to inform him, first to excite his curiosity ; delay as long as possible the satisfying it ; and by that means raise his anxiety and impatience to the utmost, before they give him a full insight into the business. They know that his curiosity will precipitate him into the passion they design to raise, and assist the object in its influence on the mind. A soldier advancing to the battle, is naturally inspir'd with courage and confidence, when he thinks on his friends and fellow-soldiers ; and is struck with fear and terror, when he reflects on the enemy. Whatever new emotion, therefore, proceeds from the former naturally encreases the courage ; as the same emotion, proceeding from the latter, augments the fear ; by the relation of ideas, and the conversion of the inferior emotion into the predominant. Hence it is that in martial discipline, the uniformity and lustre of our habit, the regularity of our figures and motions, with all the pomp and majesty of war, encourage ourselves and allies ; while the same objects in the enemy strike terror into us, tho' agreeable and beautiful in themselves.

Since passions, however independent, are naturally transfus'd into each other, if they are both present at the same time ; it follows, that when good or evil is plac'd in such a situation, as to cause any particular emotion, beside its direct passion of desire or aversion, that latter passion must acquire new force and violence.

This happens, among other cases, whenever any object excites contrary passions. For 'tis observable that an opposition of passions commonly causes a new emotion in the spirits, and produces more disorder, than the concurrence of any two affections of equal force. This new emotion is easily converted into the predominant passion, and encreases its violence, beyond the pitch it wou'd have ariv'd at had it met with no opposition. Hence we naturally desire what is forbid, and take a pleasure in performing actions, merely because they are unlawful. The notion of duty, when opposite to the passions, is seldom able to overcome them; and when it fails of that effect, is apt rather to encrease them, by producing an opposition in our motives and principles.

The same effect follows whether the opposition arises from internal motives or external obstacles. The passion commonly acquires new force and violence in both cases. The efforts, which the mind makes to surmount the obstacle, excite the spirits and enliven the passion.

Uncertainty has the same influence as opposition. The agitation of the thought; the quick turns it makes from one view to another; the variety of passions, which succeed each other, according to the different views: All these produce an agitation in the mind, and transfuse themselves into the predominant passion.

There is not in my opinion any other natural cause, why security diminishes the passions, than because it removes that uncertainty, which encreases them. The mind, when left to itself, immediately languishes; and in order to preserve its ardour, must be every moment supported by a new flow of passion. For the same reason, despair, tho' contrary to security, has a like influence.

'Tis certain nothing more powerfully animates any affection, than to conceal some part of its object by throwing it into a kind of shade, which at the same time that it shews enough to pre-possess us in favour of the object, leaves still some work for the imagination. Besides that obscurity is always attended with a kind of uncertainty; the effort, which the fancy makes to compleat the idea, rouzes the spirits, and gives an additional force to the passion.

As despair and security, tho' contrary to each other, produce the same effects; so absence is observ'd to have contrary effects, and in different circumstances either encreases or diminishes our affections. The *Duc de la Rochefoucault* has very well observ'd, that absence destroys weak passions, but encreases strong ; as the wind extinguishes a candle, but blows up a fire. Long absence naturally weakens our idea, and diminishes the passion : But where the idea is so strong and lively as to support itself, the uneasiness, arising from absence, encreases the passion, and gives it new force and violence.

SECTION V.

Of the effects of custom.

But nothing has a greater effect both to encrease and diminish our passions, to convert pleasure into pain, and pain into pleasure, than custom and repetition. Custom has two *original* effects upon the mind, in bestowing a *facility* in the performance of any action or the conception of any object; and afterwards a *tendency or inclination* towards it ; and from these we may account for all its other effects, however extraordinary.

When the soul applies itself to the performance of any action, or the conception of any object, to which it is not accustom'd, there is a certain unpliableness in the faculties, and a difficulty of the spirit's moving in their new direction. As this difficulty excites the spirits, 'tis the source of wonder, surprise, and of all the emotions, which arise from novelty; and is in itself very agreeable, like every thing, which inlivens the mind to a moderate degree. But tho' surprize be agreeable in itself, yet as it puts the spirits in agitation, it not only augments our agreeable affections, but also our painful, according to the foregoing principle, *that every emotion, which precedes or attends a passion, is easily converted into it.* Hence every thing, that is new, is most affecting, and gives us either more pleasure or pain, than what, strictly speaking, naturally belongs to it. When it often returns upon us, the novelty wears off ; the passions subside ; the hurry of the spirits is over ; and we survey the objects with greater tranquillity.

By degrees the repetition produces a facility, which is another very powerful principle of the human mind, and an infallible source of pleasure, where the facility goes not beyond a certain degree. And here 'tis remarkable that the pleasure, which arises from a moderate facility, has not the same tendency with that which arises from novelty, to augment the painful, as well as the agreeable affections, The pleasure of facility does not so much consist in any ferment of the spirits, as in their orderly motion ; which will sometimes be so powerful as even to convert pain into pleasure, and give us a relish in time for what at first was most harsh and disagreeable.

But again, as facility converts pain into pleasure, so it often converts pleasure into pain, when it is too great, and renders the actions of the mind so faint and languid, that they are no longer able to interest and support it. And indeed, scarce any other objects become disagreeable thro' custom ; but such as are naturally attended with some emotion or affection, which is destroy'd by the too frequent repetition. One can consider the clouds, and heavens, and trees, and stones, however frequently repeated, without ever feeling any aversion. But when the fair sex, or music, or good cheer, or any thing, that naturally ought to be agreeable, becomes indifferent, it easily produces the opposite affection.

But custom not only gives a facility to perform any action, but likewise an inclination and tendency towards it, where it is not entirely disagreeable, and can never be the object of inclination. And this is the reason why custom encreases all *active* habits, but diminishes *passive*, according to the observation of a late eminent philosopher. The facility takes off from the force of the passive habits by rendering the motion of the spirits faint and languid. But as in the active, the spirits are sufficiently supported of themselves, the tendency of the mind gives them new force, and bends them more strongly to the action.

[Section VI., which is a very short one, examines the influence of the imagination on the passions. The general view advanced is that an idea of particular pleasures exercises a stronger influence than a general idea. "Any pleasure, with which we are acquainted, affects us more than any other, which we own to be superior, but of whose nature we are wholly ignorant. Of the one we can form a particular and determinate idea : the other we conceive under the general notion of pleasure ; and 'tis certain, that the more general and universal any of our ideas are, the less influence they have upon the imagination," and hence have less upon the passions and the will.

"Contiguity and distance in space and time," as characteristic of objects of the mind show the same difference of influence as "particular" and "general" ideas. Objects at a distance which if present would move our desires are more or less ineffective, and those remote in time have the same effect, past time being less influential than the present. "Contiguous objects must have an influence much superior to the distant and remote. Accordingly we find in common life, that men are principally concern'd about those objects,

which are not much removed in space or time, enjoying the
present and leaving what is afar off to the care of chance
and fortune. Talk to a man of his condition thirty years
hence, and he will not regard you. Speak of what is to
happen to-morrow, and he will lend you attention. The
breaking of a mirror gives us more concern when at home,
than the burning of a house when abroad, and some hundred leagues distant." This difference of attractive and
stimulating effect avails to influence the imagination and the
passions according to the same law, and hence the will is
influenced in a way to show which is the stronger motive to
volition.

The ninth section is a consideration of the direct passions
grief and sorrow, fear and hope, desire and aversion, which
had been mentioned and discussed briefly when treating of
the will. But nothing is remarked of any importance either
to the free will controversy or having any bearing upon subsequent questions. Hume himself remarks of them : "None
of the direct affections seem to merit our particular attention, except hope and fear, which we shall here endeavor to
account for." He regards them both as mixtures of joy and
grief, their difference being determined by the different proportions in which they are combined, or by the degree of
probability connected with a prospective event. They affect
the will according to their intensity.

The last section treats of " curiosity or the love of truth "
as a passion. The only interest which attaches to his treatment of it is his comparison of it to the passion of hunting.
It affects the will merely as all other passions.]

BOOK III.

OF MORALS.

PART I.

OF VIRTUE AND VICE IN GENERAL.

SECTION I.

Moral Distinctions not deriv'd from Reason.

THERE is an inconvenience which attends all abstruse reasoning, that it may silence, without convincing an antagonist, and requires the same intense study to make us sensible of its force, that was at first requisite for its invention. When we leave our closet, and engage in the common affairs of life, its conclusions seem to vanish, like the phantoms of the night on the appearance of the morning ; and 'tis difficult for us to retain even that conviction, which we had attain'd with difficulty. This is still more conspicuous in a long chain of reasoning, where we must preserve to the end the evidence of the first propositions, and where we often lose sight of all the most receiv'd maxims, either of philosophy or common life. I am not, however, without hopes, that the present system of philosophy will acquire new force as it advances ; and that our reasonings concerning *morals* will corroborate whatever has been said concerning the *understanding* and the *passions*. Morality is a subject that interests us above all others : We fancy the peace of society to be at stake in every decision concerning it ; and 'tis evident, that this concern must make our speculations appear more real and solid, than where the subject is, in a great measure, indifferent to us. What affects us, we conclude can never be a chimera ; and as our passion is engag'd on the one side or the other, we naturally think that the question lies within human comprehension ; which, in other cases of this nature, we are apt to entertain some doubt of. Without this advantage I never should have ventur'd upon a third volume of such abstruse philosophy, in an age, wherein the greatest part of men seem agreed to convert reading into an amusement, and to reject every thing that requires any considerable degree of attention to be comprehended.

It has been observ'd, that nothing is ever present to the mind but its perceptions ; and that all the actions of seeing, hearing, judging, loving, hating, and thinking, fall under this denomination. The mind can never exert itself in any action, which we may not comprehend under the term of *perception;* and consequently that term is no less applicable to those judgments, by which we distinguish moral good and evil, than to every other operation of the mind. To approve of one character, to condemn another, are only so many different perceptions.

Now as perceptions resolve themselves into two kinds, viz., *impressions* and *ideas*, this distinction gives rise to a question, with which we shall open up our present enquiry concerning morals, *Whether 'tis by means of our* ideas *or* impressions *we distinguish betwixt vice and virtue, and pronounce an action blameable or praise-worthy?* This will immediately cut off all loose discourses and declamations, and reduce us to something precise and exact on the present subject.

Those who affirm that virtue is nothing but a conformity to reason ; that there are eternal fitnesses and unfitnesses of things, which are the same to every rational being that considers them ; that the immutable measures of right and wrong impose an obligation, not only on human creatures, but also on the Deity himself : All these systems concur in the opinion, that morality, like truth, is discern'd merely by ideas, and by their juxta-position and comparison. In order, therefore, to judge of these systems, we need only consider, whether it be possible, from reason alone, to distinguish betwixt moral good and evil, or whether there must concur some other principles to enable us to make that distinction.

If morality had naturally no influence on human passions and actions, 'twere in vain to take such pains to inculcate it ; and nothing wou'd be more fruitless than that multitude of rules and precepts, with which all moralists abound. Philosophy is commonly divided into *speculative* and *practical;* and as morality is always comprehended under the latter division, 'tis supposed to influence our passions and actions, and to go beyond the calm and indolent judgments of the understanding. And this is confirm'd by common experience, which informs us, that men are often govern'd by their duties, and are deter'd from some actions by the opinion of injustice, and impell'd to others by that of obligation.

Since morals, therefore, have an influence on the actions and affections, it follows, that they cannot be deriv'd from reason ; and that because reason alone, as we have already prov'd, can never have any such influence. Morals excite passions, and produce or prevent actions. Reason of itself is utterly impotent in this particular. The rules of morality, therefore, are not conclusions of our reason.

No one, I believe, will deny the justness of this inference ; nor is there any other means of evading it, than by denying that principle, on which it is founded. As long as it is allow'd, that reason has no influence on our passions and actions, 'tis in vain to pretend, that morality is discover'd only by a deduction of reason. An active principle can never be founded on an inactive ; and if reason be inactive in itself, it must remain so in all its shapes and appearances, whether it exerts itself in natural or moral subjects, whether it considers the powers of external bodies, or the actions of rational beings.

It would be tedious to repeat all the arguments, by which I have prov'd[1], that reason is perfectly inert, and can never either prevent or produce any action or affection. "Twill be easy to recollect what has been said upon that subject. I shall only recal on this occasion one of these arguments, which I shall endeavour to render still more conclusive, and more applicable to the present subject.

Reason is the discovery of truth or falsehood. Truth or falsehood consists in an agreement or disagreement either to the *real* relations of ideas, or to *real* existence and matter of fact. Whatever, therefore, is not susceptible of this agreement or disagreement, is incapable of being true or false, and can never be an object of our reason. Now 'tis evident our passions, volitions, and actions, are not susceptible of any such agreement or disagreement ; being original facts and realities, compleat in themselves, and implying no reference to other passions, volitions, and actions. 'Tis impossible, therefore, they can be pronounced either true or false, and be either contrary or comformable to reason.

This argument is of double advantage to our present purpose. For it proves *directly*, that actions do not derive their merit from a conformity to reason, nor their blame from a contrariety to it ; and it proves the same truth more *indirectly*, by shewing us, that as reason can never immediately prevent or produce any action by contradicting or approving of it, it cannot be the source of moral good and evil, which are found to have that influence. Actions may be laudable or blameable ; but they cannot be reasonable or unreasonable : Laudable or blameable, therefore, are not the same with reasonable or unreasonable. The merit and demerit of actions frequently contradict, and sometimes con-

[1] Book II. Part III. sect. 3.

troul our natural propensities. But reason has no such influence. Moral distinctions, therefore, are not the offspring of reason. Reason is wholly inactive, and can never be the source of so active a principle as conscience, or a sense of morals.

But perhaps it may be said, that tho' no will or action can be immediately contradictory to reason, yet we may find such a contradiction in some of the attendants of the action, that is, in its causes or effects. The action may cause a judgment, or may be *obliquely* caus'd by one, when the judgment concurs with a passion ; and by an abusive way of speaking, which philosophy will scarce allow of, the same contrariety may, upon that account, be ascrib'd to the action. How far this truth or falshood may be the source of morals, 'twill now be proper to consider.

It has been observ'd, that reason, in a strict and philosophical sense, can have an influence on our conduct only after two ways : Either when it excites a passion by informing us of the existence of something which is a proper object of it ; or when it discovers the connexion of causes and effects, so as to afford us means of exerting any passion. These are the only kinds of judgment, which can accompany our actions, or can be said to produce them in any manner ; and it must be allow'd, that these judgments may often be false and erroneous. A person may be affected with passion, by supposing a pain or pleasure to lie in an object, which has no tendency to produce either of these sensations, or which produces the contrary to what is imagin'd. A person may also take false measures for the attaining his end, and may retard, by his foolish conduct, instead of forwarding the execution of any project. These false judgments may be thought to affect the passions and actions, which are connected with them, and may be said to render them unreasonable, in a figurative and improper way of speaking. But tho' this be acknowledg'd, 'tis easy to observe, that these errors are so far from being the source of all immorality, that they are commonly very innocent, and draw no manner of guilt upon the person who is so unfortunate as to fall into them. They extend not beyond a mistake of *fact*, which moralists have not generally suppos'd criminal, as being perfectly involuntary. I am more to be lamented than blam'd if I am mistaken with regard to the influence of objects in producing pain or pleasure, or if I know not the proper means of satisfying my desires. No one can ever regard such errors as a defect in my moral character. A fruit, for instance, that is really disagreeable, appears to me at a distance, and thro' mistake I fancy it to be pleasant and delicious. Here is one error. I choose certain means of reaching this fruit, which are not proper for my end. Here is a second error; nor is there any third one, which can ever possibly enter into our reasonings concerning actions. I ask, therefore, if a man, in this situation, and guilty of these two errors, is to be regarded as vicious and criminal, however unavoidable they might have been? Or if it be possible to imagine, that such errors are the sources of all immorality?

And here it may be proper to observe, that if moral distinctions be deriv'd from the truth or falshood of those judgments, they must take place wherever we form the judgments; nor will there be any difference, whether the question be concerning an apple or a kingdom, or whether the error be avoidable or unavoidable. For as the very essence of morality is suppos'd to consist in an agreement or disagreement to reason, the other circumstances are entirely arbitrary, and can never either bestow on any action the character of virtuous or vicious, or deprive it of that character. To which we may add, that this agreement or disagreement, not admitting of degrees, all virtues and vices wou'd of course be equal.

Shou'd it be pretended, that tho' a mistake of *fact* be not criminal, yet a mistake of *right* often is; and that this may be the source of immorality : I would answer, that 'tis impossible such a mistake can ever be the original source of immorality, since it supposes a real right and wrong ; that is, a real distinction in morals, independent of these judgments. A mistake, therefore, of right may become a species of immorality ; but 'tis only a secondary one, and is founded on some other, antecedent to it.

As to those judgments which are the *effects* of our actions, and which, when false, give occasion to pronounce the actions contrary to truth and reason ; we may observe, that our actions never cause any judgment, either true or false, in ourselves, and that 'tis only on others they have such an influence. 'Tis certain, that an action, on many occasions, may give rise to false conclusions in others ; and that a person, who thro' a window sees any lewd behaviour of mine with my neighbour's wife, may be so simple as to imagine she is certainly my own. In this respect my action resembles somewhat a lye or falshood ; only with this difference, which is material, that I perform not the action with any intention of giving rise to a false judgment in another, but merely to satisfy my lust and passion. It causes, however, a mistake and false judgment by accident ; and the falshood of its effects may be ascribed, by some odd figurative way of speaking, to the action itself. But still I can see no pretext of reason for asserting, that the tendency to cause such an error is the first spring or original source of all immorality [1].

[1] One might think it were entirely superfluous to prove this, if a late author [Wollaston], who has had the good fortune to obtain some reputation, had not seriously affirmed, that such a falshood is the foundation of all guilt and moral deformity. That we may discover the fallacy of his hypothesis, we need only consider, that a false conclusion is drawn from an action, only by means of an obscurity of natural principles, which makes a cause be secretly interrupted in its operation, by contrary causes, and renders the connection betwixt two objects uncertain and variable. Now, as a like uncertainty and variety of causes take place, even in natural objects, and produce a like error in our judgment, if that tendency to produce error were the very essence of vice and

Thus upon the whole, 'tis impossible, that the distinction betwixt moral good and evil, can be made by reason ; since that distinction has an influence upon our actions, of which reason alone is incapable. Reason and judgment may, indeed, be the mediate cause of an action, by prompting, or by directing a passion : But it is not pretended, that a judgment of this kind, either in its truth or falshood, is attended with virtue or vice. And as to the judgments which are caused by our judgments, they can still less bestow those moral qualities on the actions, which are their causes.

But to be more particular, and to shew, that those eternal immutable fitnesses and unfitnesses of things cannot be defended by sound philosophy, we may weigh the following considerations.

If the thought and understanding were alone capable of fixing the boundaries of right and wrong, the character of immorality, it shou'd follow, that even inanimate objects might be vicious and immoral.

'Tis in vain to urge, that inanimate objects act without liberty and choice. For as liberty and choice are not necessary to make an action produce in us an erroneous conclusion, they can be, in no respect, essential to morality ; and I do not readily perceive, upon this system, how they can ever come to be regarded by it. If the tendency to cause error be the origin of immorality, that tendency and immorality wou'd in every case be inseparable.

Add to this, that if I had used the precaution of shutting the windows, while I indulg'd myself in those liberties with my neighbour's wife, I should have been guilty of no immorality ; and that because my action, being perfectly conceal'd, wou'd have had no tendency to produce any false conclusion.

For the same reason, a thief, who steals in by a ladder at a window, and takes all imaginable care to cause no disturbance, is in no respect criminal. For either he will not be perceiv'd, or if he be, 'tis impossible he can produce any error, nor will anyone, from these circumstances, take him to be other than what he really is.

'Tis well known, that those who are squint-sighted, do very readily cause mistakes in others, and that we imagine they salute or are talking to one person, while they address themselves to another. Are they therefore, upon that account, immoral ?

Besides, we may easily observe, that in all those arguments there is an evident reasoning in a circle. A person who takes possession of *another's* goods, and uses them as his *own*, in a manner declares them virtuous and vicious either must lie in some relations of objects, or must be a matter of fact, which is discovered by our reasoning. This consequence is evident. As the operations of human understanding divide themselves into two kinds, the comparing of ideas, and the inferring of matter of fact ; were virtue discover'd by the understanding ; it must be an object of one of these operations, nor is there any third operation of the understanding, which can discover it. There has been an opinion very industriously propagated by certain philosophers, that morality is susceptible of demonstration ; and tho' no one has ever been able to advance a single step in those demonstrations ; yet 'tis taken for granted, that this science may be brought to an equal certainty with geometry or algebra. Upon this supposition, vice and virtue must consist in some relations ; since 'tis allow'd on all hands, that no matter of fact is

to be his own ; and this falshood is the source of the immorality of injustice. But is property, or right, or obligation, intelligible, without an antecedent morality?

A man that is ungrateful to his benefactor, in a manner affirms, that he never received any favours from him. But in what manner? Is it because 'tis his duty to be grateful? But this supposes, that there is some antecedent rule of duty and morals. Is it because human nature is generally grateful, and makes us conclude, that a man who does any harm never received any favour from the person he harm'd? But human nature is not so generally grateful, as to justify such a conclusion. Or if it were, is an exception to a general rule in every case criminal, for no other reason than because it is an exception?

But what may suffice entirely to destroy this whimsical system is, that it leaves us under the same difficulty to give a reason why truth is virtuous and falshood vicious, as to account for the merit or turpitude of any other action. I shall allow, if you please, that all immorality is derived from this supposed falsehood in action, provided you can give me any plausible reason, why such a falshood is immoral. If you consider rightly of the matter, you will find yourself in the same difficulty as at the beginning.

This last argument is very conclusive ; because, if there be not an evident merit or turpitude annex'd to this species of truth or falshood, it can never have any influence upon our actions. For, who ever thought of forbearing any action, because others might possibly draw false conclusions from it? Or, who ever perform'd any, that he might give rise to true conclusions?

capable of being demonstrated. Let us, therefore, begin with examining this hypothesis, and endeavour, if possible, to fix those moral qualities, which have been so long the objects of our fruitless researches. Point out distinctly the relations, which constitute morality or obligation, that we may know wherein they consist, and after what manner we must judge of them.

If you assert that vice and virtue consist in relations susceptible of certainty and demonstration, you must confine yourself to those *four* relations, which alone admit of that degree of evidence ; and in that case you run into absurdities, from which you will never be able to extricate yourself. For as you make the very essence of morality to lie in the relations, and as there is no one of these relations but what is applicable, not only to an irrational, but also to an inanimate object ; it follows, that even such objects must be susceptible of merit or demerit. *Resemblance, contrariety, degrees in quality,* and *proportions in quantity and number ;* all these relations belong as properly to matter, as to our actions, passions, and volitions. 'Tis unquestionable, therefore, that morality lies not in any of these relations, nor the sense of it in their discovery.[1]

[1] As a proof, how confus'd our way of thinking on this subject commonly is, we may observe, that those who assert, that morality is demonstrable, do not say, that morality lies in the relations, and that the relations are distinguishable by reason. They only say, that reason can discover such an action, in such relations, to be virtuous, and such another vicious. It seems they thought it sufficient, if they cou'd bring the word, Relation, into the proposition, without troubling themselves whether it was to the purpose or not. But here, I think, is plain argument. Demonstrative reason discovers only relations. But that reason, according to this hypothesis, discovers also vice and virtue. These moral qualities, therefore, must be relations. When we blame any action, in any situation, the whole complicated object, of action and situation, must form certain relations, wherein the essence of vice consists. This hypothesis is not otherwise intelligible. For what does reason discover, when it pronounces any action vicious? Does it discover a relation or a matter of fact? These questions are decisive, and must not be eluded.

Shou'd it be asserted, that the sense of morality consists in the discovery of some relation, distinct from these, and that our enumeration was not compleat, when we comprehended all demonstrable relations under four general heads : To this I know not what to reply, till some one be so good as to point out to me this new relation.   'Tis impossible to refute a system, which has never yet been explain'd.   In such a manner of fighting in the dark, a man loses his blows in the air, and often places them where the enemy is not present.

I must, therefore, on this occasion, rest contented with requiring the two following conditions of any one that wou'd undertake to clear up this system. *First,* As moral good and evil belong only to the actions of the mind, and are deriv'd from our situation with regard to external objects, the relations from which these moral distinctions arise, must lie only betwixt internal actions, and external objects, and must not be applicable either to internal actions, compared among themselves, or to external objects, when placed in opposition to other external objects.   For as morality is supposed to attend certain relations, if these relations cou'd belong to internal actions consider'd singly, it wou'd follow, that we might be guilty of crimes in ourselves, and independent of our situation, with respect to the universe : And in like manner, if these moral relations cou'd be apply'd to external objects, it would follow, that even inanimate beings wou'd be susceptible of moral beauty and deformity.   Now it seems difficult to imagine, that any relation can be discover'd betwixt our passions, volitions and actions, compared to external objects, which relation might not belong either to these passions and volitions, or to these external objects, compar'd among *themselves.*

But it will be still more difficult to fulfil the *second* condition, requisite to justify this system.   According to the principles of those who maintain an abstract rational difference betwixt moral good and evil, and a natural fitness and unfitness of things, 'tis not only suppos'd, that these relations, being eternal and immutable, are the same, when consider'd by every rational creature, but their *effects* are also suppos'd to be necessarily the same ; and 'tis concluded they have no less, or rather a greater, influence in directing the will of the diety, than in governing the rational and virtuous of our own species. These two particulars are evidently distinct. 'Tis one thing to know virtue, and another to conform the will to it. In order, therefore, to prove, that the measures of right and wrong are eternal laws, *obligatory* on every rational mind, 'tis not sufficient to shew the relations upon which they are founded : We must also point out the connexion betwixt the relation, and the will ; and must prove that this connexion is so necessary, that in every well-disposed mind, it must take place and have its influence ; tho' the difference betwixt these minds be in other respects immense and infinite. Now besides what I have already prov'd, that even in human nature no relation can ever alone produce any action ; besides this, I say, it has been shewn, in treating of the understanding, that there is no connexion of cause and effect, such as this is suppos'd to be, which is discoverable otherwise than by experience, and of which we can pretend to have any security by the simple consideration of the objects. All beings in the universe, consider'd in themselves, appear entirely loose and independent of each other. 'Tis only by experience we learn their influence and connexion ; and this influence we ought never to extend beyond experience.

Thus it will be impossible to fulfil the *first* condition required to the system of eternal rational measures of right and wrong ; because it is impossible to shew those relations, upon which such a distinction may be 'founded : And 'tis as impossible to fulfil the *second* condition ; because we cannot prove *a priori*, that these relations, if they really existed and were perceiv'd, wou'd be universally forcible and obligatory.

But to make these general reflections more clear and convincing, we may illustrate them by some particular instances, wherein this character of moral good or evil is the most universally acknowledged. Of all crimes that human creatures are capable of committing, the most horrid and unnatural is ingratitude, especially when it is committed against parents, and appears in the more flagrant instances of wounds and death. This is acknowledg'd by all mankind, philosophers as well as the people ; the question only arises among philosophers, whether the guilt or moral deformity of this action be discover'd by demonstrative reasoning, or be felt by an internal sense, and by means of some sentiment, which the reflecting on such an action naturally occasions. This question will soon be decided against the former opinion, if we can shew the same relations in other objects, without the notion of any guilt or iniquity attending them. Reason or science is nothing but the comparing of ideas, and the discovery of their relations ; and if the same relations have different characters, it must evidently follow, that those characters are not discover'd merely by reason. To put the affair, therefore, to this trial, let us chuse any inanimate object, such as an oak or elm ; and let us suppose, that by the dropping of its seed, it produces a sapling below it, which springing up by degrees, at last overtops and destroys the parent tree : I ask, if in this instance there be wanting any relation, which is discoverable in parricide or ingratitude ? Is not the one tree the cause of the other's existence ; and the latter the cause of the destruction of the former, in the same manner as when a child murders his parents? 'Tis not sufficient to reply, that a choice or will is wanting. For in the case of parricide, a will does not give rise to any *different* relations, but is only the cause from which the action is deriv'd ; and consequently produces the *same* relations, that in the oak or elm arise from some other principles. 'Tis a will or choice, that determines a man to kill his parent ; and they are the laws of matter and motion, that determine a sapling to destroy the oak, from which it sprung. Here then the same relations have different causes ; but still the relations are the same : And as their discovery is not in both cases attended with a notion of immorality, it follows, that that notion does not arise from such a discovery.

But to chuse an instance, still more resembling ; I would fain ask any one, why incest in the human species is criminal, and why the very same action, and the same relations in animals have not the smallest moral turpitude and deformity? If it be answer'd, that this action is innocent in animals, because they have not reason sufficient to discover its turpitude ; but that man, being endow'd with that faculty, which *ought* to restrain him to his duty, the same action instantly becomes criminal to him ; should this be said, I would reply, that this is evidently arguing in a circle. For before reason can perceive this turpitude, the turpitude must exist ; and consequently is independent of the decisions of our reason, and is their object more properly than their effect. According to this system, then, every animal, that has sense, and appetite, and will ; that is, every animal must be susceptible of all the same virtues and vices, for which we ascribe praise and blame to human creatures. All the difference is, that our superior reason may serve to discover the vice or virtue, and by that means may augment the blame or praise : But still this discovery supposes a separate being in these moral distinctions, and a being, which depends only on the will and appetite, and which, both in thought and reality, may be distinguish'd from the reason. Animals are susceptible of the same relations, with respect to each other, as the human species, and therefore wou'd also be susceptible of the same morality, if the essence of morality consisted in these relations. Their want of a sufficient degree of reason may hinder them from perceiving the duties and obligations of morality, but can never hinder these duties from existing; since they must antecedently exist, in order to their being perceiv'd. Reason must find them, and can never produce them. This argument deserves to be weigh'd, as being, in my opinion, entirely decisive.

Nor does this reasoning only prove, that morality consists not in any relations, that are the objects of science; but if examin'd, will prove with equal certainty, that it consists not in any *matter of fact*, which can be discover'd by the understanding. This is the *second* part of our argument; and if it can be made evident, we may conclude, that morality is not an object of reason. But can there be any difficulty in proving, that vice and virtue are not matters of fact, whose existence we can infer by reason? Take any action allowed to be vicious: Wilful murder, for instance. Examine it in all lights, and see if you can find that matter of fact, or real existence, which you call *vice*. In which-ever way you take it, you find only certain passions, motives, volitions and thoughts. There is no other matter of fact in the case. The vice entirely escapes you, as long as you consider the object. You never can find it, till you turn your reflection into your own breast, and find a sentiment of disapprobation, which arises in you, towards this action. Here is a matter of fact; but 'tis the object of feeling, not of reason. It lies in yourself, not in the object. So that when you pronounce any action or character to be vicious, you mean nothing, but that from the constitution of your nature you have a feeling or sentiment of blame from the contemplation of it. Vice and virtue, therefore, may be compar'd to sounds, colours, heat and cold, which, according to modern philosophy, are not qualities in objects, but perceptions in the mind: And this discovery in morals, like that other in physics, is to be regarded as a considerable advancement of the speculative sciences ; tho', like that too, it has little or no influence on practice. Nothing can be more real, or concern us more, than our own sentiments of pleasure and uneasiness ; and if these be favourable to virtue, and unfavourable to vice, no more can be requisite to the regulation of our conduct and behaviour.

I cannot forbear adding to these reasonings an observation, which may, perhaps, be found of some importance. In every system of morality, which I have hitherto met with, I have always remark'd, that the author proceeds for some time in the ordinary way of reasoning, and establishes the being of a God, or makes observations concerning human affairs ; when of a sudden I am surpriz'd to find, that instead of the usual copulation of propositions, *is*, and *is not*, I meet with no proposition that is not connected with an *ought*, or an *ought not*. This change is imperceptible ; but is, however, of the last consequence. For as this *ought*, or *ought not*, expresses some new relation or affirmation, 'tis necessary that it shou'd be observ'd and explain'd ; and at the same time that a reason should be given, for what seems altogether inconceivable, how this new relation can be a deduction from others, which are entirely different from it. But as authors do not commonly use this precaution, I shall presume to recommend it to the readers ; and am persuaded, that this small attention wou'd subvert all the vulgar systems of morality, and let us see, that the distinction of vice and virtue is not founded merely on the relations of objects, nor is perceiv'd by reason.

SECTION II

Moral distinctions deriv'd from a moral sense.

THUS the course of the argument leads us to conclude, that since vice and virtue are not discoverable merely by reason, or the comparison of ideas, it must be by means of some impression or sentiment they occasion, that we are able to mark the difference betwixt them. Our decisions concerning moral rectitude and depravity are evidently perceptions ; and as all perceptions are either impressions or ideas, the exclusion of the one is a convincing argument for the other. Morality, therefore, is more properly felt than judg'd of ; tho' this feeling or sentiment is commonly so soft and gentle, that we are apt to confound it with an idea, according to our common custom of taking all things for the same, which have any near resemblance to each other.

The next question is, Of what nature are these impressions, and after what manner do they operate upon us? Here we cannot remain long in suspense, but must pronounce the impression arising from virtue, to be agreeable, and that proceeding from vice to be uneasy. Every moment's experience must convince us of this. There is no spectacle so fair and beautiful as a noble and generous action ; nor any which gives us more abhorrence than one that is cruel and treacherous. No enjoyment equals the satisfaction we receive from the company of those we love and esteem ; as the greatest of all punishments is to be oblig'd to pass our lives with those we hate or contemn. A very play or romance may afford us instances of this pleasure, which virtue conveys to us ; and pain, which arises from vice.

Now since the distinguishing impressions, by which moral good or evil is known, are nothing but *particular* pains or pleasures ; it follows, that in all enquiries concerning these moral distinctions, it will be sufficient to shew the principles, which make us feel a satisfaction or uneasiness from the survey of any character, in order to satisfy us why the character is laudable or blameable. An action, or sentiment, or character is virtuous or vicious ; why? because its view causes a pleasure or uneasiness of a particular kind. In giving a reason, therefore, for the pleasure or uneasiness, we sufficiently explain the vice or virtue. To have the sense of virtue, is nothing but to *feel* a satisfaction of a particular kind from the contemplation of a character. The very *feeling* constitutes our praise or admiration. We go no farther; nor do we enquire into the cause of the satisfaction. We do not infer a character to be virtuous, because it pleases : But in feeling that it pleases after such a particular manner, we in effect feel that it is virtuous. The case is the same as in our judgments concerning all kinds of beauty, and tastes, and sensations. Our approbation is imply'd in the immediate pleasure they convey to us.

I have objected to the system, which establishes eternal rational measures of right and wrong, that 'tis impossible to shew, in the actions of reasonable creatures, any relations, which are not found in external objects ; and therefore, if morality always attended these relations, 'twere possible for inanimate matter to become virtuous or vicious. Now it may, in like manner, be objected to the present system, that if virtue and vice be determin'd by pleasure and pain, these qualities, must, in every case, arise from the sensations ; and consequently any object, whether animate or inanimate, rational or irrational, might become morally good or evil, provided it can excite a satisfaction or uneasiness. But tho' this objection seems to be the very same, it has by no means the same force, in the one case as in the other. For, *first*, 'tis evident, that under the term *pleasure*, we comprehend sensations, which are very different from each other, and which have only such a distant resemblance, as is requisite to make them be express'd by the same abstract term. A good composition of music and a bottle of good wine equally produce pleasure ; and what is more, their goodness is determin'd merely by the pleasure. But shall we say upon that account, that the wine is harmonious, or the music of a good flavour? In like manner an inanimate object, and the character or sentiments of any person may, both of them, give satisfaction ; but as the satisfaction is different, this keeps our sentiments concerning them from being confounded, and makes us ascribe virtue to the one, and not to the other. Nor is every sentiment of pleasure or pain, which arises from characters and actions, of that *peculiar* kind, which makes us praise or condemn. The good qualities of an enemy are hurtful to us ; but may still command our esteem and respect. 'Tis only when a character is considered in general, without reference to our particular interest, that it causes such a feeling or sentiment, as denominates it morally good or evil. 'Tis true, those sentiments, from interest and morals, are apt to be confounded, and naturally run into one another.   It seldom happens, that we do not think an enemy vicious, and can distinguish betwixt his opposition to our interest and real villainy or baseness.   But this hinders not, but that the sentiments are, in themselves, distinct ; and a man of temper and judgment may preserve himself from these illusions. In like manner, tho' 'tis certain a musical voice is nothing but one that naturally gives a *particular* kind of pleasure ; yet 'tis difficult for a man to be sensible, that the voice of an enemy is agreeable, or to allow it to be musical.   But a person of a fine ear, who has the command of himself, can separate these feelings, and give praise to what deserves it.

Secondly, We may call to remembrance the preceding system of the passions, in order to remark a still more considerable difference among our pains and pleasures.   Pride and humility, love and hatred are excited, when there is any thing presented to us, that both bears a relation to the object of the passion, and produces a separate sensation related to the sensation of the passion.   Now virtue and vice are attended with these circumstances.   They must necessarily be plac'd either in ourselves or others, and excite either pleasure or uneasiness ; and therefore must give rise to one of these four passions ; which clearly distinguishes them from the pleasure and pain arising from inanimate objects, that often bear no relation to us : And this is, perhaps, the most considerable effect that virtue and vice have upon the human mind.

It may now be ask'd *in general*, concerning this pain or pleasure, that distinguishes moral good and evil, *From what principles is it derived, and whence does it arise in the human mind?* To this I reply, *first*, that 'tis absurd to imagine, that in every particular instance, these sentiments are produc'd by an *original* quality and *primary* constitution. For as the number of our duties is, in a manner, infinite, 'tis impossible that our original instincts should extend to each of them, and from our very first infancy impress on the human mind all that multitude of precepts, which are contain'd in the compleatest system of ethics. Such a method of proceeding is not conformable to the usual maxims, by which nature is conducted, where a few principles produce all that variety we observe in the universe, and every thing is carry'd on in the easiest and most simple manner. 'Tis necessary, therefore, to abridge these primary impulses, and find some more general principles, upon which all our notions of morals are founded.

But in the *second* place, should it be ask'd, Whether we ought to search for these principles in *nature*, or whether we must look for them in some other origin ? I wou'd reply, that our answer to this question depends upon the definition of the word, Nature, than which there is none more ambiguous and equivocal. If *nature* be oppos'd to miracles, not only the distinction betwixt vice and virtue is natural, but also every event, which has ever happen'd in the world, *excepting those miracles, on which our religion is founded.* In saying, then, that the sentiments of vice and virtue are natural in this sense, we make no very extraordinary discovery.

But *nature* may also be opposed to rare and unusual ; and in this sense of the word, which is the common one, there may often arise disputes concerning what is natural or unnatural; and one may in general affirm, that we are not possess'd of any very precise standard, by which these disputes can be decided. Frequent and rare depend upon the number of examples we have observ'd; and as this number may gradually encrease or diminish, 'twill be impossible to fix any exact boundaries betwixt them. We may only affirm on this head, that if ever there was any thing, which cou'd be call'd natural in this sense, the sentiments of morality certainly may; since there never was any nation of the world, nor any single person in any nation, who was utterly depriv'd of them, and who never, in any instance, shew'd the least approbation or dislike of manners. These sentiments are so rooted in our constitution and temper, that without entirely confounding the human mind by disease or madness, 'tis impossible to extirpate and destroy them.

But *nature* may also be opposed to artifice, as well as to what is rare and unusual; and in this sense it may be disputed, whether the notions of virtue be natural or not. We readily forget, that the designs, and projects, and views of men are principles as necessary in their operation as heat and cold, moist and dry: But taking them to be free and entirely our own, 'tis usual for us to set them in opposition to the other principles of nature. Shou'd it, therefore, be demanded, whether the sense of virtue be natural or artificial, I am of opinion, that 'tis impossible for me at present to give any precise answer to this question. Perhaps it will appear afterwards, that our sense of some virtues is artificial, and that of others natural. The discussion of this question will be more proper, when we enter upon an exact detail of each particular vice and virtue.[1]

[1] In the following discourse *natural* is also opposed sometimes to *civil*, sometimes to *moral*. The opposition will always discover the sense, in which it is taken.

Mean while it may not be amiss to observe from these definitions of *natural* and *unnatural*, that nothing can be more unphilosophical than those systems, which assert, that virtue is the same with what is natural, and vice with what is unnatural. For in the first sense of the word, Nature, as opposed to miracles, both vice and virtue are equally natural; and in the second sense, as oppos'd to what is unusual, perhaps virtue will be found to be the most unnatural. At least it must be own'd, that heroic virtue, being as unusual, is as little natural as the most brutal barbarity. As to the third sense of the word, 'tis certain, that both vice and virtue are equally artificial, and out of nature. For however it may be disputed, whether the notion of a merit or demerit in certain actions be natural or artificial, 'tis evident, that the actions themselves are artificial, and are perform'd with a certain design and intention; otherwise they cou'd never be rank'd under any of these denominations. 'Tis impossible, therefore, that the character of natural and unnatural can ever, in any sense, mark the boundaries of vice and virtue.

Thus we are still brought back to our first position, that virtue is distinguished by the pleasure, and vice by the pain, that any action, sentiment or character gives us by the mere view and contemplation. This decision is very commodious; because it reduces us to this simple question, *Why any action or sentiment upon the general view or survey, gives a certain satisfaction or uneasiness*, in order to shew the origin of its moral rectitude or depravity, without looking for any incomprehensible relations and qualities, which never did exist in nature, nor even in our imagination, by any clear and distinct conception. I flatter myself I have executed a great part of my present design by a state of the question, which appears to me so free from ambiguity and obscurity.

PART II.

OF JUSTICE AND INJUSTICE.

SECTION I.

Justice, whether a natural or artificial virtue?

I HAVE already hinted, that our sense of every kind of virtue is not natural ; but that there are some virtues, that produce pleasure and approbation by means of an artifice or contrivance, which arises from the circumstances and necessity of mankind.   Of this kind I assert *justice* to be ; and shall endeavor to defend this opinion by a short, and, I hope, convincing argument, before I examine the nature of the artifice, from which the sense of that virtue is derived.

'Tis evident, that when we praise any actions, we regard only the motives that produced them, and consider the actions as signs or indications of certain principles in the mind and temper.   The external performance has no merit. We must look within to find the moral quality.   This we cannot do directly ; and therefore fix our attention on actions, as on external signs.   But these actions are still considered as signs ; and the ultimate object of our praise and approbation is the motive, that produc'd them.

After the same manner, when we require any action, or blame a person for not performing it, we always suppose, that one in that situation shou'd be influenc'd by the proper motive of that action, and we esteem it vicious in him to be regardless of it.   If we find, upon enquiry, that the virtuous motive was still powerful over his breast, tho' check'd in its operation by some circumstances unknown to us, we retract our blame, and have the same esteem for him, as if he had actually perform'd the action, which we require of him.

It appears, therefore, that all virtuous actions derive their merit only from virtuous motives, and are consider'd merely as signs of those motives. From this principle I conclude, that the first virtuous motive, which bestows a merit on any action, can never be a regard to the virtue of that action, but must be some other natural motive or principle. To suppose, that the mere regard to the virtue of the action, may be the first motive, which‘ produced the action, and render'd it virtuous, is to reason in a circle. Before we can have such a regard, the action must be really virtuous ; and this virtue must be deriv'd from some virtuous motive : And consequently the virtuous motive must be different from the regard to the virtue of the action. A virtuous motive is requisite to render an action virtuous. An action must be virtuous, before we can have a regard to its virtue. Some virtuous motive, therefore, must be antecedent to that regard.

Nor is this merely a metaphysical subtilty; but enters into all our reasonings in common life, tho' perhaps we may not be able to place it in such distinct philosophical terms. We blame a father for neglecting his child. Why? because it shews a want of natural affection, which is the duty of every parent. Were not natural affection a duty, the care of children cou'd not be a duty ; and 'twere impossible we cou'd have the duty in our eye in the attention we give to our offspring. In this case, therefore, all men suppose a motive to the action distinct from a sense of duty.

Here is a man, that does many benevolent actions ; re-lieves the distress'd, comforts the afflicted, and extends his bounty even to the greatest strangers. No character can be more amiable and virtuous. We regard these actions as proofs of the greatest humanity. This humanity bestows a merit on the actions. A regard to this merit is, therefore, a secondary consideration, and deriv'd from the antecedent principle of humanity, which is meritorious and laudable.

In short, it may be establish'd as an undoubted maxim, *that no action can be virtuous, or morally good, unless there be in human nature some motive to produce it, distinct from the sense of its morality.*

But may not the sense of morality or duty produce an action, without any other motive? I answer, It may : But this is no objection to the present doctrine. When any virtuous motive or principle is common in human nature, a person, who feels his heart devoid of that motive, may hate himself upon that account, and may perform the action without the motive, from a certain sense of duty, in order to acquire by practice, that virtuous principle, or at least, to disguise to himself, as much as possible, his want of it. A man that really feels no gratitude in his temper, is still pleas'd to perform grateful actions, and thinks he has, by that means, fulfill'd his duty. Actions are at first only consider'd as signs of motives : But 'tis usual, in this case, as in all others, to fix our attention on the signs, and neglect, in some measure, the thing signify'd. But tho', on some occasions, a person may perform an action merely out of regard to its moral obligation, yet still this supposes in human nature some distinct principles, which are capable of producing the action, and whose moral beauty renders the action meritorious.

Now to apply all this to the present case ; I suppose a person to have lent me a sum of money, on condition that it be restor'd in a few days ; and also suppose, that after the expiration of the term agreed on, he demands the sum ; I ask, *What reason or motive have I to restore the money?* It will, perhaps, be said, that my regard to justice, and abhorrence to villainy and knavery, are sufficient reasons for me, if I have the least grain of honesty, or sense of duty or obligation. And this answer, no doubt, is just and satisfactory

to man in his civiliz'd state, and when train'd up according
to a certain discipline and education. But in his rude and
more *natural* condition, if you are pleas'd to call such a
condition natural, this answer wou'd be rejected as perfectly
unintelligible and sophistical. For one in that situation
wou'd immediately ask you, *Wherein consists this honesty and
justice, which you find in restoring a loan, and abstaining from
the property of others?* It does not surely lie in the external
action. It must, therefore, be plac'd in the motive, from
which the external action is deriv'd. This motive can never
be a regard to the honesty of the action. For 'tis a plain
fallacy to say, that a virtuous motive is requisite to render an
action honest, and at the same time that a regard to the
honesty is the motive of the action. We can never have a
regard to the virtue of an action, unless the action be antecedently virtuous. No action can be virtuous, but so far as
it proceeds from a virtuous motive. A virtuous motive,
therefore, must precede the regard to the virtue ; and 'tis
impossible, that the virtuous motive and the regard to the
virtue can be the same.

'Tis requisite, then, to find some motive to acts of justice
and honesty, distinct from our regard to the honesty ; and
in this lies the great difficulty. For shou'd we say, that a
concern for our private interest or reputation is the legitimate
motive to all honest actions : it wou'd follow, that wherever
that concern ceases, honesty can no longer have place. But
'tis certain, that self-love, when it acts at its liberty, instead
of engaging us to honest actions, is the source of all injustice
and violence ; nor can a man ever correct those vices, without correcting and restraining the *natural* movements of
that appetite.

But shou'd it be affirm'd, that the reason or motive of
such actions is the *regard to publick interest,* to which nothing is more contrary than examples of injustice and dis-
honesty ; shou'd this be said, I wou'd propose the three

following considerations, as worthy of our attention. *First*, public interest is not naturally attach'd to the observation of the rules of justice ; but is only connected with it, after an artificial convention for the establishment of these rules, as shall be shewn more at large hereafter. *Secondly*, if we suppose, that the loan was secret, and that it is necessary for the interest of the person, that the money be restor'd in the same manner (as when the lender wou'd conceal his riches) in that case the example ceases, and the public is no longer interested in the actions of the borrower ; tho' I suppose there is no moralist, who will affirm, that the duty and obligation ceases. *Thirdly*, experience sufficiently proves, that men, in the ordinary conduct of life, look not so far as the public interest, when they pay their creditors, perform their promises, and abstain from theft, and robbery, and injustice of every kind. That is a motive too remote and too sublime to affect the generality of mankind, and operate with any force in actions so contrary to private interest as are frequently those of justice and common honesty.

In general, it may be affirm'd, that there is no such passion in human minds, as the love of mankind, merely as such, independent of personal qualities, of services, or of relation to ourself. 'Tis true, there is no human, and indeed no sensible, creature, whose happiness or misery does not, in some measure, affect us, when brought near to us, and represented in lively colours : But this proceeds merely from sympathy, and is no proof of such an universal affection to mankind, since this concern extends itself beyond our own species. An affection betwixt the sexes is a passion evidently implanted in human nature ; and this passion not only appears in its peculiar symptoms, but also in inflaming every other principle of affection, and raising a stronger love from beauty, wit, kindness, than what wou'd otherwise flow from them. Were there an universal love among all human creatures, it wou'd appear after the same manner. Any degree of a good quality wou'd cause a stronger affection than the same degree of a bad quality wou'd cause hatred ; contrary to what we find by experience. Men's tempers are different, and some have a propensity to the tender, and others to the rougher, affections : But in the main, we may affirm, that man in general, or human nature, is nothing but the object both of love and hatred, and requires some other cause, which by a double relation of impressions and ideas, may excite these passions. In vain wou'd we endeavour to elude this hypothesis. There are no phænomena that point out any such kind affection to men, independent of their merit, and every other circumstance. We love company in general ; but 'tis as we love any other amusement. An *Englishman* in *Italy* is a friend : A *Europæan* in *China ;* and perhaps a man wou'd be belov'd as such, were we to meet him in the moon. But this proceeds only from the relation to ourselves ; which in these cases gathers force by being confined to a few persons.

If public benevolence, therefore, or a regard to the interests of mankind, cannot be the original motive to justice, much less can *private benevolence,* or a *regard to the interests of the party concern'd,* be this motive. For what if he be my enemy, and has given me just cause to hate him ? What if he be a vicious man, and deserves the hatred of all mankind ? What if he be a miser, and can make no use of what I wou'd deprive him of ? What if he be a profligate debauchee, and wou'd rather receive harm than benefit from large possessions ? What if I be in necessity, and have urgent motives to acquire something to my family ? In all these cases, the original motive to justice wou'd fail ; and consequently the justice itself, and along with it all property, right, and obligation.

A rich man lies under a moral obligation to communicate to those in necessity a share of his superfluities. Were private benevolence the original motive to justice, a man wou'd not be oblig'd to leave others in the possession of more than he is oblig'd to give them. At least the difference wou'd be very inconsiderable. Men generally fix their affections more on what they are possess'd of, than on what they never enjoy'd : For this reason, it wou'd be greater cruelty to dispossess a man of anything, than not to give it him. But who will assert, that this is the only foundation of justice ?

Besides, we must consider, that the chief reason, why men attach themselves so much to their possessions is, that they consider them as their property, and as secur'd to them inviolably by the laws of society. But this is a secondary consideration, and dependent on the preceding notions of justice and property.

A man's property is suppos'd to be fenc'd against every mortal, in every possible case. But private benevolence is, and ought to be, weaker in some persons, than in others : And in many, or indeed in most persons, must absolutely fail. Private benevolence, therefore, is not the original motive of justice.

From all this it follows, that we have no real or universal motive for observing the laws of equity, but the very equity and merit of that observance ; and as no action can be equitable or meritorious, where it cannot arise from some separate motive, there is here an evident sophistry and reasoning in a circle. Unless, therefore, we will allow, that nature has establish'd a sophistry, and render'd it necessary and unavoidable, we must allow, that the sense of justice and injustice is not deriv'd from nature, but arises artificially, tho' necessarily from education, and human conventions.

I shall add, as a corollary to this reasoning, that since no action can be laudable or blameable, without some motives or impelling passions, distinct from the sense of morals, these distinct passions must have a great influence on that sense.

'Tis according to their general force in human nature, that we blame or praise. In judging of the beauty of animal bodies, we always carry in our eye the œconomy of a certain species ; and where the limbs and features observe that proportion, which is common to the species, we pronounce them handsome and beautiful. In like manner we always consider the *natural* and *usual* force of the passions, when we determine concerning vice and virtue ; and if the passions depart very much from the common measures on either side, they are always disapprov'd as vicious. A man naturally loves his children better than his nephews, his nephews better than his cousins, his cousins better than strangers, where every thing else is equal. Hence arise our common measures of duty, in preferring the one to the other. Our sense of duty always follows the common and natural course of our passions.

To avoid giving offence, I must here observe, that when I deny justice to be a natural virtue, I make use of the word, *natural*, only as oppos'd to *artifical*. In another sense of the word ; as no principle of the human mind is more natural than a sense of virtue ; so no virtue is more natural than justice. Mankind is an inventive species ; and where an invention is obvious and absolutely necessary, it may as properly be said to be natural as anything that proceeds immediately from original principles, without the intervention of thought or reflection. 'Tho the rules of justice be *artificial*, they are not *arbitrary*. Nor is the expression improper to call them *Laws of Nature;* if by natural we understand what is common to any species, or even if we confine it to mean what is inseparable from the species.

SECTION II.

Of the origin of justice and property.

WE now proceed to examine two questions, viz. *concerning the manner, in which the rules of justice are establish'd by the*

*artifice of men; and concerning the reasons which determine us
to attribute to the observance or neglect of these rules a moral
beauty and deformity.* These questions will appear afterwards
to be distinct. We shall begin with the former.

Of all the animals, with which this globe is peopled, there
is none towards whom nature seems, at first sight to have
exercis'd more cruelty than towards man, in the numberless
wants and necessities, with which she has loaded him, and in
the slender means, which she affords to the relieving these
necessities. In other creatures these two particulars generally compensate each other. If we consider the lion as a
voracious and carnivorous animal, we shall easily discover
him to be very necessitous ; but if we turn our eye to his
make and temper, his agility, his courage, his arms, and his
force, we shall find, that his advantages hold proportion with
his wants. The sheep and ox are depriv'd of all these
advantages ; but their appetites are moderate, and their food
is of easy purchase. In man alone, this unnatural conjunction of infirmity, and of necessity, may be observ'd in its
greatest perfection. Not only the food, which is requir'd
for his sustenance, flies his search and approach, or at least
requires his labour to be produc'd, but he must be possess'd
of cloaths and lodging, to defend him against the injuries of
the weather ; tho' to consider him only in himself, he is
provided, neither with arms, nor force, nor other natural
abilities, which are in any degree answerable to so many
necessities.

'Tis by society alone he is able to supply his defects, and
raise himself up to an equality with his fellow-creatures, and
even acquire a superiority above them. By society all his
infirmities are compensated ; and tho' in that situation his
wants multiply every moment upon him, yet his abilities are
still more augmented, and leave him in every respect more
satisfied and happy, than 'tis possible for him, in his savage
and solitary condition, ever to become. When every indi-

vidual person labours a-part, and only for himself, his force is too small to execute any considerable work ; his labour being employ'd in supplying all his different necessities, he never attains a perfection in any particular art ; and as his force and success are not at all times equal, the least failure in either of these particulars must be attended with inevitable ruin and misery. Society provides a remedy for these *three* inconveniences. By the conjunction of forces, our power is augmented : By the partition of employments, our ability encreases : And by mutual succour we are less expos'd to fortune and accidents. 'Tis by this additional *force, ability,* and *security,* that society becomes advantageous.

But in order to form society, 'tis requisite not only that it be advantageous, but also that men be sensible of these advantages ; and 'tis impossible, in their wild uncultivated state, that by study and reflection alone, they should ever be able to attain this knowledge. Most fortunately, therefore, there is conjoin'd to those necessities, whose remedies are remote and obscure, another necessity, which having a present and more obvious remedy, may justly be regarded as the first and original principle of human society. This necessity is no other than that natural appetite betwixt the sexes, which unites them together, and preserves their union, till a new tye takes place in their concern for their common offspring. This new concern becomes also a principle of union betwixt the parents and offspring, and forms a more numerous society ; where the parents govern by the advantage of their superior strength and wisdom, and at the same time are restrain'd in the exercise of their authority by that natural affection, which they bear their children. In a little time, custom and habit operating on the tender minds of the children, makes them sensible of the advantages, which they may reap from society, as well as fashions them by degrees for it, by rubbing off those rough corners and untoward affections, which prevent their coalition.

For it must be confest, that however the circumstances of human nature may render an union necessary, and however those passions of lust and natural affection may seem to render it unavoidable ; yet there are other particulars in our *natural temper*, and in our *outward circumstances*, which are very incommodious, and are even contrary to the requisite conjunction. Among the former, we may justly esteem our *selfishness* to be the most considerable. I am sensible, that, generally speaking, the representations of this quality have been carried much too far ; and that the descriptions, which certain philosophers delight so much to form of mankind in this particular, are as wide of nature as any accounts of monsters, which we meet with in fables and romances. So far from thinking, that men have no affection for anything beyond themselves, I am of opinion, that tho' it be rare to meet with one, who loves any single person better than himself ; yet 'tis as rare to meet with one, in whom all the kind affections, taken together, do not over-balance all the selfish. Consult common experience : Do you not see, that tho' the whole expence of the family be generally under the direction of the master of it, yet there are few that do not bestow the largest part of their fortunes on the pleasures of their wives, and the education of their children, reserving the smallest portion for their own proper use and entertainment. This is what we may observe concerning such as have those endearing ties ; and may presume, that the case would be the same with others, were they plac'd in a like situation.

But tho' this generosity must be acknowledg'd to the honour of human nature, we may at the same time remark, that so noble an affection, instead of fitting men for large societies, is almost as contrary to them, as the most narrow selfishness. For while each person loves himself better than any other single person, and in his love to others bears the greatest affection to his relations and acquaintance, this must necessarily produce an opposition of passions, and a consequent opposition of actions ; which cannot but be dangerous to the new-establish'd union.

'Tis however worth while to remark, that this contrariety of passions wou'd be attended with but small danger, did it not concur with a peculiarity in our *outward circumstances*, which affords it an opportunity of exerting itself. There are three different species of goods, which we are possess'd of ; the internal satisfaction of our minds, the external advantages of our body, and the enjoyment of such possessions as we have acquir'd by our industry and good fortune. We are perfectly secure in the enjoyment of the first. The second may be ravish'd from us, but can be of no advantage to him who deprives us of them. The last only are both expos'd to the violence of others, and may be transferr'd without suffering any loss or alteration ; while at the same time, there is not a sufficient quantity of them to supply every one's desires and necessities. As the improvement, therefore, of these goods is the chief advantage of society, so the *instability* of their possession, along with their *scarcity*, is the chief impediment.

In vain shou'd we expect to find, in *uncultivated nature*, a remedy to this inconvenience ; or hope for any inartificial principle of the human mind, which might controul those partial affections, and make us overcome the temptations arising from our circumstances. The idea of justice can never serve to this purpose, or be taken for a natural principle, capable of inspiring men with an equitable conduct towards each other. That virtue, as it is now understood, wou'd never have been dream'd of among rude and savage men. For the notion of the injury or injustice implies an immorality or vice committed against some other person : And as every immorality is deriv'd from some defect or unsoundness of the passions, and as this defect must be judg'd of, in a great measure, from the ordinary course of nature in the constitution of the mind ; 'twill be easy to know, whether we be guilty of any immorality, with regard to others, by considering the natural, and usual force of those several affections, which are directed towards them.   Now it appears, that in the original frame of our mind, our strongest attention is confin'd to ourselves ; our next is extended to our relations and acquaintance ; and 'tis only the weakest which reaches to strangers and indifferent persons.   This partiality, then, and unequal affection, must not only have an influence on our behaviour and conduct in society but even on our ideas of vice and virtue ; so as to make us regard any remarkable transgression of such a degree of partiality, either by too great an enlargement, or contraction of the affections, as vicious and immoral.   This we may observe in our common judgments concerning actions, where we blame a person, who either centers all his affections in his family, or is so regardless of them, as, in any opposition of interest, to give the preference to a stranger, or mere chance acquaintance.   From all which it follows, that our natural uncultivated ideas of morality, instead of providing a remedy for the partiality of our affections, do rather conform themselves to that partiality, and give it an additional force and influence.

The remedy, then, is not deriv'd from nature, but from *artifice* ; or more properly speaking, nature provides a remedy in the judgment and understanding, for what is irregular and incommodious in the affections.   For when men, from their early education in society, have become sensible of the infinite advantages that result from it, and have besides acquir'd a new affection to company and conversation ; and when they have observ'd, that the principal disturbance in society arises from those goods, which we call external, and from their looseness and easy transition from one person to another ; they must seek for a remedy, by putting these goods, as far as possible, on the same footing with with the fix'd and constant advantages of the mind and body. This can be done after no other manner, than by a convention enter'd into by all the members of the society to bestow stability on the possession of those external goods, and leave every one in the peaceable enjoyment of what he may acquire by his fortune and industry. By this means, every one knows what he may safely possess ; and the passions are restrain'd in their partial and contradictory motions. Nor is such a restraint contrary to these passions ; for if so, it cou'd never be entered into, nor maintain'd ; but it is only contrary to their heedless and impetuous movement. Instead of departing from our own interest, or from that of our nearest friends, by abstaining from the possessions of others, we cannot better consult both these interests, than by such a convention ; because it is by that means we maintain society, which is so necessary to their well-being and subsistence, as well as to our own.

This convention is not of the nature of a *promise* : For even promises themselves, as we shall see afterwards, arise from human conventions. It is only a general sense of common interest ; which sense all the members of the society express to one another, and which induces them to regulate their conduct by certain rules. I observe, that it will be for my interest to leave another in the possession of his goods, *provided* he will act in the same manner with regard to me. He is sensible of a like interest in the regulation of his conduct. When this common sense of interest is mutually express'd, and is known to both, it produces a suitable resolution and behaviour. And this may properly enough be call'd a convention or agreement betwixt us, tho' without the interposition of a promise ; since the actions of each of us have a reference to those of the other, and are perform'd upon the supposition, that something is to be perform'd on the other part. Two men, who pull the oars of a boat, do it by an agreement or convention, tho' they have never given promises to each other.

Nor is the rule concerning the stability of possession the less deriv'd from human conventions, that it arises gradually, and acquires force by a slow progression, and by our repeated experience of the inconveniences of transgressing it. On the contrary, this experience assures us still more, that the sense of interest has become common to all our fellows, and gives us a confidence of the future regularity of their conduct : And 'tis only on the expectation of this, that our moderation and abstinence are founded. In like manner are languages gradually establish'd by human conventions without any promise. In like manner do gold and silver become the common measures of exchange, and are esteem'd sufficient payment for what is of a hundred times their value.

After this convention, concerning abstinence from the possessions of others, is enter'd into, and every one has acquir'd a stability in his possessions, there immediately arise the ideas of justice and injustice ; as also those of *property*, *right*, and *obligation*. The latter are altogether unintelligible without first understanding the former. Our property is nothing but those goods, whose constant possession is establish'd by the laws of society ; that is, by the laws of justice. Those, therefore, who make use of the words *property*, or *right*, or *obligation*, before they have explain'd the origin of justice, or even make use of them in that explication, are guilty of a very gross fallacy, and can never reason upon any solid foundation. A man's property is some object related to him. This relation is not natural, but moral, and founded on justice. 'Tis very preposterous, therefore, to imagine, that we can have any idea of property, without fully comprehending the nature of justice, and shewing its origin in the artifice and contrivance of men. The origin of justice explains that of property. The same artifice gives rise to both. As our first and most natural sentiment of morals is founded on the nature of our passions, and gives the preference to ourselves and friends, above strangers ; 'tis impossible there can be naturally any such thing as a fix'd right or property, while the opposite passions of men impel them in contrary directions, and are not restrain'd by any convention or agreement.

No one can doubt, that the convention for the distinction of property, and for the stability of possession, is of all circumstances the most necessary to the establishment of human society, and that after the agreement for the fixing and observing of this rule, there remains little or nothing to be done towards settling a perfect harmony and concord. All the other passions, beside this of interest, are either easily restrain'd, or are not of such pernicious consequence, when indulg'd. *Vanity* is rather to be esteem'd a social passion, and a bond of union among men. *Pity* and *love* are to be consider'd in the same light. And as to *envy* and *revenge*, tho' pernicious, they operate only by intervals, and are directed against particular persons, whom we consider as our superiors or enemies. This avidity alone, of acquiring goods and possessions for ourselves and our nearest friends, is insatiable, perpetual, universal, and directly destructive of society. There scarce is any one, who is not actuated by it ; and there is no one, who has not reason to fear from it, when it acts without any restraint, and gives way to its first and most natural movements. So that upon the whole, we are to esteem the difficulties in the establishment of society, to be greater or less, according to those we encounter in regulating and restraining this passion.

'Tis certain, that no affection of the human mind has both a sufficient force, and a proper direction to counter-balance the love of gain, and render men fit members of society, by making them abstain from the possessions of others. Benevolence to strangers is too weak for this purpose ; and as to the other passions, they rather inflame this avidity, when we observe, that the larger our possessions are, the more ability we have of gratifying all our appetites. There is no passion, therefore, capable of controlling the interested affection, but the very affection itself, by an alteration of its direction. Now this alteration must necessarily take place upon the least reflection; since 'tis evident, that the passion is much better satisfy'd by its restraint, than by its liberty, and that in preserving society, we make much greater advances in the acquiring possessions, than in the solitary and forlorn condition, which must follow upon violence and an universal licence. The question, therefore, concerning the wickedness or goodness of human nature, enters not in the least into that other question concerning the origin of society; nor is there any thing to be consider'd but the degrees of men's sagacity or folly. For whether the passion of self-interest be esteemed vicious or virtuous, 'tis all a case; since itself alone restrains it: So that if it be virtuous, men become social by their virtue; if vicious, their vice has the same effect.

Now as 'tis by establishing the rule for the stability of possession, that this passion restrains itself; if that rule be very abstruse, and of difficult invention; society must be esteem'd, in a manner, accidental, and the effect of many ages. But if it be found, that nothing can be more simple and obvious than that rule; that every parent, in order to preserve peace among his children, must establish it; and that these first rudiments of justice must every day be improv'd, as the society enlarges: If all this appear evident, as it certainly must, we may conclude, that 'tis utterly impossible for men to remain any considerable time in that savage condition, which precedes society; but that his very first state and situation may justly be esteem'd social. This, however, hinders not, but that philosophers may, if they please, extend their reasoning to the suppos'd *state of nature;* provided they allow it to be a mere philosophical fiction, which never had, and never cou'd have any reality. Human nature being compos'd of two principal parts, which are requisite in all its actions, the affections and understanding ; 'tis certain, that the blind motions of the former, without the direction of the latter, incapacitate men for society : And it may be allow'd us to consider separately the effects, that result from the separate operations of these two component parts of the mind. The same liberty may be permitted to moral, which is allow'd to natural philosophers ; and 'tis very usual with the latter to consider any motion as compounded and consisting of two parts separate from each other, tho' at the same time they acknowledge it to be in itself uncompounded and inseparable.

This *state of nature*, therefore, is to be regarded as a mere fiction, not unlike that of the *golden age*, which poets have invented ; only with this difference, that the former is describ'd as full of war, violence and injustice ; whereas the latter is painted out to us, as the most charming and most peaceable condition that can possibly be imagin'd. The seasons, in that first age of nature, were so temperate, if we may believe the poets, that there was no necessity for men to provide themselves with cloaths and houses as a security against the violence of heat and cold. The rivers flow'd with wine and milk : The oaks yielded honey ; and nature spontaneously produc'd her greatest delicacies. Nor were these the chief advantages of that happy age. The storms and tempests were not alone removed from nature ; but those more furious tempests were unknown to human breasts, which now cause such uproar, and engender such confusion. Avarice, ambition, cruelty, selfishness, were never heard of ; Cordial affection, compassion, sympathy, were the only movements, with which the human mind was yet acquainted. Even the distinction of *mine* and *thine* was banish'd from that happy race of mortals, and carry'd with them the very notions of property and obligation, justice and injustice.

This, no doubt, is to be regarded as an idle fiction ; but yet deserves our attention, because nothing can more evidently shew the origin of those virtues, which are the subjects of our present enquiry.   I have already observ'd, that justice takes its rise from human conventions ; and that these are intended as a remedy to some inconveniences, which proceed from the concurrence of certain *qualities* of the human mind with the *situation* of external objects.   The qualities of the mind are *selfishness* and *limited generosity :* And the situation of external objects is their *easy change*, join'd to their *scarcity* in comparison of the wants and desires of men.   But however philosophers may have been bewilder'd in those speculations, poets have been guided more infallibly, by a certain taste or common instinct, which in most kinds of reasoning goes farther than any of that art and philosophy, with which we have been yet acquainted. They easily perceiv'd, if every man had a tender regard for another, or if nature supplied abundantly all our wants and desires, that the jealousy of interest, which justice supposes, could no longer have place ; nor would there be any occasion for those distinctions and limits of property and possession, which at present are in use among mankind. Encrease to a sufficient degree the benevolence of men, or the bounty of nature, and you render justice useless, by supplying its place with much nobler virtues, and more valuable blessings.   The selfishness of men is animated by the few possessions we have, in proportion to our wants ; and 'tis to restrain this selfishness, that men have been oblig'd to separate themselves from the community, and to distinguish betwixt their own goods and those of others.

Nor need we have recourse to the fictions of poets to learn this ; but beside the reason of the thing, may discover the same truth by common experience and observation.   'Tis easy to remark, that a cordial affection renders all things common among friends ; and that married people in particular mutually lose their property, and are unacquainted with the *mine* and *thine*, which are so necessary, and yet cause such disturbance in human society. The same effect arises from any alteration in the circumstances of mankind ; as when there is such a plenty of anything as satisfies all the desires of men : In which case the distinction of property is entirely lost, and every thing remains in common. This we may observe with regard to air and water, tho' the most valuable of all external objects ; and may easily conclude, that if men were supplied with every thing in the same abundance, or if *every one* had the same affection and tender regard for *every one* as for himself ; justice and injustice would be equally unknown among mankind.

Here then is a proposition, which, I think, may be regarded as certain, *that 'tis only from the selfishness and confin'd generosity of men, along with the scanty provision nature has made for his wants, that justice derives its origin.* If we look backward we shall find, that this proposition bestows an additional force on some of those observations, which we have already made on this subject.

First, we may conclude from it, that a regard to public interest, or a strong extensive benevolence, is not our first and original motive for the observation of the rules of justice ; since 'tis allow'd, that if men were endow'd with such a benevolence, these rules would never have been dreamt of.

Secondly, we may conclude from the same principle, that the sense of justice is not founded on reason, or on the discovery of certain connexions and relations of ideas, which are eternal, immutable, and universally obligatory. For since it is confest, that such an alteration as that above-mention'd, in the temper and circumstances of mankind, wou'd entirely alter our duties and obligations, 'tis necessary upon the common system, *that the sense of virtue is deriv'd from reason*, to shew the change which this must produce in the relations and ideas. But 'tis evident, that the only cause, why the extensive generosity of man, and the perfect abundance of every thing, wou'd destroy the very idea of justice, is because they render it useless ; and that, on the other hand, his confin'd benevolence, and his necessitous condition, give rise to that virtue, only by making it requisite to the publick interest, and to that of every individual. 'Twas therefore a concern for our own, and the publick interest, which made us establish the laws of justice ; and nothing can be more certain, than that it is not any relation of ideas, which gives us this concern, but our impressions and sentiments, without which every thing in nature is perfectly indifferent to us, and can never in the least affect us. The sense of justice, therefore, is not founded on our ideas, but on our impressions.

Thirdly, we may farther confirm the foregoing proposition, *that those impressions, which give rise to this sense of justice, are not natural to the mind of man, but arise from artifice and human conventions.* For since any considerable alteration of temper and circumstances destroys equally justice and injustice ; and since such an alteration has an effect only by changing our own and the publick interest ; it follows, that the first establishment of the rules of justice depends on these different interests. But if men pursu'd the publick interest naturally, and with a hearty affection, they wou'd never have dream'd of restraining each other by these rules ; and if they pursu'd their own interest, without any precaution, they wou'd run head-long into every kind of injustice and violence. These rules, therefore, are artificial, and seek their end in an oblique and indirect manner; nor is the interest, which gives rise to them, of a kind that cou'd be pursu'd by the natural and inartificial passions of men.

To make this more evident, consider, that tho' the rules of justice are establish'd merely by interest, their connexion with interest is somewhat singular, and is different from what may be observ'd on other occasions. A single act of justice is frequently contrary to *public interest;* and were it to stand alone, without being follow'd by other acts, may, in itself, be very prejudicial to society. When a man of merit, of a beneficent disposition, restores a great fortune to a miser, or a seditious bigot, he has acted justly and laudably, but the public is a real sufferer. Nor is every single act of justice, consider'd apart, more conducive to private interest, than to public ; and 'tis easily conceiv'd how a man may impoverish himself by a signal instance of integrity, and have reason to wish, that with regard to that single act, the laws of justice were for a moment suspended in the universe. But however single acts of justice may be contrary, either to public or private interest, 'tis certain, that the whole plan or scheme is highly conducive, or indeed absolutely requisite, both to the support of society, and the well-being of every individual. 'Tis impossible to separate the good from the ill. Property must be stable, and must be fix'd by general rules. Tho' in one instance the public be a sufferer, this momentary ill is amply compensated by the steady prosecution of the rule, and by the peace and order, which it establishes in society. And even every individual person must find himself a gainer, on ballancing the account ; since, without justice, society must immediately dissolve, and every one must fall into that savage and solitary condition, which is infinitely worse than the worse situation that can possibly be suppos'd in society. When therefore men have had experience enough to observe, that whatever may be the consequence of any single act of justice, perform'd by a single person, yet the whole system of actions, concurr'd in by the whole society, is infinitely advantageous to the whole, and to every part ; it is not long before justice and property take place. Every member of society is sensible of this interest : Every one expresses this sense to his fellows, along with the resolution he has taken of squaring his actions by it, on condition that others will do the same. No more is requisite to induce any one of them to perform an act of justice, who has the first opportunity. This becomes an example to others. And thus justice establishes itself by a kind of convention or agreement ; that is, by a sense of interest, suppos'd to be common to all, and where every single act is perform'd in expectation that others are to perform the like. Without such a convention, no one wou'd ever have dream'd, that there was such a virtue as justice, or have been induced to conform his actions to it. Taking any single act, my justice may be pernicious in every respect ; and 'tis only upon the supposition, that others are to imitate my example, that I can be induc'd to embrace that virtue ; since nothing but this combination can render justice advantageous, or afford me any motives to conform myself to its rules.

We come now to the *second* question we propos'd, *viz. Why we annex the idea of virtue to justice, and of vice to injustice.* This question will not detain us long after the principles, which we have already establish'd. All we can say of it at present will be dispatch'd in a few words : And for farther satisfaction, the reader must wait till we come to the *third* part of this book. The *natural* obligation to justice, *viz.* interest, has been fully explain'd ; but as to the *moral* obligation, or the sentiment of right and wrong, 'twill first be requisite to examine the natural virtues, before we can give a full and satisfactory account of it.

After men have found by experience, that their selfishness and confin'd generosity, acting at their liberty, totally incapacitate them for society ; and at the same time have observ'd. that society is necessary to the satisfaction of those very passions, they are naturally induc'd to lay themselves under the restraint of such rules, as may render their commerce more safe and commodious. To the imposition then, and observance of these rules, both in general, and in every particular instance, they are at first induc'd only by a regard to interest ; and this motive, on the first formation of society, is sufficiently strong and forcible. But when society has become numerous, and has encreas'd to a tribe or nation, this interest is more remote ; nor do men so readily perceive, that disorder and confusion follow upon every breach of these rules, as in a more narrow and contracted society. But tho' in our own actions we may frequently lose sight of that interest, which we have in maintaining order, and may follow a lesser and more present interest, we never fail to observe the prejudice we receive, either mediately or immediately, from the injustice of others ; as not being in that case either blinded by passion, or byass'd by any contrary temptation. Nay when the injustice is so distant from us, as no way to affect our interest, it still displeases us ; because we consider it as prejudicial to human society, and pernicious to every one that approaches the person guilty of it. We partake of their uneasiness by *sympathy;* and as every thing, which gives uneasiness in human actions, upon the general survey, is call'd Vice, and whatever produces satisfaction, in the same manner, is denominated Virtue ; this is the reason why the sense of moral good and evil follows upon justice and in-justice. And tho' this sense, in the present case, be deriv'd only from contemplating the actions of others, yet we fail not to extend it even to our own actions. The *general rule* reaches beyond those instances, from which it arose ; while at the same time we naturally *sympathize* with others in the sentiments they entertain of us. *Thus self-interest is the original motive to the* establishment *of justice: but a* sympathy *with public interest is the source of the* moral approbation, *which attends that virtue.*

Tho' this progress of the sentiments be *natural,* and even necessary, 'tis certain, that it is here forwarded by the artifice of politicians, who, in order to govern men more easily, and preserve peace in human society, have endeavour'd to pro-duce an esteem for justice, and an abhorrence of injustice.

This, no doubt, must have its effect : but nothing can be more evident, than that the matter has been carry'd too far by certain writers on morals, who seem to have employ'd their utmost efforts to extirpate all sense of virtue from among mankind. Any artifice of politicians may assist nature in the producing of those sentiments, which she suggests to us, and may even on some occasions, produce alone an approbation or esteem for any particular action ; but 'tis impossible it should be the sole cause of the distinction we make betwixt vice and virtue. For if nature did not aid us in this particular, 'twou'd be in vain for politicians to talk of *honourable* or *dishonourable*, *praiseworthy* or *blameable*. These words wou'd be perfectly unintelligible, and wou'd no more have any idea annex'd to them, than if they were of a tongue perfectly unknown to us. The utmost politicians can perform, is, to extend the natural sentiments beyond their original bounds ; but still nature must furnish the materials, and give us some notion of moral distinctions.

As publick praise and blame encrease our esteem for justice ; so private education and instruction contribute to the same effect. For as parents easily observe, that a man is the more useful, both to himself and others, the greater degree of probity and honour he is endow'd with ; and that those principles have greater force, when custom and education assist interest and reflection : For these reasons they are induc'd to inculcate on their children, from their earliest infancy, the principles of probity, and teach them to regard the observance of those rules, by which society is maintain'd, as worthy and honourable, and their violation as base and infamous. By this means the sentiments of honour may take root in their tender minds, and acquire such firmness and solidity, that they may fall little short of those principles, which are the most essential to our natures, and the most deeply radicated in our internal constitution.

What farther contributes to encrease their solidity, is the interest of our reputation, after the opinion, *that a merit or demerit attends justice or injustice*, is once firmly establish'd among mankind. There is nothing, which touches us more nearly than our reputation, and nothing on which our reputation more depends than our conduct, with relation to the property of others. For this reason, every one, who has any regard to his character, or intends to live on good terms with mankind, must fix an inviolable law to himself, never, by any temptation, to be induc'd to violate those principles, which are essential to a man of probity and honour.

I shall make only one observation before I leave this subject, *viz.* that tho' I assert, that in the *state of nature*, or that imaginary state, which preceded society, there be neither justice nor injustice, yet I assert not, that it was allowable, in such a state, to violate the property of others. I only maintain, that there was no such thing as property ; and consequently cou'd be no such thing as justice or injustice. I shall have occasion to make a similar reflection with regard to *promises*, when I come to treat of them ; and I hope this reflection, when duly weigh'd, will suffice to remove all odium from the foregoing opinions, with regard to justice and injustice.

SECTION III.

Of the rules, which determine property.

THO' the establishment of the rule, concerning the stability of possession, be not only useful, but even absolutely necessary to human society, it can never serve to any purpose, while it remains in such general terms. Some method must be shewn, by which we may distinguish what particular goods are to be assign'd to each particular person, while the rest of mankind are excluded from their possession and enjoyment. Our next business, then, must be to discover the reasons which modify this general rule, and fit it to the common use and practice of the world.

'Tis obvious, that those reasons are not deriv'd from any utility or advantage, which either the *particular* person or the public may reap from his enjoyment of any *particular* goods, beyond what wou'd result from the possession of them by any other person. 'Twere better, no doubt, that every one were possess'd of what is most suitable to him, and proper for his use : But besides, that this relation of fitness may be common to several at once, 'tis liable to so many controversies, and men are so partial and passionate in judging of these controversies, that such a loose and uncertain rule would be absolutely incompatible with the peace of human society. The convention concerning the stability of possession is enter'd into, in order to cut off all occasions of discord and contention ; and this end wou'd never be attain'd, were we allowed to apply this rule differently in every particular case, according to every particular utility, which might be discover'd in such an application. Justice, in her decisions, never regards the fitness or unfitness of objects to particular persons, but conducts herself by more extensive views. Whether a man be generous, or a miser, he is equally well receiv'd by her, and obtains with the same facility a decision in his favour, even for what is entirely useless to him.

It follows, therefore, that the general rule, *that possession must be stable*, is not apply'd by particular judgments, but by other general rules, which must extend to the whole society, and be inflexible either by spite or favour. To illustrate this, I propose the following instance. I first consider men in their savage and solitary condition ; and suppose, that being sensible of the misery of that state, and foreseeing the advantages that wou'd result from society, they seek each other's company, and make an offer of mutual protection and assistance. I also suppose, that they are endow'd with such sagacity as immediately to perceive, that the chief impediment to this project of society and partnership lies in the avidity and selfishness of their natural temper ; to remedy which, they enter into a convention for the stability of possession, and for mutual restraint and forbearance. I am sensible, that this method of proceeding is not altogether natural ; but besides that I here only suppose those reflections to be form'd at once, which in fact arise insensibly and by degrees ; besides this, I say, 'tis very possible, that several persons, being by different accidents separated from the societies, to which they formerly belong'd, may be oblig'd to form a new society among themselves ; in which case they are entirely in the situation above-mentioned.

'Tis evident, then, that their first difficulty, in this situation, after the general convention for the establishment of society, and for the constancy of possession, is, how to separate their possessions, and assign to each his particular portion, which he must for the future inalterably enjoy. This difficulty will not detain them long ; but it must immediately occur to them, as the most natural expedient, that every one continue to enjoy what he is at present master of, and that property or constant possession be conjoin'd to the immediate possession. Such is the effect of custom, that it not only reconciles us to any thing we have long enjoy'd, but even gives us an affection for it, and makes us prefer it to other objects, which may be more valuable, but are less known to us. What has long lain under our eye, and has often been employ'd to our advantage, *that* we are always the most unwilling to part with ; but can easily live without possessions, which we never have enjoy'd, and are not accustom'd to. 'Tis evident, therefore, that men would easily acquiesce in this expedient, *that every one continue to enjoy what he is at present possess'd of ;* and this is the reason, why they wou'd so naturally agree in preferring it.[1]

[1] No questions in philosophy are more difficult, than when a number of causes present themselves for the same phænomenon, to determine which is the principal and predominant. There seldom is any very precise argument to fix our choice, and men must be contented to be guided by a kind of taste or fancy, arising from analogy, and a comparison of similar instances. Thus, in the present case, there are, no doubt, motives of public interest for most of the rules, which determine property ; but still I suspect, that these rules are principally fix'd by the imagination, or the more frivolous properties of our thought and conception. I shall continue to explain these causes, leaving it to the reader's choice, whether he will prefer those deriv'd from publick utility, or those deriv'd from the imagination. We shall begin with the right of the present possessor.

'Tis a quality, which (*a*) I have already observ'd in human nature, that when two objects appear in a close relation to each other, the mind is apt to ascribe to them any additional relation in order to compleat the union ; and this inclination is so strong, as often to make us run into errors (such as that of the conjunction of thought and matter) if we find that they can serve to that purpose. Many of our impressions are incapable of place or local position ; and yet those very impressions we suppose to have a local conjuction with the impressions of sight and touch, merely because they are conjoin'd by causation, and are already united in the imagination. Since, therefore, we can feign a new relation, and even an absurd one, in order to compleat any union, 'twill easily be imagin'd that if there be any relations, which depend on the mind, 'twill readily conjoin them to any preceding relation, and unite by a new bond such objects as have already an union in the fancy. Thus for instance, we never fail, in our arrangement of bodies, to place those which are *resembling* in *contiguity* to each other, or at least in *correspondent* points of view ; because we feel a satisfaction in joining the relation of contiguity to that of resemblance, or the resemblance of situation to that of qualities. And this is easily accounted for from the known properties of human nature. When the mind is determin'd to join certain objects, but undetermin'd in its choice of the particular objects, it naturally turns its eye to such as are related together. They are already united in the mind : They present themselves at the same time to the conception , and instead of requiring any new reason for their conjunction, it wou'd require a very powerful reason to make us over-look this natural affinity. This we shall have occasion to explain more fully afterwards, when we come to treat of *beauty*. In the mean time, we may content ourselves with observing, that the same love of order and uniformity, which arranges the books in a library, and the chairs in a parlour, contribute to the formation of society, and to the

(*a*) *Book* I. *Part* IV. *sect.* 5.

But we may observe, that tho' the rule of the assignment of property to the present possessor be natural, and by that means useful, yet its utility extends not beyond the first formation of society ; nor wou'd any thing be more pernicious, than the constant observance of it ; by which restitution wou'd be excluded, and every injustice wou'd be authoriz'd and rewarded. We must, therefore, seek for some other circumstance, that may give rise to property after society is once established ; and of this kind, I find four most considerable, *viz.* Occupation, Prescription, Accession, and Succession. We shall briefly examine each of these, beginning with *Occupation.*

The possession of all external goods is changeable and uncertain ; which is one of the most considerable impediments to the establishment of society, and is the reason why, by universal agreement, express or tacite, men restrain themselves by what we now call the rules of justice and equity. The misery of the condition, which precedes this restraint, is the cause why we submit to that remedy as quickly as possible ; and this affords us any easy reason, why we annex the idea of property to the first possession, or to *occupation.* Men are unwilling to leave property in suspence, even for the shortest time, or open the least door to violence and disorder. To which we may add, that the first possession always engages the attention most ; and did we neglect it, there wou'd be no colour of reason for assigning property to any succeeding possession.[1]

well-being of mankind, by modifying the general rule concerning the stability of possession. And as property forms a relation betwixt a person and an object, 'tis natural to found it on some preceding relation ; and as property is nothing but a constant possession, secur'd by the laws of society, 'tis natural to add it to the present possession, which is a relation that resembles it. For this also has its influence. If it be natural to conjoin all sorts of relations, 'tis more so to conjoin such relations as are resembling, and are related together.

[1] Some philosophers account for the right of occupation, by saying, that every one has a property in his own labour; and when he joins that

There remains nothing, but to determine exactly, what is meant by possession ; and this is not so easy as may at first sight be imagin'd. We are said to be in possession of any thing, not only when we immediately touch it, but also when we are so situated with respect to it, as to have it in our power to use it ; and may move, alter, or destroy it, according to our present pleasure or advantage. This relation, then, is a species of cause and effect ; and as property is nothing but a stable possession, deriv'd from the rules of justice, or the conventions of men, 'tis to be consider'd as the same species of relation. But here we may observe, that as the power of using any object becomes more or less certain, according as the interruptions we may meet with are more or less probable ; and as this probability may increase by insensible degrees ; 'tis in many cases impossible to determine when possession begins or ends ; nor is there any certain standard, by which we can decide such controversies. A wild boar, that falls into our snares, is deem'd to be in our possession, if it be impossible for him to escape. But what do we mean by impossible? How do we separate this impossibility from an improbability? And how distinguish that exactly from a probability? Mark the precise limits of the one and the other, and show the standard, by which we may decide all disputes that may arise, and, as we find by experience, frequently do arise upon this subject.[1]

labour to any thing, it gives him the property of the whole: But, 1. There are several kinds of occupation, where we cannot be said to join our labour to the object we acquire: As when we possess a meadow by grazing our cattle upon it. 2. This accounts for the matter by means of *accession;* which is taking a needless circuit. 3. We cannot be said to join our labour to any thing but in a figurative sense. Properly speaking, we only make an alteration on it by our labour. This forms a relation betwixt us and the object; and thence arises the property, according to the preceding principles.

[1] If we seek a solution of these difficulties in reason and public interest, we never shall find satisfaction; and if we look for it in the imagination, 'tis evident, that the qualities, which operate upon that faculty, run so insensibly and gradually into each other, that 'tis impos-

But such disputes may not only arise concerning the real existence of property and possession, but also concerning their extent ; and these disputes are often susceptible of no decision, or can be decided by no other faculty than the imagination. A person who lands on the shore of a small island, that is desart and uncultivated, is deem'd its possessor from the very first moment, and acquires the property of the whole ; because the object is there bounded and circumscrib'd in the fancy, and at the same time is proportioned to the new possessor. The same person landing on a desart island, as large as *Great Britain*, extends his property no farther than his immediate possession ; tho' a

sible to give them any precise bounds or termination. The difficulties on this head must encrease, when we consider, that our judgment alters very sensibly, according to the subject, and that the same power and proximity will be deem'd possession in one case, which is not esteem'd such in another. A person, who has hunted a hare to the last degree of weariness, wou'd look upon it as an injustice for another to rush in before him, and seize his prey. But the same person, advancing to pluck an apple, that hangs within his reach, has no reason to complain, if another, more alert, passes him, and takes possession. What is the reason of this difference, but that immobility, not being natural to the hare, but the effect of industry, forms in that case a strong relation with the hunter, which is wanting in the other?

Here then it appears, that a certain and infallible power of enjoyment, without touch or some other sensible relation, often produces not property: And I farther observe, that a sensible relation, without any present power, is sometimes sufficient to give a title to any object. The sight of a thing is seldom a considerable relation, and is only regarded as such, when the object is hidden, or very obscure; in which case we find, that the view alone conveys a property; according to that maxim, *that even a whole continent belongs to the nation, which first discover'd it.* 'Tis however remarkable, that both in the case of discovery and that of possession, the first discoverer and possessor must join to the relation an intention of rendering himself proprietor, otherwise the relation will not have its effect; and that because the connexion in our fancy betwixt the property and the relation is not so great, but that it requires to be help'd by such an intention.

From all these circumstances, 'tis easy to see how perplex'd many questions may become concerning the acquisition of property by occupation; and the least effort of thought may present us with instances, which are not susceptible of any reasonable decision. If we prefer examples, which are real, to such as are feign'd, we may consider the numerous colony are esteem'd the proprietors of the whole from the instant of their debarkment.

But it often happens, that the title of the first possession becomes obscure thro' time ; and that 'tis impossible to determine many controversies, which may arise concerning it. In that case long possession or *prescription* naturally takes place, and gives a person a sufficient property in any thing he enjoys. The nature of human society admits not of any great accuracy ; nor can we always remount to the first origin of things, in order to determine their present condition. Any considerable space of time sets objects at such a distance, that they seem, in a manner, to lose their

following one, which is to be met with in almost every writer, that has treated of the laws of nature. Two *Grecian* colonies, leaving their native country, in search of new seats, were inform'd that a city near them was deserted by its inhabitants. To know the truth of this report, they dispatch'd at once two messengers, one from each colony; who finding on their approach, that their information was true, begun a race together with an intention to take possession of the city, each of them for his countrymen. One of these messengers, finding that he was not an equal match for the other, launch'd his spear at the gates of the city, and was so fortunate as to fix it there, before the arrival of his companion. This produc'd a dispute betwixt the two colonies, which of them was the proprietor of the empty city; and this dispute still subsists among philosophers. For my part I find the dispute impossible to be decided, and that because the whole question hangs upon the fancy, which in this case is not possess'd of any precise or determinate standard, upon which it can give sentence. To make this evident, let us consider, that if these two persons had been simply members of the colonies, and not messengers or deputies, their actions wou'd not have been of any consequence; since in that case their relation to the colonies wou'd have been but feeble and .imperfect. Add to this, that nothing determin'd them to run to the gates rather than the walls, or any other part of the city, but that the gates, being the most obvious and remarkable part, satisfy the fancy best in taking them for the whole ; as we find by the poets, who frequently draw their images and metaphors from them. Besides we may consider, that the touch or contact of the one messenger is not properly possession, no more than the piercing the gates with a spear; but only forms a relation ; and there is a relation, in the other case, equally obvious, tho' not, perhaps, of equal force. Which of these relations, then, conveys a right and property, or whether any of them be sufficient for that effect, I leave to the decision of such as are wiser than myself.

reality, and have as little influence on the mind, as if they never had been in being. A man's title, that is clear and certain at present, will seem obscure and doubtful fifty years hence, even tho' the facts, on which it is founded, shou'd be prov'd with the greatest evidence and certainty. The same facts have not the same influence after so long an interval of time. And this may be received as a convincing argument for our preceding doctrine with regard to property and justice. Possession during a long tract of time conveys a title to any object. But as 'tis certain, that, however every thing be produc'd in time, there is nothing real, that is produc'd by time ; it follows, that property being produc'd by time, is not any thing real in the objects, but is the offspring of the sentiments, on which alone time is found to have any influence.[1]

We acquire the property of objects by *accession*, when they are connected in an intimate manner with objects that are already our property, and at the same time are inferior to them. Thus the fruits of our garden, the offspring of our cattle, and the work of our slaves, are all of them esteem'd our property, even before possession. Where objects are connected together in the imagination, they are apt to be put on the same footing, and are commonly suppos'd to be endow'd with the same qualities. We readily pass from one to the other, and make no difference in our judgments concerning them ; especially if the latter be inferior to the former.[2]

[1] Present possession is plainly a relation betwixt a person and an object ; but is not sufficient to counter-ballance the relation of first possession, unless the former be long and uninterrupted : In which case the relation is encreas'd on the side of the present possession, by the extent of time, and diminish'd on that of first possession, by the distance. This change in the relation produces a consequent change in the property.

[2] This source of property can never be explain'd but from the imaginations ; and one may affirm, that the causes are here unmix'd. We shall proceed to explain them more particularly, and illustrate them by examples from common life and experience.

It has been observ'd above, that the mind has a natural propensity to join relations, especially resembling ones, and finds a kind of fitness and

The right of *succession* is a very natural one, from the presum'd consent of the parent or near relation, and from the
general interest of mankind, which requires, that men's

uniformity in such an union. From this propensity are deriv'd these
laws of nature, *that upon the first formation of society, property always
follows the present possession ;* and afterwards, *that it arises from first
or from long possession.* Now we may easily observe, that relation is
not confin'd merely to one degree ; but that from an object, that is
related to us, we acquire a relation to every other object which is related
to it, and so on, till the thought loses the chain by too long a progress.
However the relation may weaken by each remove, 'tis not immediately
destroy'd ; but frequently connects two objects by means of an intermediate one, which is related to both. And this principle is of such
force as to give rise to the right of *accession*, and causes us to acquire
the property not only of such objects as we are immediately possess'd
of, but also of such as are closely connected with them.

Suppose a *German*, a *Frenchman*, and a *Spaniard* to come into a
room, where there are plac'd upon the table three bottles of wine,
Rhenish, *Burgundy* and *Port*; and suppose they shou'd fall a quarrelling about the division of them ; a person who was chosen for umpire,
wou'd naturally, to shew his impartiality, give every one the product of
his own country : And this from a principle, which in some measure, is
the source of those laws of nature, that ascribe property to occupation,
prescription and accession.

In all these cases and particularly that of accession, there is first a
natural union betwixt the idea of the person and that of the object, and
afterwards a new and *moral* union produc'd by the right or property,
which we ascribe to the person. But here there occurs a difficulty,
which merits our attention, and may afford us an opportunity of putting
to tryal that singular method of reasoning, which has been employ'd on
the present subject. I have already observ'd, that the imagination
passes with greater facility from little to great, than from great to little,
and that the transition of ideas is always easier and smoother in the
former case than in the latter. Now as the right of accession arises
from the easy transition of ideas, by which related objects are connected
together, it shou'd naturally be imagin'd, that the right of accession
must encrease in strength, in proportion as the transition of ideas is perform'd with greater facility. It may, therefore, be thought, that when
we have acquir'd the property of any small object, we shall readily
consider any great object related to it as an accession, and as belonging
to the proprietor of the small one ; hence the transition is in that case
very easy from the small object to the great one, and shou'd connect
them together in the closest manner. But in fact the case is always
found to be otherwise. The empire of *Great Britain* seems to draw
along with it the dominion of the *Orkneys*, the *Hebrides*, the isle of *Man*,
and the isle of *Wight;* but the authority over those lesser islands does
not naturally imply any title to *Great Britain*. In short, a small object

possessions shou'd pass to those, who are dearest to them, in order to render them more industrious and frugal. Perhaps these causes are seconded by the influence of *relation*,

naturally follows a great one as its accession ; but a great one is never suppos'd to belong to the proprietor of a small one related to it, merely on account of that property and relation. Yet in this latter case the transition of ideas is smoother from the proprietor to the small object, which is his property, and from the small object to the great one, than in the former case from the proprietor to the great object, and from the great one to the small. It may therefore be thought, that these phænomena are objections to the foregoing hypothesis, *that the ascribing of property to accession is nothing but an effect of the relations of ideas, and of the smooth transition of the imagination.*

'Twill be easy to solve this objection, if we consider the agility and unsteadiness of the imagination, with the different views, in which it is continually placing its objects. When we attribute to a person a property in two objects, we do not always pass from the person to one object, and from that to the other related to it. The objects being here to be consider'd as the property of the person, we are apt to join them together, and place them in the same light. Suppose, therefore, a great and a small object to be related together; if a person be strongly related to the great object, he will likewise be strongly related to both the objects, consider'd together, because he is related to the most considerable part. On the contrary, if he be only related to the small object, he will not be strongly related to both, consider'd together, since his relation lies only with the most trivial part, which is not apt to strike us in any great degree, when we consider the whole. And this is the reason, why small objects become accessions to great ones, and not great to small.

'Tis the general opinion of philosophers and civilians, that the sea is incapable of becoming the property of any nation; and that because 'tis impossible to take possession of it, or form any such distinct relation with it, as may be the foundation of property. Where this reason ceases, property immediately takes place. Thus the most strenuous advocates for the liberty of the seas universally allow, that friths and bays naturally belong as an accession to the proprietors of the surrounding continent. These have properly no more bond or union with the land, than the *pacific* ocean wou'd have; but having an union in the fancy, and being at the same time *inferior*, they are of course regarded as an accession.

The property of rivers, by the laws of most nations, and by the natural turn of our thought, is attributed to the proprietors of their banks, excepting such vast rivers as the *Rhine* or the *Danube*, which seem too large to the imagination to follow as an accession the property of the neighboring fields. Yet even these rivers are consider'd as the property of that nation, thro' whose dominions they run; the idea of a or the association of ideas, by which we are naturally directed to consider the son after the parent's decease, and ascribe to him a title to his father's possessions. Those

nation being of a suitable bulk to correspond with them, and bear them such a relation in the fancy.

The accessions, which are made to lands bordering upon rivers, follow the land, say the civilians, provided it be made by what they call *alluvion*, that is, insensibly and imperceptibly; which are circumstances that mightily assist the imagination in the conjunction. Where there is any considerable portion torn at once from one bank, and join'd to another, it becomes not his property, whose land it falls on, till it unite with the land, and till the trees or plants have spread their roots into both. Before that, the imagination does not sufficiently join them.

There are other cases, which somewhat resemble this of accession, but which, at the bottom, are considerably different, and merit our attention. Of this kind is the conjunction of the properties of different persons, after such a manner as not to admit of *separation*. The question is, to whom the united mass must belong.

Where this conjunction is of such a nature as to admit of *division*, but not of *separation*, the decision is natural and easy. The whole mass must be suppos'd to be common betwixt the proprietors of the several parts, and afterwards must be divided according to the proportions of these parts. But hear I cannot forbear taking notice of a remarkable subtilty of the *Roman* law, in distinguishing betwixt *confusion* and *commixtion*. Confusion is an union of two bodies, such as different liquors, where the parts become entirely undistinguishable. Commixtion is the blending of two bodies, such as two bushels of corn, where the parts remain separate in an obvious and visible manner. As in the latter case the imagination discovers not so entire an union as in the former, but is able to trace and preserve a distinct idea of the property of each; this is the reason, why the *civil* law, tho' it establish'd an entire community in the case of *confusion*, and after that a proportional division, yet in the case of *commixtion*, supposes each of the proprietors to maintain a distinct right; however necessity may at last force them to submit to the same division.

Quod si frumentum Titii frumento tuo mistum fuerit: siquidem ex voluntate vestra, commune est: quia singula corpora, id est, singula grana, quæ cujusque propria fuerunt, ex consensu vestro communicata sunt. Quod si casu id mistum fuerit, vel Titius id miscuerit sine tua voluntate, non videtur id commune esse: quia singula corpora in sua substantia durant. Sed nec magis istis casibus commune sit frumentum quam grex intelligitur esse communis, si pecora Titii tuis pecoribus mista fuerint. Sed si ab alterutro vestrûm totum id frumentum retineatur, in rem quidem actio pro modo frumenti cujusque competit. Arbitrio autem judicis, ut ipse æstimet quale cujusque frumentum fuerit. Inst. Lib. II. Tit. 1. § 28.

Where the properties of two persons are united after such a manner as neither to admit of *division* nor *separation*, as when one builds a goods must become the property of some body : But *of whom* is the question.   Here 'tis evident the person's children naturally present themselves to the mind ; and

house on another's ground, in that case, the whole must belong to one of the proprietors: And here I assert, that it naturally is conceiv'd to belong to the proprietor of the most considerable part.   For however the compound object may have a relation to two different persons, and carry our view at once to both of them, yet as the most considerable part principally engages our attention, and by the strict union draws the inferior along it; for this reason, the whole bears a relation to the proprietor of that part, and is regarded as his property.   The only difficulty is, what we shall be pleas'd to call the most considerable part, and most attractive to the imagination.

This quality depends on several different circumstances, which have little connexion with each other.   One part of a compound object may become more considerable than another, either because it is more constant and durable; because it is of greater value; because it is more obvious and remarkable; because it is of greater extent; or because its existence is more separate and independent.   'Twill be easy to conceive, that, as these circumstances may be conjoin'd and oppos'd in all the different ways, and according to all the different degrees, which can be imagin'd, there will result many cases, where the reasons on both sides are so equally balanc'd, that 'tis impossible for us to give any satisfactory decision.   Here then is the proper business of municipal laws, to fix what the principles of human nature have left undetermin'd.   The superficies yields to the soil, says the civil law : The writing to the paper : The canvas to the picture.   These decisions do not well agree together, and are a proof of the contrariety of those principles, from which they are deriv'd.

But of all the questions of this kind the most curious is that, which for so many ages divided the disciples of *Proculus* and *Sabinus*.   Suppose a person shou'd make a cup from the metal of another, or a ship from his wood, and suppose the proprietor of the metal or wood shou'd demand his goods, the question is, whether he acquires a title to the cup or ship.   *Sabinus* maintain'd the affirmative, and asserted that the substance or matter is the foundation of all the qualities ; that it is incorruptible and immortal, and therefore superior to the form, which is casual and dependent.   On the other hand, *Proculus* observ'd, that the form is the most obvious and remarkable part, and that from it bodies are denominated of this or that particular species.   To which he might have added, that the matter or substance is in most bodies so fluctuating and uncertain, that 'tis utterly impossible to trace it in all its changes.   For my part, I know not from what principles such a controversy can be certainly determin'd.   I shall therefore content my self with observing, that the decision of *Trebonian* seems to me pretty ingenious; that the cup belongs to the proprietor of the metal, because it can be brought back to its first form: But that the ship belongs to being already connected to those possessions by means of their deceas'd parent, we are apt to connect them still farther by the relation of property. Of this there are many parallel instances.[1]

SECTION IV.

Of the transference of property by consent.

HOWEVER useful, or even necessary, the stability of possession may be to human society, 'tis attended with very considerable inconveniences. The relation of fitness or suitableness ought never to enter into consideration, in distributing the properties of mankind; but we must govern ourselves by rules, which are more general in their application, and more free from doubt and uncertainty. Of this kind is *present* possession upon the first establishment of society; and afterwards *occupation*, *prescription*, *accession*, and *succession*. As these depend very much on chance, they must frequently

the author of its form for a contrary reason. But however ingenious this reason may seem, it plainly depends upon the fancy, which by the possibility of such a reduction, finds a closer connexion and relation betwixt a cup and the proprietor of its metal, than betwixt a ship and the proprietor of its wood, where the substance is more fix'd and unalterable.

[1] In examining the different titles to authority in government, we shall meet with many reasons to convince us, that the right of succession depends, in a great measure, on the imagination. Mean while I shall rest contented with observing one example, which belongs to the present subject. Suppose that a person die without children, and that a dispute arises among his relations concerning his inheritance; 'tis evident, that if his riches be deriv'd partly from his father, partly from his mother, the most natural way of determining such a dispute, is, to divide his possessions, and assign each part to the family, from whence it is deriv'd. Now as the person is suppos'd to have been once the full and entire proprietor of those goods; I ask, what is it makes us find a certain equity and natural reason in this partition, except it be the imagination? His affection to these families does not depend upon his possessions; for which reason his consent can never be presum'd precisely for such a partition. And as to the public interest, it seems not to be in the least concern'd on the one side or the other.

prove contradictory both to men's wants and desires ; and persons and possessions must often be very ill adjusted. This is a grand inconvenience, which calls for a remedy. To apply one directly, and allow every man to seize by violence what he judges to be fit for him, wou'd destroy society ; and therefore the rules of justice seek some medium betwixt a rigid stability, and this changeable and uncertain adjustment. But there is no medium better than that obvious one, that possession and property shou'd always be stable, except when the proprietor consents to bestow them on some other person. This rule can have no ill consequence, in occasioning wars and dissentions ; since the proprietor's consent, who alone is concern'd, is taken along in the alienation : And it may serve to many good purposes in adjusting property to persons. Different parts of the earth produce different commodities ; and not only so, but different men both are by nature fitted for different employments, and attain to greater perfection in any one, when they confine themselves to it alone. All this requires a mutual exchange and commerce ; for which reason the translation of property by consent is founded on a law of nature, as well as its stability without such a consent.

So far is determin'd by a plain utility and interest. But perhaps 'tis from more trivial reasons, that *delivery*, or a sensible tranference of the object is commonly requir'd by civil laws, and also by the laws of nature, according to most authors, as a requisite circumstance in the translation of property. The property of an object, when taken for something real, without any reference to morality, or the sentiments of the mind, is a quality perfectly insensible, and even inconceivable ; nor can we form any distinct notion, either of its stability or translation. This imperfection of our ideas is less sensibly felt with regard to its stability, as it engages less our attention, and is easily past over by the mind, without any scrupulous examination. But as the translation of property from one person to another is a more remarkable event, the defect of our ideas becomes more sensible on that occasion, and obliges us to turn ourselves on every side in search of some remedy.   Now as nothing more enlivens any idea than a present impression, and a relation betwixt that impression and the idea ; 'tis natural for us to seek some false light from this quarter.   In order to aid the imagination in conceiving the transference of property, we take the sensible object, and actually transfer its possession to the person, on whom we wou'd bestow the property.   The suppos'd resemblance of the actions, and the presence of this sensible delivery, deceive the mind, and make it fancy, that it conceives the mysterious transition of the property.   And that this explication of the matter is just, appears hence, that men have invented a *symbolical* delivery, to satisfy the fancy, where the real one is impracticable.   Thus the giving the keys of a granary is understood to be the delivery of the corn contain'd in it :   The giving of stone and earth represents the delivery of a mannor.   This is a kind of superstitious practice in civil laws, and in the laws of nature, resembling the *Roman catholic* superstitions in religion.   As the *Roman catholics* represent the inconceivable mysteries of the *Christian* religion, and render them more present to the mind, by a taper, or habit, or grimace, which is suppos'd to resemble them ;   so lawyers and moralists have run into like inventions for the same reason, and have endeavour'd by those means to satisfy themselves concerning the transference of property by consent.

SECTION V.

Of the obligation of promises.

THAT the rule of morality, which enjoins the performance of promises, is not *natural*, will sufficiently appear from these two propositions, which I proceed to prove, viz. *that a promise wou'd not be intelligible, before human conventions had establish'd it;* and *that even if it were intelligible, it wou'd not be attended with any moral obligation.*

I say, *first,* that a promise is not intelligible naturally, nor antecedent to human conventions ; and that a man, unacquainted with society, could never enter into any engagements with another, even tho' they could perceive each other's thoughts by intuition. If promises be natural and intelligible, there must be some act of the mind attending these words, *I promise;* and on this act of the mind must the obligation depend. Let us, therefore, run over all the faculties of the soul, and see which of them is exerted in our promises. The act of the mind, exprest by a promise, is not a *resolution* to perform any thing : For that alone never imposes any obligation. Nor is it a *desire* of such a performance : For we may bind ourselves without such a desire, or even with an aversion, declar'd and avow'd. Neither is it the *willing* of that action, which we promise to perform : For a promise always regards some future time, and the will has an influence only on present actions. It follows, therefore, that since the act of the mind, which enters into a promise, and produces its obligation, is neither the resolving, desiring, nor willing any particular performance, it must necessarily be the *willing* of that *obligation,* which arises from the promise. Nor is this only a conclusion of philosophy; but is entirely conformable to our common ways of thinking and of expressing ourselves, when we say that we are bound by our own consent, and that the obligation arises from our mere will and pleasure. The only question, then, is, whether there be not a manifest absurdity in supposing this act of the mind, and such an absurdity as no man cou'd fall into, whose ideas are not confounded with prejudice and the fallacious use of language.

All morality depends upon our sentiments ; and when any action, or quality of the mind, pleases us *after a certain manner*, we say it is virtuous ; and when the neglect, or non-performance of it, displeases us *after a like manner*, we say that we lie under an obligation to perform it.   A change of the obligation supposes a change of the sentiment ; and a creation of a new obligation supposes some new sentiment to arise.   But 'tis certain we can naturally no more change our own sentiments, than the motions of the heavens ; nor by a single act of our will, that is, by a promise, render any action agreeable or disagreeable, moral or immoral ; which, without that act, wou'd have produc'd contrary impressions, or have been endow'd with different qualities.   It wou'd be absurd, therefore, to will any new obligation, that is, any new sentiment of pain or pleasure ; nor is it possible, that men cou'd naturally fall into so gross an absurdity.   A promise, therefore, is *naturally* something altogether unintelligible, nor is there any act of the mind belonging to it.[1]

[1] Were morality discoverable by reason, and not by sentiment, 'twou'd be still more evident, that promises cou'd make no alteration upon it.   Morality is suppos'd to consist in relation.   Every new imposition of morality, therefore, must arise from some new relation of objects; and consequently the will cou'd not produce *immediately* any change in morals, but cou'd have that effect only by producing a change upon the objects.   But as the moral obligation of a promise is the pure effect of the will, without the least change in any part of the universe; it follows, that promises have no *natural* obligation.

Shou'd it be said, that this act of the will being in effect a new object, produces new relations and new duties; I wou'd answer, that this is a pure sophism, which may be detected by a very moderate share of accuracy and exactness.   To will a new obligation, is to will a new relation of objects; and therefore, if this new relation of objects were form'd by the volition itself, we shou'd in effect will the volition; which is plainly absurd and impossible.   The will has here no object to which it cou'd tend; but must return upon itself *in infinitum*.   The new obligation depends upon new relations.   The new relations depend upon a new volition.   The new volition has for object a new obligation, and consequently new relations, and consequently a new volition; which volition again has in view a new obligation, relation and volition, without any termination.   'Tis impossible, therefore, we cou'd ever will a new obligation; and consequently 'tis impossible the will cou'd ever accompany a promise, or produce a new obligation of morality.

But, *secondly*, if there was any act of the mind belonging to it, it could not *naturally* produce any obligation. This appears evidently from the foregoing reasoning. A promise creates a new obligation. A new obligation supposes new sentiments to arise. The will never creates new sentiments. There could not naturally, therefore, arise any obligation from a promise, even supposing the mind could fall into the absurdity of willing that obligation.

The same truth may be prov'd still more evidently by that reasoning, which prov'd justice in general to be an artificial virtue. No action can be requir'd of us as our duty, unless there be implanted in human nature some actuating passion or motive, capable of producing the action. This motive cannot be the sense of duty. A sense of duty supposes an antecedent obligation : And where an action is not requir'd by any natural passion, it cannot be requir'd by any natural obligation ; since it may be omitted without proving any defect or imperfection in the mind and temper, and con-sequently without any vice. Now 'tis evident we have no motive leading us to the performance of promises, distinct from a sense of duty. If we thought, that promises had no moral obligation, we never shou'd feel any inclination to observe them. This is not the case with the natural virtues. Tho' there was no obligation to relieve the miserable, our humanity wou'd lead us to it ; and when we omit that duty, the immorality of the omission arises from its being a proof, that we want the natural sentiments of humanity. A father knows it to be his duty to take care of his children : But he has also a natural inclination to it. And if no human creature had that inclination, no one cou'd lie under any such obligation. But as there is naturally no inclination to observe promises, distinct from a sense of their obligation ; it follows, that fidelity is no natural virtue, and that promises have no force, antecedent to human conventions.

If any one dissent from this, he must give a regular proof of these two propositions, viz. *that there is a peculiar act of the mind, annext to promises;* and *that consequent to this act of the mind, there arises an inclination to perform, distinct from a sense of duty.* I presume, that it is impossible to prove either of these two points ; and therefore I venture to conclude, that promises are human inventions, founded on the necessities and interests of society.

In order to discover these necessities and interests, we must consider the same qualities of human nature, which we have already found to give rise to the preceding laws of society. Men being naturally selfish, or endow'd only with a confin'd generosity, they are not easily induc'd to perform any action for the interest of strangers, except with a view to some reciprocal advantage, which they have no hope of obtaining but by such a performance. Now as it frequently happens, that these mutual performances cannot be finish'd at the same instant, 'tis necessary, that one party be contented to remain in uncertainty, and depend upon the gratitude of the other for a return of kindness. But so much corruption is there among men, that, generally speaking, this becomes but a slender security ; and as the benefactor is here suppos'd to bestow his favours with a view to self-interest, this both takes off from the obligation, and sets an example of selfishness, which is the true mother of ingratitude. Were we, therefore, to follow the natural course of our passions and inclinations, we shou'd perform but few actions for the advantage of others, from disinterested views ; because we are naturally very limited in our kindness and affection: And we shou'd perform as few of that kind, out of a regard to interest ; because we cannot depend upon their gratitude. Here then is the mutual commerce of good offices in a manner lost among mankind and every one reduc'd to his own skill and industry for his well-being and subsistence. The invention of the law of nature, concerning

the *stability* of possession; has already render'd men tolerable
to each other ; that of the *transference* of property and possession by consent has begun to render them mutually
advantageous : But still these laws of nature, however strictly
observ'd, are not sufficient to render them so serviceable to
each other, as by nature they are fitted to become. Tho'
possession be *stable*, men may often reap but small advantage
from it, while they are possess'd of a greater quantity of any
species of goods than they have occasion for, and at the same
time suffer by the want of others. The *transference* of
property, which is the proper remedy for this inconvenience,
cannot remedy it entirely ; because it can only take place
with regard to such objects as are *present* and *individual*, but
not to such as are *absent* or *general*. One cannot transfer the
property of a particular house, twenty leagues distant ;
because the consent cannot be attended with delivery, which
is a requisite circumstance. Neither can one transfer the
property of ten bushels of corn, or five hogsheads of wine, by
the mere expression and consent ; because these are only
general terms, and have no direct relation to any particular
heap of corn, or barrels of wine. Besides, the commerce of
mankind is not confin'd to the barter of commodities, but
may extend to services and actions, which we may exchange
to our mutual interest and advantage. Your corn is ripe
to-day ; mine will be so to-morrow. 'Tis profitable for us
both, that I shou'd labour with you to-day, and that you
shou'd aid me to-morrow. I have no kindness for you, and
know you have as little for me. I will not, therefore, take
any pains upon your account ; and should I labour with you
upon my own account, in expectation of a return, I know I
shou'd be disappointed, and that I shou'd in vain depend
upon your gratitude. Here then I leave you to labour
alone : You treat me in the same manner. The seasons
change ; and both of us lose our harvests for want of mutual
confidence and security.

All this is the effect of the natural and inherent principles and passions of human nature ; and as these passions and principles are inalterable, it may be thought, that our conduct, which depends on them, must be so too, and that 'twou'd be in vain, either for moralists or politicians, to tamper with us, or attempt to change the usual course of our actions, with a view to public interest. And indeed, did the success of their designs depend upon their success in correcting the selfishness and ingratitude of men, they wou'd never make any progress, unless aided by omnipotence, which is alone able to new-mould the human mind, and change its character in such fundamental articles. All they can pretend to, is, to give a new direction to those natural passions, and teach us that we can better satisfy our appetites in an oblique and artificial manner, than by their headlong and impetuous motion. Hence I learn to do a service to another, without bearing him any real kindness ; because I forsee, that he will return my service, in expectation of another of the same kind, and in order to maintain the same correspondence of good offices with me or with others. And accordingly, after I have serv'd him, and he is in possession of the advantage arising from my action, he is induc'd to perform his part, as forseeing the consequences of his refusal.

But tho' this self-interested commerce of men begins to take place, and to predominate in society, it does not entirely abolish the more generous and noble intercourse of friendship and good offices. I may still do services to such persons as I love, and am more particularly acquainted with, without any prospect of advantage ; and they make me a return in the same manner, without any view but that of recompensing my past services. In order, therefore, to distinguish those two different sorts of commerce, the interested and the disinterested, there is a *certain form of words* invented for the former, by which we bind ourselves to the performance of ·

any action. This form of words constitutes what we call a *promise*, which is the sanction of the interested commerce of mankind. When a man says *he promises any thing*, he in effect expresses a *resolution* of performing it; and along with that, by making use of this *form of words*, subjects himself to the penalty of never being trusted again in case of failure. A resolution is the natural act of the mind, which promises express : But were there no more than a resolution in the case, promises wou'd only declare our former motives, and wou'd not create any new motive or obligation. They are the conventions of men, which create a new motive, when experience has taught us, that human affairs wou'd be conducted much more for mutual advantage, were there certain *symbols* or *signs* instituted, by which we might give each other security of our conduct in any particular incident. After these signs are instituted, whoever uses them is immediately bound by his interest to execute his engagements, and must never expect to be trusted any more, if he refuse to perform what he promis'd.

Nor is that knowledge, which is requisite to make mankind sensible of this interest in the *institution* and *observance* of promises, to be esteem'd superior to the capacity of human nature, however savage and uncultivated. There needs but a very little practice of the world, to make us perceive all these consequences and advantages. The shortest experience of society discovers them to every mortal ; and when each individual perceives the same sense of interest in all his fellows, he immediately performs his part of any contract, as being assur'd, that they will not be wanting in theirs. All of them, by concert, enter into a scheme of actions, calculated for common benefit, and agree to be true to their word ; nor is there any thing requisite to form this concert or convention, but that every one have a sense of interest in the faithful fulfilling of engagements, and express that sense to other members of the society. This immediately causes that interest to operate upon them ; and interest is the *first* obligation to the performance of promises.

Afterwards a sentiment of morals concurs with interest, and becomes a new obligation upon mankind. This sentiment of morality, in the performance of promises, arises from the same principles as that in the abstinence from the property of others. *Public interest, education*, and *the artifices of politicians*, have the same effect in both cases. The difficulties, that occur to us, in supposing a moral obligation to attend promises, we either surmount or elude. For instance; the expression of a resolution is not commonly suppos'd to be obligatory; and we cannot readily conceive how the making use of a certain form of words shou'd be able to cause any material difference. Here, therefore, we *feign* a new act of the mind, which we call the *willing* an obligation; and on this we suppose the morality to depend. But we have prov'd already, that there is no such act of the mind, and consequently that promises impose no natural obligation.

To confirm this, we may subjoin some other reflections concerning that will, which is suppos'd to enter into a promise, and to cause its obligation. 'Tis evident, that the will alone is never suppos'd to cause the obligation, but must be express'd by words or signs, in order to impose a tye upon any man. The expression being once brought in as subservient to the will, soon becomes the principal part of the promise; nor will a man be less bound by his word, tho' he secretly give a different direction to his intention, and with-hold himself both from a resolution, and from willing an obligation. But tho' the expression makes on most occasions the whole of the promise, yet it does not always so; and one, who should make use of any expression, of which he knows not the meaning, and which he uses without any intention of binding himself, wou'd not certainly be bound by it. Nay, tho' he knows its meaning, yet if he uses it in jest only, and with such signs as shew evidently he has no serious intention of binding himself, he wou'd not lie under any obligation of performance ; but 'tis necessary, that the words be a perfect expression of the will, without any contrary signs. Nay, even this we must not carry so far as to imagine, that one, whom, by our quickness of understanding, we conjecture, from certain signs, to have an intention of deceiving us, is not bound by his expression or verbal promise, if we accept of it; but must limit this conclusion to those cases, where the signs are of a different kind from those of deceit. All these contradictions are easily accounted for, if the obligation of promises be merely a human invention for the convenience of society; but will never be explain'd, if it be something *real* and *natural*, arising from any action of the mind or body.

I shall farther observe, that since every new promise imposes a new obligation of morality on the person who promises, and since this new obligation arises from his will; 'tis one of the most mysterious and incomprehensible operations that can possibly be imagin'd, and may even be compar'd to *transubstantiation*, or *holy orders*,[1] where a certain form of words, along with a certain intention, changes entirely the nature of an external object, and even of a human creature. But tho' these mysteries be so far alike, 'tis very remarkable, that they differ widely in other particulars, and that this difference may be regarded as a strong proof of the difference of their origins. As the obligation of promises is an invention for the interest of society, 'tis warp'd into as many different forms as that interest requires, and even runs into direct contradictions, rather than lose sight of its object. But as those other monstrous doctrines are merely priestly inventions, and have no public interest in view, they are less disturb'd in their progress by new obstacles;

[1] I mean so far, as holy orders are suppos'd to produce the *indelible character*. In other respects they are only a legal qualification.

and it must be own'd, that, after the first absurdity, they follow more directly the current of reason and good sense. Theologians clearly perceiv'd, that the external form of words, being mere sound, require an intention to make them have any efficacy; and that this intention being once consider'd as a requisite circumstance, its absence must equally prevent the effect, whether avow'd or conceal'd, whether sincere or deceitful. Accordingly they have commonly determin'd, that the intention of the priest makes the sacrament, and that when he secretly withdraws his intention, he is highly criminal in himself; but still destroys the baptism, or communion, or holy orders. The terrible consequences of this doctrine were not able to hinder its taking place; as the inconvenience of a similar doctrine, with regard to promises, have prevented that doctrine from establishing itself. Men are always more concern'd about the present life than the future; and are apt to think the smallest evil, which regards the former, more important than the greatest, which regards the latter.

We may draw the same conclusion, concerning the origin of promises, from the *force*, which is suppos'd to invalidate all contracts, and to free us from their obligation. Such a principle is a proof, that promises have no natural obligation, and are mere artificial contrivances for the convenience and advantage of society. If we consider aright of the matter, force is not essentially different from any other motive of hope or fear, which may induce us to engage our word, and lay ourselves under any obligation. A man, dangerously wounded, who promises a competent sum to a surgeon to cure him, wou'd certainly be bound to performance ; tho' the case be not so much different from that of one, who promises a sum to a robber, as to produce so great a difference in our sentiments of morality, if these sentiments were not built entirely on public interest and convenience.

SECTION VI.

Some farther reflections concerning justice and injustice.

WE have now run over the three fundamental laws of nature, *that of the stability of possession, of its transference by consent,* and *of the performance of promises.* 'Tis on the strict observance of those three laws, that the peace and security of human society entirely depend ; nor is there any possibility of establishing a good correspondence among men, where these are neglected. Society is absolutely necessary for the well-being of men ; and these are as necessary to the support of society. Whatever restraint they may impose on the passions of men, they are the real offspring of those passions, and are only a more artful and more refin'd way of satisfying them. Nothing is more vigilant and inventive than our passions ; and nothing is more obvious, than the convention for the observance of these rules. Nature has, therefore, trusted this affair entirely to the conduct of men, and has not plac'd in the mind any peculiar original principles, to determine us to a set of actions, into which the other principles of our frame and constitution were sufficient to lead us. And to convince us the more fully of this truth, we may here stop a moment, and from a review of the preceding reasonings may draw some new arguments, to prove that those laws, however necessary, are entirely artificial, and of human invention ; and consequently that justice is an artificial, and not a natural virtue.

I. The first argument I shall make use of is deriv'd from the vulgar definition of justice. Justice is commonly defin'd to be *a constant and perpetual will of giving every one his due.* In this definition 'tis supposed, that there are such things as right and property, independent of justice, and antecedent to it ; and that they wou'd have subsisted, tho' men had never dreamt of practicing such a virtue. I have already observ'd, in a cursory manner, the fallacy of this opinion, and shall here continue to open up a little more distinctly my sentiments on that subject.

I shall begin with observing, that this quality, which we call *property*, is like many of the imaginary qualities of the *peripatetic* philosophy, and vanishes upon a more accurate inspection into the subject, when consider'd a-part from our moral sentiments. 'Tis evident property does not consist in any of the sensible qualities of the object. For these may continue invariably the same, while the property changes. Property, therefore, must consist in some relation of the object. But 'tis not in its relation with regard to other external and inanimate objects. For these may also continue invariably the same, while the property changes. This quality, therefore, consists in the relations of objects to intelligent and rational beings. But 'tis not the external and corporeal relation, which forms the essence of property. For that relation may be the same betwixt inanimate objects, or with regard to brute creatures ; tho' in those cases it forms no property. 'Tis, therefore, in some internal relation, that the property consists ; that is, in some influence, which the external relations of the object have on the mind and actions. Thus the external relation, which we call *occupation* or first possession, is not of itself imagin'd to be the property of the object, but only to cause its property. Now 'tis evident, this external relation causes nothing in external objects, and has only an influence on the mind, by giving us a sense of duty in abstaining from that object, and in restoring it to the first possessor. These actions are properly what we call *justice;* and consequently 'tis on that virtue that the nature of property depends, and not the virtue on the property.

If any one, therefore, wou'd assert, that justice is a natural virtue, and injustice a natural vice, he must assert, that abstracting from the notions of *property*, and *right* and *obligation*, a certain conduct and train of actions, in certain external relations of objects, has naturally a moral beauty or deformity, and causes an original pleasure or uneasiness. Thus the restoring a man's goods to him is consider'd as virtuous, not because nature has annex'd a certain sentiment of pleasure to such a conduct, with regard to the property of others, but because she has annex'd that sentiment to such a conduct, with regard to those external objects, of which others have had the first or long possession, or which they have receiv'd by the consent of those, who have had first or long possession. If nature has given us no such sentiment, there is not, naturally, nor antecedent to human conventions, any such thing as property. Now, tho' it seems sufficiently evident, in this dry and accurate consideration of the present subject, that nature has annex'd no pleasure or sentiment of approbation to such a conduct ; yet that I may leave as little room for doubt as possible, I shall subjoin a few more arguments to confirm my opinion.

First, If nature had given us a pleasure of this kind, it wou'd have been as evident and discernible as on every other occasion ; nor shou'd we have found any difficulty to perceive, that the consideration of such actions, in such a situation, gives a certain pleasure and sentiment of approbation. We shou'd not have been oblig'd to have recourse to notions of property in the definition of justice, and at the same time make use of the notions of justice in the definition of property. This deceitful method of reasoning is a plain proof, that there are contain'd in the subject some obscurities and difficulties, which we are not able to surmount, and which we desire to evade by this artifice.

Secondly, Those rules, by which properties, rights, and obligations are determin'd, have in them no marks of a natural origin, but many of artifice and contrivance. They are too numerous to have proceeded from nature : They are

changeable by human laws : And have all of them a direct
and evident tendency to public good, and the support of
civil society.   This last circumstance is remarkable upon two
accounts.   *First,* because, tho' the cause of the establishment of these laws had been a *regard* for the public good, as
much as the public good is their natural tendency, they
wou'd still have been artificial, as being purposely contriv'd
and directed to a certain end.   *Secondly,* because, if men
had been endow'd with such a strong regard for public
good, they wou'd never have restrain'd themselves by these
rules ; so that the laws of justice arise from natural principles in a manner still more oblique and artificial.   'Tis self-
love which is their real origin ; and as the self-love of one
person is naturally contrary to that of another, these several
interested passions are oblig'd to adjust themselves after
such a manner as to concur in some system of conduct and
behaviour.   This system, therefore, comprehending the
interest of each individual, is of course advantageous to the
public ; tho' it be not intended for that purpose by the
inventors.

II. In the second place we may observe, that all kinds of
vice and virtue run insensibly into each other, and may
approach by such imperceptible degrees as will make it very
difficult, if not absolutely impossible, to determine when the
one ends, and the other begins ; and from this observation
we may derive a new argument for the foregoing principle.
For whatever may be the case, with regard to all kinds of
vice and virtue, 'tis certain, that rights, and obligations, and
property, admit of no such insensible gradation, but that a
man either has a full and perfect property, or none at all ;
and is either entirely oblig'd to perform any action, or lies
under no manner of obligation.   However civil laws may
talk of a perfect *dominion*, and of an imperfect, 'tis easy to
observe, that this arises from a fiction, which has no founda-

tion in reason, and can never enter into our notions of natural justice and equity. A man that hires a horse, tho' but for a day, has as full a right to make use of it for that time, as he whom we call its proprietor has to make use of it any other day ; and 'tis evident, that however the use may be bounded in time or degree, the right itself is not susceptible of any such gradation, but is absolute and entire, so far as it extends. Accordingly we may observe, that this right both arises and perishes in an instant ; and that a man entirely acquires the property of any object by occupation, or the consent of the proprietor ; and loses it by his own consent ; without any of that insensible gradation, which is remarkable in other qualities and relations. Since, therefore, this is the case with regard to property, and rights, and obligations, I ask, how it stands with regard to justice and injustice ? After whatever manner you answer this question, you run into inextricable difficulties. If you reply, that justice and injustice admit of degree, and run insensibly into each other, you expressly contradict the foregoing position, that obligation and property are not susceptible of such a gradation. These depend entirely upon justice and injustice, and follow them in all their variations. Where the justice is entire, the property is also entire : Where the justice is imperfect, the property must also be imperfect. And *vice versa*, if the property admit of no such variations, they must also be incompatible with justice. If you assent, therefore, to this last proposition, and assert that justice and injustice are not susceptible of degrees, you in effect assert, that they are not *naturally* either vicious or virtuous ; since vice and virtue, moral good and evil, and indeed all *natural* qualities, run insensibly into each other, and are, on many occasions, undistinguishable.

And here it may be worth while to observe, that tho' abstract reasoning, and the general maxims of philosophy and law establish this position, *that property, and right, and obligation admit not of degrees*, yet in our common and negligent way of thinking, we find great difficulty to entertain that opinion, and do even *secretly* embrace the contrary principle. An object must either be in the possession of one person or another. An action must either be perform'd or not. The necessity there is of choosing one side in these dilemmas, and the impossibility there often is of finding any just medium, oblige us, when we reflect on the matter, to acknowledge, that all property and obligations are entire. But on the other hand, when we consider the origin of property and obligation, and find that they depend on public utility, and sometimes on the propensities of the imagination, which are seldom entire on any side ; we are naturally inclin'd to imagine, that these moral relations admit of an insensible gradation. Hence it is, that in references, where the consent of the parties leave the referees entire masters of the subject, they commonly discover so much equity and justice on both sides, as induces them to strike a medium, and divide the difference betwixt the parties. Civil judges, who have not this liberty, but are oblig'd to give a decisive sentence on some one side, are often at a loss how to determine, and are necessitated to proceed on the most frivolous reasons in the world. Half rights and obligations, which seem so natural in common life, are perfect absurdities in their tribunal ; for which reason they are often oblig'd to take half arguments for whole ones, in order to terminate the affair one way or other.

III. The third argument of this kind I shall make use of may be explain'd thus. If we consider the ordinary course of human actions, we shall find, that the mind restrains not itself by any general and universal rules ; but acts on most occasions as it is determin'd by its present motives and inclination. As each action is a particular individual event, it must proceed from particular principles, and from

our immediate situation within ourselves, and with respect
to the rest of the universe. If on some occasions we extend
our motives beyond those very circumstances, which gave rise
to them, and form something like *general rules* for our conduct, 'tis easy to observe that these rules are not perfectly
inflexible, but allow of many exceptions. Since, therefore, this
is the ordinary course of human actions, we may conclude
that the laws of justice, being universal and perfectly inflexible,
can never be deriv'd from nature, nor be the immediate offspring of any natural motive or inclination. No action can
be either morally good or evil, unless there be some natural
passion or motive to impel us to it, or deter us from it ; and
'tis evident, that the morality must be susceptible of all
the same variations, which are natural to the passion. Here
are two persons, who dispute for an estate ; of whom one is
rich, a fool, and a batchelor ; the other poor, a man of sense,
and has a numerous family : The first is my enemy ; the
second my friend. Whether I be actuated in this affair by
a view to public or private interest, by friendship or enmity,
I must be induc'd to do my utmost to procure the estate to
the latter. Nor wou'd any consideration of the right and
property of the persons be able to restrain me, were I actuated only by natural motives, without any combination or
convention with others. For as all property depends on
morality ; and as all morality depends on the ordinary course
of our passions and actions ; and as these again are only
directed by particular motives ; 'tis evident, such a partial
conduct must be suitable to the strictest morality, and cou'd
never be a violation of property. Were men, therefore, to
take the liberty of acting with regard to the laws of society,
as they do in every other affair, they wou'd conduct themselves, on most occasions, by particular judgments, and wou'd
take into consideration the characters and circumstances of
the persons, as well as the general nature of the question.
But 'tis easy to observe, that this wou'd produce an infinite

confusion in human society, and that the avidity and partiality of men wou'd quickly bring disorder into the world,
if not restrain'd by some general and inflexible principles.
'Twas, therefore, with a view to this inconvenience, that men
have establish'd those principles, and have agreed to restrain
themselves by general rules which are unchangeable by spite
and favour, and by particular views of private or public
interest. These rules, then, are artificially invented for a
certain purpose, and are contrary to the common principles of
human nature, which accommodate themselves to circumstances, and have no stated invariable method of operation.

Nor do I perceive how I can easily be mistaken in this
matter. I see evidently, that when any man imposes on
himself general inflexible rules in his conduct with others, he
considers certain objects as their property, which he supposes
to be sacred and inviolable. But no proposition can be more
evident, than that property is perfectly unintelligible without
first supposing justice and injustice; and that these virtues
and vices are as unintelligible, unless we have motives,
independent of the morality, to impel us to just actions, and
deter us from unjust ones. Let those motives therefore, be
what they will, they must accommodate themselves to circumstances, and must admit of all the variations, which
human affairs, in their incessant revolutions are susceptible
of. They are consequently a very improper foundation for
such rigid inflexible rules as the laws of [justice?]; and 'tis
evident these laws can only be deriv'd from human conventions, when men have perceiv'd the disorders that result
from following their natural and variable principles.

Upon the whole, then, we are to consider this distinction
betwixt justice and injustice, as having two different
foundations, *viz.* that of *interest*, when men observe, that 'tis
impossible to live in society without restraining themselves
by certain rules; and that of *morality*, when this interest is

once observ'd, and men receive a pleasure from the view of such actions as tend to the peace of society, and an uneasiness from such as are contrary to it. 'Tis the voluntary convention and artifice of men, which makes the first interest take place ; and therefore those laws of justice are so far to be consider'd as *artificial.* After that interest is once establish'd and acknowledg'd, the sense of morality in the observance of these rules follows *naturally*, and of itself ; tho' 'tis certain, that it is also augmented by a new *artifice*, and that the public instructions of politicians, and the private education of parents, contribute to the giving us a sense of honour and duty in the strict regulation of our actions with regard to the properties of others.

SECTION VII.

Of the origin of government.

NOTHING is more certain, than that men are, in a great measure, govern'd by interest, and that even when they extend their concern beyond themselves, 'tis not to any great distance ; nor is it usual for them, in common life, to look farther than their nearest friends and acquaintance. 'Tis no less certain, that 'tis impossible for men to consult their interest in so effectual a manner, as by an universal and inflexible observance of the rules of justice, by which alone they can preserve society, and keep themselves from falling into that wretched and savage condition, which is commonly represented as the *state of nature.* And as this interest, which all men have in the upholding of society, and the observation of the rules of justice, is great, so is it palpable and evident, even to the most rude and uncultivated of the human race ; and 'tis almost impossible for any one, who has had experience of society, to be mistaken in this particular. Since, therefore, men are so sincerely attach'd to their interest, and their interest is so much concern'd in the observance of justice, and this interest is so certain and avow'd ; it may be ask'd, how any disorder can ever arise in society, and what principle there is in human nature so *powerful* as to overcome so strong a passion, or so *violent* as to obscure so clear a knowledge?

It has been observ'd, in treating of the passions, that men are mightily govern'd by the imagination, and proportion their affections more to the light, under which any object appears to them, than to its real and intrinsic value. What strikes upon them with a strong and lively idea commonly prevails above what lies in a more obscure light ; and it must be a great superiority of value, that is able to compensate this advantage. Now as every thing, that is contiguous to us, either in space or time, strikes upon us with such an idea, it has a proportional effect on the will and passions, and commonly operates with more force than any object, that lies in a more distant and obscure light. Tho' we may be fully convinc'd, that the latter object excels the former, we are not able to regulate our actions by this judgment ; but yield to the sollicitations of our passions, which always plead in favour of whatever is near and contiguous.

This is the reason why men so often act in contradiction to their known interest ; and in particular why they prefer any trivial advantage, that is present, to the maintenance of order in society, which so much depends on the observance of justice. The consequences of every breach of equity seem to lie very remote, and are not able to counterballance any immediate advantage, that may be reap'd from it. They are, however, never the less real for being remote ; and as all men are, in some degree, subject to the same weakness, it necessarily happens, that the violations of equity must become very frequent in society, and the commerce of men, by that means, be render'd very dangerous and uncertain. You have the same propension, that I have, in favour of

what is contiguous above what is remote. You are, therefore, naturally carried to commit acts of injustice as well as
me. Your example both pushes me forward in this way by
imitation, and also affords me a new reason for any breach
of equity, by shewing me, that I should be the cully of my
integrity, if I alone shou'd impose on myself a severe
restraint amidst the licentiousness of others.

This quality, therefore, of human nature, not only is very
dangerous to society, but also seems, on a cursory view, to
be incapable of any remedy. The remedy can only come
from the consent of men ; and if men be incapable of themselves to prefer remote to contiguous, they will never consent to any thing, which wou'd oblige them to such a choice,
and contradict, in so sensible a manner, their natural principles and propensities. Whoever chuses the means, chuses
also the end ; and if it be impossible for us to prefer what
is remote, 'tis equally impossible for us to submit to any
necessity, which wou'd oblige us to such a method of acting.

But here 'tis observable, that this infirmity of human
nature becomes a remedy to itself, and that we provide
against our negligence about remote objects, merely because
we are naturally inclin'd to that negligence. When we consider any objects at a distance, all their minute distinctions
vanish, and we always give the preference to whatever is in
itself preferable, without considering its situation and circumstances. This gives rise to what in an improper sense we
call *reason,* which is a principle, that is often contradictory
to those propensities that display themselves upon the
approach of the object. In reflecting on any action, which
I am to perform a twelve-month hence, I always resolve to
prefer the greater good, whether at that time it will be more
contiguous or remote ; nor does any difference in that particular make a difference in my present intentions and
resolutions. My distance from the final determination
makes all those minute differences vanish, nor am I affected

by any thing, but the general and more discernable qualities of good and evil. But on my nearer approach, those circumstances, which I at first over-look'd, begin to appear, and have an influence on my conduct and affections. A new inclination to the present good springs up, and makes it difficult for me to adhere inflexibly to my first purpose and resolution. This natural infirmity I may very much regret, and I may endeavour, by all possible means, to free my self from it. I may have recourse to study and reflection within myself; to the advice of friends; to frequent meditation, and repeated resolution: And having experienc'd how ineffectual all these are, I may embrace with pleasure any other expedient, by which I may impose a restraint upon myself, and guard against this weakness.

The only difficulty, therefore, is to find out this expedient, by which men cure their natural weakness, and lay themselves under the necessity of observing the laws of justice and equity, notwithstanding their violent propension to prefer contiguous to remote. 'Tis evident such a remedy can never be effectual without correcting this propensity; and as 'tis impossible to change or correct any thing material in our nature, the utmost we can do is to change our circumstances and situation, and render the observance of the laws of justice our nearest interest, and their violation our most remote. But this being impracticable with respect to all mankind, it can only take place with respect to a few, whom we thus immediately interest in the execution of justice. These are the persons, whom we call civil magistrates, kings and their ministers, our governors and rulers, who being indifferent persons to the greatest part of the state, have no interest, or but a remote one, in any act of injustice; and being satisfied with their present condition, and with their part in society, have an immediate interest in every execution of justice, which is so necessary to the upholding of society. Here then is the origin of civil government and society. Men are not able radically to cure, either in themselves or others, that narrowness of soul, which makes them prefer the present to the remote. They cannot change their natures. All they can do is to change their situation, and render the observance of justice the immediate interest of some particular persons, and its violation their more remote. These persons, then, are not only induc'd to observe those rules in their own conduct, but also to constrain others to a like regularity, and inforce the dictates of equity thro' the whole society. And if it be necessary, they may also interest others more immediately in the execution of justice, and create a number of officers, civil and military, to assist them in their government.

But this execution of justice, tho' the principal, is not the only advantage of government. As violent passion hinders men from seeing distinctly the interest they have in an equitable behaviour towards others; so it hinders them from seeing that equity itself, and gives them a remarkable partiality in their own favours. This inconvenience is corrected in the same manner as that above-mention'd. The same persons, who execute the laws of justice, will also decide all controversies concerning them; and being indifferent to the greatest part of the society, will decide them more equitably than every one wou'd in his own case.

By means of these two advantages, in the *execution* and *decision* of justice, men acquire a security against each others weakness and passion, as well as against their own, and under the shelter of their governors, begin to taste at ease the sweets of society and mutual assistance. But government extends farther its beneficial influence; and not contented to protect men in those conventions they make for their mutual interest, it often obliges them to make such conventions, and forces them to seek their own advantage, by a concurrence in some common end or purpose. There is no quality in human nature, which causes more fatal errors in our conduct, than that which leads us to prefer whatever is present to the distant and remote, and makes us desire objects more according to their situation than their intrinsic value. Two neighbours may agree to drain a meadow, which they possess in common; because 'tis easy for them to know each others mind; and each must perceive, that the immediate consequence of his failing in his part, is the abandoning the whole project. But 'tis very difficult, and indeed impossible, that a thousand persons shou'd agree in any such action; it being difficult for them to concert so complicated a design, and still more difficult for them to execute it; while each seeks a pretext to free himself of the trouble and expence, and wou'd lay the whole burden on others. Political society easily remedies both these inconveniences. Magistrates find an immediate interest in the interest of any considerable part of their subjects. They need consult no body but themselves to form any scheme for the promoting of that interest. And as the failure of any one piece in the execution is connected, tho' not immediately, with the failure of the whole, they prevent that failure, because they find no interest in it, either immediate or remote. Thus bridges are built; harbours open'd ramparts rais'd; canals form'd; fleets equip'd; and armies disciplin'd; every where, by the care of government, which, tho' compos'd of men subject to all human infirmities, becomes, by one of the finest and most subtle inventions imaginable, a composition, which is, in some measures exempted from all these infirmities.

SECTION VIII.

Of the source of allegiance.

THOUGH government be an invention very advantageous, and even in some circumstances absolutely necessary to mankind ; it is not necessary in all circumstances, nor is it impossible for men to preserve society for some time, without having recourse to such an invention. Men, 'tis true, are always much inclin'd to prefer present interest to distant and remote ; nor is it easy for them to resist the temptation of any advantage, that they may immediately enjoy, in apprehension of an evil, that lies at a distance from them: But still this weakness is less conspicuous, where the possessions, and the pleasures of life are few, and of little value, as they always are in the infancy of society. An *Indian* is but little tempted to dispossess another of his hut, or to steal his bow as being already provided of the same advantages ; and as to any superior fortune, which may attend one above another in hunting and fishing, 'tis only carnal and temporary, and will have but small tendency to disturb society. And so far am I from thinking with some philosophers, that men are utterly incapable of society without government, that I assert the first rudiments of government to arise from quarrels, not among men of the same society, but among those of different societies. A less degree of riches will suffice to this latter effect, than is requisite for the former. Men fear nothing from public war and violence but the resistance they meet with, which, because they share it in common, seems less terrible, and because it comes from strangers, seems less pernicious in its consequences, than when they are exposed singly against one whose commerce is advantageous to them, and without whose society 'tis impossible they can subsist. Now foreign war to a society without government necessarily produces civil war. Throw any considerable goods among men, they instantly fall a quarrelling, while each strives to get possession of what pleases him, without regard to the consequences. In a foreign war the most considerable of all goods, life and limbs, are at stake ; and as every one shuns dangerous ports, seizes the best arms, seeks excuse for the slightest wounds, the laws, which may be well enough observ'd, while men were calm, can now no longer take place, when they are in such commotion.

This we find verified in the *American* tribes, where men live in concord and amity among themselves without any establish'd government; and never pay submission to any of their fellows, except in time of war, when their captain enjoys a shadow of authority, which he loses after their return from the field, and the establishment of peace with the neighboring tribes.   This authority, however, instructs them in the advantages of government, and teaches them to have recourse to it, when either by the pillage of war, by commerce, or by any fortuitous inventions, their riches and possessions become so considerable as to make them forget, on every emergence, the interest they have in the preservation of peace and justice.   Hence we may give a plausible reason, among others, why all governments are at first monarchial, without any mixture and variety; and why republics arise only from the abuses of monarchy and despotic power.   Camps are the true mothers of cities ; and as war can not be administred, by reason of the suddenness of every exigency, without some authority in a single person, the same kind of authority naturally takes place in that civil government, which succeeds the military.   And this reason I take to be more natural, than the common one deriv'd from patriarchal government, or the authority of a father, which is said first to take place in one family, and to accustom the members of it to the government of a single person.   The state of society without government is one of the most natural states of men, and must subsist with the conjunction of many families, and long after the first generation.   Nothing but an encrease of riches and possessions cou'd oblige men to quit it ; and so barbarous and uninstructed are all societies on their first formation, that many years must elapse before these can encrease to such a degree, as to disturb men in the enjoyment of peace and concord.

But tho' it be possible for men to maintain a small uncultivated society without government, 'tis impossible they shou'd maintain a society of any kind without justice, and the observance of those three fundamental laws concerning the stability of possession, its translation by consent, and the performance of promises. These are, therefore, antecedent to government, and are suppos'd to impose an obligation before the duty of allegiance to civil magistrates has once been thought of. Nay, I shall go farther, and assert, that government, *upon its first establishment*, wou'd naturally be supposed to derive its obligation from those laws of nature, and, in particular, from that concerning the performance of promises. When men have once perceiv'd the necessity of government to maintain peace, and execute justice, they wou'd naturally assemble together, wou'd chuse magistrates, determine their power, and *promise* them obedience. As a promise is suppos'd to be a bond or security already in use, and attended with a moral obligation, 'tis to be consider'd as the original sanction of government, and as the source of the first obligation to obedience. This reasoning appears so natural, that it has become the foundation of our fashionable system of politics, and is in a manner the creed of a party amongst us, who pride themselves, with reason, on the soundness of their philosophy, and their liberty of thought. *All men*, say they, *are born free and equal: Government and superiority can only be establish'd by consent: The consent of men, in establishing government, imposes on them a new obligation, unknown to the laws of nature. Men, therefore, are bound to obey their magistrates, only because they promise it; and if they had not given their word, either expressly or tacitly, to preserve allegiance, it would never have become a part of their moral duty.* This conclusion, however, when carried so far as to comprehend government in all its ages and situations, is entirely erroneous ; and I maintain, that tho' the duty of allegiance be at first grafted on the obligation of promises, and be for some time supported by that obligation, yet it quickly takes root of itself, and has an original obligation and authority, independent of all contracts.   This is a principle of moment, which we must examine with care and attention, before we proceed any farther.

' Tis reasonable for those philosophers, who assert justice to be a natural virtue, and antecedent to human conventions, to resolve all civil allegiance into the obligation of a promise, and assert that 'tis our own consent alone, which binds us to any submission to magistracy.   For as all government is plainly an invention of men, and the origin of most governments is known in history, 'tis necessary to mount higher, in order to find the source of our political duties, if we wou'd assert them to have any *natural* obligation of morality. These philosophers, therefore, quickly observe, that society is as antient as the human species, and those three fundamental laws of nature as antient as society :   So that taking advantage of the antiquity, and obscure origin of these laws, they first deny them to be artificial and voluntary inventions of men, and then seek to ingraft on them those other duties, which are more plainly artificial.   But being once undeceiv'd in this particular, and having found that *natural*, as well as *civil* justice, derives its origin from human conventions, we shall quickly perceive, how fruitless it is to resolve the one into the other, and seek, in the laws of nature, a stronger foundation for our political duties than interest, and human conventions ; while these laws themselves are built on the very same foundation.   On which ever side we turn this subject, we shall find, that these two kinds of duty are exactly on the same footing, and have the same source both of their *first invention* and *moral obligation*.   They are contriv'd to remedy like inconveniences, and acquire their moral sanction in the same manner, from their remedying those inconveniences.   These are two points, which we shall endeavour to prove as distinctly as possible.

We have already shewn, that men *invented* the three fundamental laws of nature, when they observ'd the necessity of society to their mutual subsistance, and found, that 'twas impossible to maintain any correspondence together, without some restraint on their natural appetites. The same self-love, therefore, which renders men so incommodious to each other, taking a new and more convenient direction, produces the rules of justice, and is the *first* motive of their observance. But when men have observ'd, that tho' the rules of justice be sufficient to maintain any society, yet 'tis impossible for them, of themselves, to observe those rules, in large and polish'd societies ; they establish government, as a new invention to attain their ends, and preserve the old, or procure new advantages, by a more strict execution of justice. So far, therefore, our *civil* duties are connected with our *natural*, that the former are invented chiefly for the sake of the latter ; and that the principal object of government is to constrain men to observe the laws of nature. In this respect, however, that law of nature, concerning the performance of promises, is only compriz'd along with the rest ; and its exact observance is to be consider'd as an effect of the institution of government, and not the obedience to government as an effect of the obligation of a promise. Tho' the object of our civil duties be the enforcing of our natural, yet the *first*[1] motive of the invention, as well as performance of both, is nothing but self-interest : And since there is a separate interest in the obedience to government, from that in the performance of promises, we must also allow of a separate obligation. To obey the civil magistrate is requisite to preserve order and concord in society. To perform promises is requisite to beget mutual trust and confidence in the common offices of life. The ends, as well as the means, are perfectly distinct ; nor is the one subordinate to the other.

---

[1] First in time, not in dignity or force.

To make this more evident, let us consider, that men will often bind themselves by promises to the performance of what it wou'd have been their interest to perform, independent of these promises ; as when they wou'd give others a fuller security, by super-adding a new obligation of interest to that which they formerly lay under. The interest in the performance of promises, besides its moral obligation, is general, avow'd, and of the last consequence in life. Other interests may be more particular and doubtful ; and we are apt to entertain a greater suspicion, that men may indulge their humour, or passion, in acting contrary to them. Here, therefore, promises come naturally in play, and are often requir'd for fuller satisfaction and security. But supposing those other interests to be as general and avow'd as the interest in the performance of a promise, they will be regarded as on the same footing, and men will begin to repose the same confidence in them. Now this is exactly the case with regard to our civil duties, or obedience to the magistrate ; without which no government cou'd subsist, nor any peace or order be maintain'd in large societies, where there are so many possessions on the one hand, and so many wants, real or imaginary, on the other. Our civil duties, therefore, must soon detach themselves from our promises, and acquire a separate force and influence. The interest in both is of the very same kind : 'Tis general, avow'd, and prevails in all times and places. There is, then, no pretext of reason for founding the one upon the other ; while each of them has a foundation peculiar to itself. We might as well resolve the obligation to abstain from the possessions of others, into the obligation of a promise, as that of allegiance. The interests are not more distinct in the one case than the other. A regard to property is not more necessary to natural society, than obedience is to civil society or government ; nor is the former society more necessary to the being of mankind, than the latter to their well-being and happiness. In short, if the performance of promises be advantageous, so is obedience to government : If the former interest be general, so is the latter : If the one interest be obvious and avow'd, so is the other. And as these two rules are founded on like obligations of interest, each of them must have a peculiar authority, independent of the other. But 'tis not only the *natural* obligations of interest, which are distinct in promises and allegiance ; but also the *moral* obligations of honour and conscience : Nor does the merit or demerit of the one depend in the least upon that of the other. And indeed, if we consider the close connexion there is betwixt the natural and moral obligations, we shall find this conclusion to be entirely unavoidable. Our interest is always engag'd on the side of obedience to magistracy ; and there is nothing but a great present advantage, that can lead us to rebellion, by making us over-look the remote interest, which we have in the preserving of peace and order in society. But tho' a present interest may thus blind us with regard to our own actions, it takes not place with regard to those of others ; nor hinders them from appearing in in their true colours, as highly prejudicial to public interest, and to our own in particular. This naturally gives us an uneasiness, in considering such seditious and disloyal actions, and makes us attach to them the idea of vice and moral deformity. 'Tis the same principle, which causes us to disapprove of all kinds of private injustice, and in particular of the breach of promises. We blame all treachery and breach of faith ; because we consider, that the freedom and extent of human commerce depend entirely on a fidelity with regard to promises. We blame all disloyalty to magistrates ; because we perceive, that the execution of justice, in the stability of possession, its translation by consent, and the performance of promises, is impossible, without submission to government. As there are here two interests entirely distinct from each other, they must give rise to two moral obligations, equally separate and independant. Tho' there was no such thing as a promise in the world, government wou'd still be necessary in all large and civiliz'd societies ; and if promises had only their own proper obligation, without the separate sanction of government, they wou'd have but little efficacy in such societies.   This separates the boundaries of our public and private duties, and shews that the latter are more dependant on the former, than the former on the latter.   *Education* and *the artifice of politicians*, concur to bestow a farther morality on loyalty, and to brand all rebellion with a greater degree of guilt and infamy.   Nor is it a wonder, that politicians shou'd be very industrious in inculcating such notions, where their interest is so particularly concern'd.

Lest those arguments shou'd not appear entirely conclusive (as I think they are) I shall have recourse to authority, and shall prove, from the universal consent of mankind, that the obligation of submission to government is not deriv'd from any promise of the subjects.   Nor need any one wonder, that tho' I have all along endeavour'd to establish my system on pure reason, and have scarce ever cited the judgment even of philosophers or historians on any article, I shou'd now appeal to popular authority, and oppose the sentiments of the rabble to any philosophical reasoning. For it must be observ'd, that the opinions of men, in this case, carry with them a peculiar authority, and are, in a great measure, infallible.   The distinction of moral good and evil is founded on the pleasure or pain, which results from the view of any sentiment, or character ; and as that pleasure or pain cannot be unknown to the person who feels it, it follows,[1] that there is just so much vice or virtue in any

---

[1] This proposition must hold strictly true, with regard to every quality, that is determin'd merely by sentiment.   In what sense we can talk either of a *right* or a *wrong* taste in morals, eloquence, or beauty, shall be consider'd afterwards.   In the mean time, it may be observ'd, that there is such an uniformity in the *general* sentiments of mankind, as to render such questions of but small importance.

character, as every one places in it, and that 'tis impossible in this particular we can ever be mistaken. And tho' our judgments concerning the *origin* of any vice or virtue, be not so certain as those concerning their *degrees ;* yet, since the question in this case regards not any philosophical origin of an obligation, but a plain matter of fact, 'tis not easily conceiv'd how we can fall into an error. A man, who acknowledges himself to be bound to another, for a certain sum, must certainly know whether it be by his own bond, or that of his father ; whether it be of his mere good-will, or for money lent him ; and under what conditions, and for what purposes he has bound himself. In like manner, it being certain, that there is a moral obligation to submit to government, because every one thinks so ; it must be as certain, that this obligation arises not from a promise; since no one, whose judgment has not been led astray by too strict adherence to a system of philosophy, has ever yet dreamt of ascribing it to that origin. Neither magistrates nor subjects have form'd this idea of our civil duties.

We find, that magistrates are so far from deriving their authority, and the obligation to obedience in their subjects, from the foundation of a promise or original contract, that they conceal, as far as possible, from their people, especially from the vulgar, that they have their origin from thence. Were this the sanction of government, our rulers wou'd never receive it tacitly, which is the utmost that can be pretended ; since what is given tacitly and insensibly can never have such influence on mankind, as what is perform'd expressly and openly. A tacit promise is, where the will is signified by other more diffuse signs than those of speech ; but a will there must certainly be in the case, and that can never escape the person's notice, who exerted it, however silent or tacit. But were you to ask the far greatest part of the nation, whether they had ever consented to the authority of their rulers, or promis'd to obey them they wou'd be inclin'd to think very strangely of you ; and wou'd certainly reply, that the affair depended not on their consent, but that they were born to such an obedience.   In consequence of this opinion, we frequently see them imagine such persons to be their natural rulers, as are at that time depriv'd of all power and authority, and whom no man, however foolish, wou'd voluntarily chuse ; and this merely because they are in that line, which rul'd before, and in that degree of it, which us'd to succeed ; tho' perhaps in so distant a period, that scarce any man alive cou'd ever have given any promise of obedience.   Has a government, then, no authority over such as these, because they never consented to it, and wou'd esteem the very attempt of such a free choice, a piece of arrogance and impiety?   We find by experience, that it punishes them very freely for what it calls treason and rebellion, which, it seems, according to this system, reduces itself to common injustice.   If you say, that by dwelling in its dominions, they in effect consented to the establish'd government ; I answer, that this can only be, where they think the affair depends on their choice, which few or none, besides those philosophers, have ever yet imagin'd.   It never was pleaded as an excuse for a ʼrebel, that the first act he perform'd, after he came to years of discretion, was to levy war against the sovereign of the state ; and that while he was a child he cou'd not bind himself by his own consent, and having become a man, show'd plainly by the first act he perform'd, that he had no design to impose on himself any obligation to obedience.   We find, on the contrary, that civil laws punish this crime at the same age as any other, which is criminal, of itself, without our consent ; that is, when the person is come to the full use of reason : Whereas to this crime they ought in justice to allow some intermediate time, in which a tacit consent at least might be suppos'd.   To which we may add, that a man living under an absolute government, wou'd owe it no allegiance ; since, by its very nature, it depends not on consent. But as that is as *natural* and *common* a government as any, it must certainly occasion some obligation ; and 'tis plain from experience, that men, who are subjected to it, do always think so. This is a clear proof, that we do not commonly esteem our allegiance to be deriv'd from our consent or promise and a farther proof is, that when our promise is upon any account expressly engag'd, we always distinguish exactly betwixt the two obligations, and believe the one to add more force to the other, than in a repetition of the same promise. Where no promise is given, a man looks not on his faith as broken in private matters, upon account of rebellion ; but keeps those two duties of honour and allegiance perfectly distinct and separate. As the uniting of them was thought by these philosophers a very subtile invention, this is a convincing proof, that 'tis not a true one ; since no man can either give a promise, or be restrain'd by its sanction and obligation unknown to himself.

SECTION IX.

Of the measures of allegiance.

THOSE political writers, who have had recourse to a promise, or original contract, as the source of our allegiance to government, intended to establish a principle, which is perfectly just and reasonable ; tho' the reasoning, upon which they endeavour'd to establish it, was fallacious and sophistical. They wou'd prove, that our submission to government admits of exceptions, and that an egregious tyranny in the rulers is sufficient to free the subjects from all ties of allegiance. Since men enter into society, say they, and submit themselves to government, by their free and voluntary consent, they must have in view certain advantages, which they propose to reap from it, and for which they are contented to resign their native liberty. There is, therefore, something mutual engag'd on the part of the magistrate, *viz.* protection and security ; and 'tis only by the hopes he affords of these advantages, that he can ever persuade men to submit to him. But when instead of protection and security, they meet with tyranny and oppression, they are free'd from their promises, (as happens in all conditional contracts) and return to that state of liberty, which preceded the institution of government. Men wou'd never be so foolish as to enter into such engagements as shou'd turn entirely to the advantage of others, without any view of bettering their own condition. Whoever proposes to draw any profit from our submission, must engage himself, either expressly or tacitly, to make us reap some advantage from his authority ; nor ought he to expect, that without the performance of his part we will ever continue in obedience.

I repeat it : This conclusion is just, tho' the principles be erroneous ; and I flatter myself, that I can establish the same conclusion on more reasonable principles. I shall not take such a compass, in establishing our political duties, as to assert, that men perceive the advantages of government ; that they institute government with a view to those advantages ; that this institution requires a promise of obedience ; which imposes a moral obligation to a certain degree, but being conditional, ceases to be binding, whenever the other contracting party performs not his part of the engagement. I perceive, that a promise itself arises entirely from human conventions, and is invented with a view to a certain interest. I seek, therefore, some such interest more immediately connected with government, and which may be at once the original motive to its institution, and the source of our obedience to it. This interest I find to consist in the security and protection, which we enjoy in political society, and which we can never attain, when perfectly free and independent. As interest, therefore, is the immediate sanction of government, the one can have no longer being than the other; and whenever the civil magistrate carries his oppression so far as to render his authority perfectly intolerable, we are no longer bound to submit to it. The cause ceases; the effect must cease also.

So far the conclusion is immediate and direct, concerning the *natural* obligation which we have to allegiance. As to the *moral* obligation, we may observe, that the maxim wou'd here be false, that *when the cause ceases, the effect must cease also.* For there is a principle of human nature, which we have frequently taken notice of, that men are mightily addicted to *general rules*, and that we often carry our maxims beyond those reasons, which first induc'd us to establish them. Where cases are similar in many circumstances, we are apt to put them on the same footing, without considering, that they differ in the most material circumstances, and that the resemblance is more apparent than real. It may, therefore, be thought, that in the case of allegiance our moral obligation of duty will not cease, even tho' the natural obligation of interest, which is its cause, has ceas'd; and that men may be bound by *conscience* to submit to a tyrannical government against their own and the public interest. And indeed, to the force of this argument I so far submit, as to acknowledge, that general rules commonly extend beyond the principles, on which they are founded; and that we seldom make any exception to them, unless that exception have the qualities of a general rule, and be founded on very numerous and common instances. Now this I assert to be entirely the present case. When men submit to the authority of others, 'tis to procure themselves some security against the wickedness and injustice of men, who are perpetually carried, by their unruly passions, and by their present and immediate interest, to the violation of all the laws of society. But as this imperfection is inherent in human nature, we know that it must attend men in all their states and conditions; and that those, whom we chuse for rulers, do not immediately become of a superior nature to the rest of mankind, upon account of their superior power and authority. What we expect from them depends not on a change of their nature but of their situation, when they acquire a more immediate interest in the preservation of order and the execution of justice. But besides that this interest is only more immediate in the execution of justice among their subjects; besides this, I say, we may often expect, from the irregularity of human nature, that they will neglect even this immediate interest, and be transported by their passions into all the excesses of cruelty and ambition. Our general knowledge of human nature, our observation of the past history of mankind, our experience of present times; all these causes must induce us to open the door to exceptions, and must make us conclude, that we may resist the more violent effects of supreme power, without any crime or injustice.

Accordingly we may observe, that this is both the general practice and principle of mankind, and that no nation, that cou'd find any remedy, ever yet suffer'd the cruel ravages of a tyrant, or were blam'd for their resistance. Those who took up arms against *Dionysius* or *Nero*, or *Philip the second*, have the favour of every reader in the perusal of their history; and nothing but the most violent perversion of common sense can ever lead us to condemn them. 'Tis certain, therefore, that in all our notions of morals we never entertain such an absurdity as that of passive obedience, but make allowances for resistance in the more flagrant instances of tyranny and oppression. The general opinion of mankind has some authority in all cases; but in this of morals 'tis perfectly infallible. Nor is it less infallible, because men cannot distinctly explain the principles, on which it is founded. Few persons can carry on this train of reasoning: 'Government is a mere human invention for the interest of society. Where the tyranny of the governor removes this interest, it also removes the natural obligation to obedience. The moral obligation is founded on the natural, and therefore must cease where *that* ceases; especially where the subject is such as makes us foresee very many occasions wherein the natural obligation may cease, and causes us to form a kind of general rule for the regulation of our conduct in such occurrences.' But tho' this train of reasoning be too subtile for the vulgar, 'tis certain, that all men have an implicit notion of it, and are sensible, that they owe obedience to government merely on account of the public interest; and at the same time, that human nature is so subject to frailties and passions, as may easily pervert this institution, and change their governors into tyrants and public enemies. If the sense of common interest were not our original motive to obedience, I wou'd fain ask, what other principle is there in human nature capable of subduing the natural ambition of men, and forcing them to such a submission? Imitation and custom are not sufficient. For the question still recurs, what motive first produces those instances of submission, which we imitate, and that train of actions, which produces the custom? There evidently is no other principle than common interest; and if interest first produces obedience to government, the obligation to obedience must cease, whenever the interest ceases, in any great degree, and in a considerable number of instances.

SECTION X.

Of the objects of allegiance.

BUT tho', on some occasions, it may be justifiable, both in sound politics and morality, to resist supreme power, 'tis certain, that in the ordinary course of human affairs nothing can be more pernicious and criminal; and that besides the convulsions, which always attend revolutions, such a practice tends directly to the subversion of all government, and the causing an universal anarchy and confusion among man-

kind.   As numerous and civiliz'd societies cannot subsist
without government, so government is entirely useless without an exact obedience.   We ought always to weigh the advantages, which we reap from authority, against the disadvantages; and by this means we shall become more
scrupulous of putting in practice the doctrine of resistance.
The common rule requires submission; and 'tis only in
cases of grievous tyranny and oppression, that the exception
can take place.

Since then such a blind submission is commonly due to
magistracy, the next question is, *to whom it is due, and whom
we are to regard as our lawful magistrates?*   In order to
answer this question, let us recollect what we have already
establish'd concerning the origin of government and political
society.   When men have once experienc'd the impossibility
of preserving any steady order in society, while every one is
his own master, and violates or observes the laws of society,
according to his present interest or pleasure, they naturally
run into the invention of government, and put it out of their
own power, as far as possible, to transgress the laws of
society.   Government, therefore, arises from the voluntary
convention of men; and 'tis evident, that the same convention, which establishes government, will also determine the
persons who are to govern, and will remove all doubt and
ambiguity in this particular.   And the voluntary consent of
men must here have the greater efficacy, that the authority
of the magistrate does *at first* stand upon the foundation of
a promise of the subjects, by which they bind themselves to
obedience; as in every other contract or engagement.   The
same promise, then, which binds them to obedience, ties
them down to a particular person, and makes him the object
of their allegiance.

But when government has been establish'd on this footing
for some considerable time, and the separate interest, which
we have in submission, has produc'd a separate sentiment of

morality, the case is entirely alter'd, and a promise is no longer able to determine the particular magistrate ; since it is no longer consider'd as the foundation of government. We naturally suppose ourselves born to submission ; and imagine, that such particular persons have a right to command, as we on our part are bound to obey. These notions of right and obligation are deriv'd from nothing but the *advantage* we reap from government, which gives us a repugnance to practise resistance ourselves, and makes us displeas'd with any instance of it in others. But here 'tis remarkable, that in this new state of affairs, the original sanction of government, which is *interest*, is not admitted to determine the persons, whom we are to obey, as the original sanction did at first, when affairs were on the footing of a *promise*. A *promise* fixes and determines the persons, without any uncertainty : But 'tis evident, that if men were to regulate their conduct in this particular, by the view of a peculiar *interest*, either public or private, they wou'd involve themselves in endless confusion, and wou'd render all government, in a great measure, ineffectual. The private interest of every one is different ; and tho' the public interest in itself be always one and the same, yet it becomes the source of as great dissentions, by reason of the different opinions of particular persons concerning it. The same interest, therefore, which causes us to submit to magistracy, makes us renounce itself in the choice of our magistrates, and binds us down to a certain form of government, and to particular persons, without allowing us to aspire to the utmost perfection in either. The case is here the same as in that law of nature concerning the stability of possession. 'Tis highly advantageous, and even absolutely necessary to society, that possession shou'd be stable ; and this leads us to the establishment of such a rule : But we find, that were we to follow the same advantage, in assigning particular possessions to particular persons, we shou'd disappoint our end, and perpetuate the confusion, which that rule is intended to prevent. We must, therefore, proceed by general rules, and regulate ourselves by general interests, in modifying the law of nature concerning the stability of possession. Nor need we fear, that our attachment to this law will diminish upon account of the seeming frivolousness of those interests, by which it is determined. The impulse of the mind is deriv'd from a very strong interest ; and those other more minute interests serve only to direct the motion, without adding any thing to it, or diminishing from it. 'Tis the same case with government. Nothing is more advantageous to society than such an invention ; and this interest is sufficient to make us embrace it with ardour and alacrity ; tho' we are oblig'd afterwards to regulate and direct our devotion to government by several considerations, which are not of the same importance, and to chuse our magistrates without having in view any particular advantage from the choice.

The *first* of those principles I shall take notice of, as a foundation of the right of magistracy, is that which gives authority to all the most establish'd governments of the world without exception : I mean, *long possession* in any one form of government, or succession of princes. 'Tis certain, that if we remount to the first origin of every nation, we shall find, that there scarce is any race of kings, or form of a commonwealth, that is not primarily founded on usurpation and rebellion, and whose title is not at first worse than doubtful and uncertain. Time alone gives solidity to their right ; and operating gradually on the minds of men, reconciles them to any authority, and makes it seem just and reasonable. Nothing causes any sentiment to have a greater influence upon us than custom, or turns our imagination more strongly to any object. When we have been long accustom'd to obey any set of men, that general instinct or tendency, which we have to suppose a moral obligation attending loyalty, takes easily this direction, and chuses that set of men for its objects. 'Tis interest which gives the general instinct; but 'tis custom which gives the particular direction.

And here 'tis observable, that the same length of time has a different influence on our sentiments of morality, according to its different influence on the mind. We naturally judge of every thing by comparison; and since in considering the fate of kingdoms and republics, we embrace a long extent of time, a small duration has not in this case a like influence on our sentiments, as when we consider any other object. One thinks he acquires a right to a horse, or a suit of cloaths, in a very short time; but a century is scarce sufficient to establish any new government, or remove all scruples in the minds of the subjects concerning it. Add to this, that a shorter period of time will suffice to give a prince a title to any additional power he may usurp, than will serve to fix his right, where the whole is an usurpation. The kings of *France* have not been possess'd of absolute power for above two reigns; and yet nothing will appear more extravagant to *Frenchmen* than to talk of their liberties. If we consider what has been said concerning *accession*, we shall easily account for this phænomenon.

When there is no form of government establish'd by *long* possession, the *present* possession is sufficient to supply its place, and may be regarded as the *second* source of all public authority. Right to authority is nothing but the constant possession of authority, maintain'd by the laws of society and the interests of mankind; and nothing can be more natural than to join this constant possession to the present one, according to the principles above-mention'd. If the same principles did not take place with regard to the property of private persons, 'twas because these principles were counter-ballanc'd by very strong considerations of interest; when we observ'd, that all restitution wou'd by that means be prevented, and every violence be authoriz'd and protected. And tho' the same motives may seem to have force, with regard to public authority, yet they are oppos'd by a contrary interest; which consists in the preservation of peace, and the avoiding of all changes, which, however they may be easily produc'd in private affairs, are unavoidably attended with bloodshed and confusion, where the public is interested.

Any one, who finding the impossibility of accounting for the right of the present possessor, by any receiv'd system of ethics, shou'd resolve to deny absolutely that right, and assert, that it is not authoriz'd by morality, wou'd be justly thought to maintain a very extravagant paradox, and to shock the common sense and judgment of mankind. No maxim is more comfortable, both to prudence and morals, than to submit quietly to the government, which we find establish'd in the country where we happen to live, without enquiring too curiously into its origin and first establishment. Few governments will bear being examin'd so rigorously. How many kingdoms are there at present in the world, and how many more do we find in history, whose governors have no better foundation for their authority than that of present possession? To confine ourselves to the *Roman* and *Grecian* empire; is it not evident, that the long succession of emperors, from the dissolution of the *Roman* liberty, to the final extinction of that empire by the *Turks*, cou'd not so much. as pretend to any other title to the empire? The election of the senate was a mere form, which always follow'd the choice of the legions; and these were almost always divided in the different provinces, and nothing but the sword was able to terminate the difference. 'Twas by the sword, therefore, that every emperor acquir'd, as well as defended his right ; and we must either say, that all the known world, for so many ages, had no government, and ow'd no allegiance to any one, or must allow, that the right of the stronger, in public affairs, is to be receiv'd as legitimate, and authoriz'd by morality, when not oppos'd by any other title.

The right of *conquest* may be consider'd as a *third* source of the title of sovereigns. This right resembles very much that of present possession; but has rather a superior force, being seconded by the notions of glory and honour, which we ascribe to *conquerors*, instead of the sentiments of hatred and detestation, which attend *usupers*. Men naturally favour those they love ; and therefore are more apt to ascribe a right to successful violence, betwixt one sovereign and another, than to the successful rebellion of a subject against his sovereign.[1]

When neither long possession, nor present possession, nor conquest take place, as when the first sovereign, who founded any monarchy, dies; in that case, the right of *succession* naturally prevails in their stead, and men are commonly induc'd to place the son of their late monarch on the throne, and suppose him to inherit his father's authority. The presum'd consent of the father, the imitation of the succession to private families, the interest, which the state has in chusing the person, who is most powerful, and has the most numerous followers; all these reasons lead men to prefer the son of their late monarch to any other person.[2]

These reasons have some weight; but I am persuaded, that to one, who considers impartially of the matter, 'twill appear, that there concur some principles of the imagination, along with those views of interest. The royal authority

---

[1] It is not here asserted, that *present possession* or *conquest* are sufficient to give a title against *long possession* and *positive laws:* But only that they have some force, and will be able to cast the balance where the titles are otherwise equal, and will even be sufficient *sometimes* to sanctify the weaker title. What degree of force they have is difficult to determine. I believe all moderate men will allow, that they have great force in all disputes concerning the rights of princes.

[2] To prevent mistakes I must observe, that this case of succession is not the same with that of hereditary monarchies, where custom has fix'd the right of succession. These depend upon the principle of long possession above explain'd.

seems to be connected with the young prince even in his
father's life-time, by the natural transition of the thought;
and still more after his death: So that nothing is more natural than to compleat this union by a new relation, and by
putting him actually in possession of what seems so naturally
to belong to him.

To confirm this we may weigh the following phænomena,
which are pretty curious in their kind. In elective monarchies
the right of succession has no place by the laws and settled
custom; and yet its influence is so natural, that 'tis impossible entirely to exclude it from the imagination, and render
the subjects indifferent to the son of their deceas'd monarch.
Hence in some governments of this kind, the choice commonly falls on one or other of the royal family; and in some
governments they are all excluded. Those contrary phænomena proceed from the same principle. Where the royal
family is excluded, 'tis from a refinement in politics, which
makes people sensible of their propensity to chuse a sovereign in that family, and gives them a jealousy of their liberty,
lest their new monarch, aided by this propensity, shou'd
establish his family, and destroy the freedom of elections for
the future.

The history of *Artaxerxes*, and the younger *Cyrus*, may
furnish us with some reflections to the same purpose. *Cyrus*
pretended a right to the throne above his elder brother,
because he was born after his father's accession. I do not
pretend, that this reason was valid. I wou'd only infer from
it, that he wou'd never have made use of such a pretext, were
it not for the qualities of the imagination above-mention'd,
by which we are naturally inclin'd to unite by a new relation
whatever objects we find already united. *Artaxerxes* had an
advantage above his brother, as being the eldest son, and
the first in succession : But *Cyrus* was more closely related
to the royal authority, as being begot after his father was
invested with it.

Shou'd it here be pretended, that the view of convenience may be the source of all the right of succession, and that men gladly take advantage of any rule, by which they can fix the successor of their late sovereign, and prevent that anarchy and confusion, which attends all new elections: To this I wou'd answer, that I readily allow, that this motive may contribute something to the effect ; but at the same time I assert, that without another principle, 'tis impossible such a motive shou'd take place. The interest of a nation requires, that the succession to the crown shou'd be fix'd one way or other; but 'tis the same thing to its interest in what way it be fix'd : So that if the relation of blood had not an effect independent of public interest, it wou'd never have been regarded, without a positive law ; and 'twou'd have been impossible, that so many positive laws of different nations cou'd ever have concur'd precisely in the same views and intentions.

This leads us to consider the *fifth* source of authority, viz. *positive laws ;* when the legislature establishes a certain form of government and succession of princes. At first sight it may be thought, that this must resolve into some of the preceding titles of authority. The legislative power, whence the positive law is deriv'd, must either be establish'd by original contract, long possession, present possession, conquest, or succession ; and consequently the positive law must derive its force from some of those principles. But here 'tis remarkable, that tho' a positive law can only derive its force from these principles, yet it acquires not all the force of the principle from whence it is deriv'd, but loses considerably in the transition ; as it is natural to imagine. For instance ; a government is establish'd for many centuries on a certain system of laws, forms, and methods of succession. The legislative power, establish'd by this long succession, changes all on a sudden the whole system of government, and introduces a new constitution in its stead.

I believe few of the subjects will think themselves bound to comply with this alteration, unless it have an evident tendency to the public good : But will think themselves still at liberty to return to the antient government. Hence the notion of *fundamental laws;* which are suppos'd to be inalterable by the will of the sovereign : And of this nature the *Salic* law is understood to be in *France.* How far these fundamental laws extend is not determin'd in any government ; nor is it possible it ever shou'd. There is such an insensible gradation from the most material laws to the most trivial, and from the most antient laws to the most modern, that 'twill be impossible to set bounds to the legislative power, and determine how far it may innovate in the principles of government. That is the work more of imagination and passion than of reason.

Whoever considers the history of the several nations of the world ; their revolutions, conquests, increase, and diminution ; the manner in which their particular governments are establish'd, and the successive right transmitted from one person to another, will soon learn to treat very lightly all disputes concerning the rights of princes, and will be convinc'd, that a strict adherence to any general rules, and the rigid loyalty to particular persons and families, on which some people set so high a value, are virtues that hold less of reason, than of bigotry and superstition. In this particular, the study of history confirms the reasonings of true philosophy ; which, shewing us the original qualities of human nature, teaches us to regard the controversies in politics as incapable of any decision in most cases, and as entirely subordinate to the interests of peace and liberty. Where the public good does not evidently demand a change ; 'tis certain, that the concurrence of all those titles, *original contract, long possession, present possession, succession,* and *positive laws*, forms the strongest title to sovereignty, and is justly regarded as sacred and inviolable. But when these

titles are mingled and oppos'd in different degrees, they
often occasion perplexity ; and are less capable of solution
from the arguments of lawyers and philosophers, than from
the swords of the soldiery. Who shall tell me, for instance,
whether *Germanicus*, or *Drusus*, ought to have succeeded
Tiberius, had he died while they were both alive, without
naming any of them for his successor? Ought the right of
adoption to be receiv'd as equivalent to that of blood in a
nation, where it had the same effect in private families, and
had already, in two instances, taken place in the public?
Ought *Germanicus* to be esteem'd the eldest son, because he
was born before *Drusus;* or the younger, because he was
adopted after the birth of his brother? Ought the right of
the elder to be regarded in a nation where the eldest brother
had no advantage in the succession to private families?
Ought the *Roman* empire at that time to be esteem'd hereditary, because of two examples ; or ought it, even so early,
to be regarded as belonging to the stronger, or the present
possessor, as being founded on so recent an usurpation?
Upon whatever principles we may pretend to answer these
and such like questions, I am afraid we shall never be able
to satisfy an impartial enquirer, who adopts no party in
political controversies, and will be satisfied with nothing but
sound reason and philosophy.

But here an *English* reader will be apt to enquire concerning that famous *revolution*, which has had such a happy
influence on our constitution, and has been attended with
such mighty consequences. We have already remark'd, that
in the case of enormous tyranny and oppression, 'tis lawful
to take arms even against supreme power ; and that as government is a mere human invention for mutual advantage
and security, it no longer imposes any obligation, either
natural or moral, when once it ceases to have that tendency.
But tho' this *general* principle be authoriz'd by common

sense, and the practice of all ages, 'tis certainly impossible for the laws, or even for philosophy, to establish any *particular* rules, by which we may know when resistance is lawful ; and decide all controversies, which may arise on that subject. This may not only happen with regard to supreme power ; but 'tis possible, even in some constitutions, where the legislative authority is not lodg'd in one person, that there may be a magistrate so eminent and powerful, as to oblige the laws to keep silence in this particular. Nor wou'd this silence be an effect only of their *respect*, but also of their *prudence;* since 'tis certain, that in the vast variety of circumstances, which occur in all governments, an exercise of power, in so great a magistrate, may at one time be beneficial to the public, which at another time wou'd be pernicious and tyrannical. But notwithstanding this silence of the laws in limited monarchies, 'tis certain, that the people still retain the right of resistance ; since 'tis impossible, even in the most despotic governments, to deprive them of it. The same necessity of self-preservation, and the same motive of public good, give them the same liberty in the one case as in the other. And we may farther observe, that in such mix'd governments, the cases, wherein resistance is lawful, must occur much oftener, and greater indulgence be given to the subjects to defend themselves by force of arms, than in arbitrary governments. Not only where the chief magistrate enters into measures, in themselves, extremely pernicious to the public, but even when he wou'd encroach on the other parts of the constitution, and extend his power beyond the legal bounds, it is allowable to resist and dethrone him ; tho' such resistance and violence may, in the general tenor of the laws, be deem'd unlawful and rebellious. For besides that nothing is more essential to public interest, than the preservation of public liberty ; 'tis evident, that if such a mix'd government be once suppos'd to be establish'd, every part or member of the constitution must have a right of self-defence,

and of maintaining its antient bounds against the encroach-
ment of every other authority. As matter would have been
created in vain, were it depriv'd of a power of resistance,
without which no part of it cou'd preserve a distinct existence, and the whole might be crowded up into a single
point : So 'tis a gross absurdity to suppose, in any government, a right without a remedy, or allow, that the supreme
power is shar'd with the people, without allowing, that 'tis
lawful for them to defend their share against every invader.
Those, therefore, who wou'd seem to respect our free government, and yet deny the right of resistance, have renounc'd
all pretensions to common sense, and do not merit a serious
answer.

It does not belong to my present purpose to shew, that
these general principles are applicable to the late *revolution;*
and that all the rights and privileges, which ought to be
sacred to a free nation, were at that time threaten'd with
the utmost danger. I am better pleas'd to leave this contro-
verted subject, if it really admits of controversy ; and to
indulge myself in some philosophical reflections, which
naturally arise from that important event.

First, We may observe, that shou'd the *lords* and *commons*
in our constitution, without any reason from public interest,
either depose the king in being, or after his death exclude
the prince, who, by laws and settled custom ought to succeed,
no one wou'd esteem their proceedings legal, or think themselves bound to comply with them. But shou'd the king,
by his unjust practices, or his attempts for a tyrannical and
despotic power, justly forfeit his legal, it then not only
becomes morally lawful and suitable to the nature of political
society to dethrone him; but what is more, we are apt likewise to think, that the remaining members of the constitution acquire a right of excluding his next heir, and of chusing whom they please for his successor. This is founded on
a very singular quality of our thought and imagination.

When a king forfeits his authority, his heir ought naturally to remain in the same situation, as if the king were remov'd by death; unless by mixing himself in the tyranny, he forfeit it for himself.   But tho' this may seem reasonable, we easily comply with the contrary opinion.   The deposition of a king, in such a government as ours, is certainly an act beyond all common authority, and an illegal assuming a power for public good, which, in the ordinary course of government, can belong to no member of the constitution.   When the public good is so great and so evident as to justify the action, the commendable use of this licence causes us naturally to attribute to the *parliament* a right of using farther licences; and the antient bounds of the laws being once transgressed with approbation, we are not apt to be so strict in confining ourselves precisely within their limits.   The mind naturally runs on with any train of action, which it has begun; nor do we commonly make any scruple concerning our duty, after the first action of any kind, which we perform.   Thus at the *revolution*, no one who thought the deposition of the father justifiable, esteem'd themselves to be confin'd to his infant son; tho' had that unhappy monarch died innocent at that time, and had his son, by any accident, been convey'd beyond seas, there is no doubt but a regency wou'd have been appointed till he shou'd come to age, and cou'd be restore'd to his dominions.   As the slightest properties of the imagination have an effect on the judgments of the people, it shews the wisdom of the laws and of the parliament to take advantage of such properties, and to chuse the magistrates either in or out of a line, according as the vulgar will most naturally attribute authority and right to them.

Secondly, Tho' the accession of the *Prince of Orange* to the throne might at first give occasion to many disputes, and his title be contested, it ought not now to appear doubtful, but must have acquir'd a sufficient authority from those three princes, who have succeeded him upon the same title.

Nothing is more usual, tho' nothing may, at first sight, appear more unreasonable, than this way of thinking. Princes often *seem* to acquire a right from their successors, as well as from their ancestors; and a king, who during his life-time might justly be deem'd an usurper, will be regarded by posterity as a lawful prince, because he has had the good fortune to settle his family on the throne, and entirely change the antient form of government. *Julius Cæsar* is regarded as the first *Roman* emperor; while *Sylla* and *Marius*, whose titles were really the same as his, are treated as tyrants and usurpers. Time and custom give authority to all forms of government, and all successions of princes; and that power, which at first was founded only on injustice and violence, becomes in time legal and obligatory. Nor does the mind rest there; but returning back upon its footsteps, transfers to their predecessors and ancestors that right, which it naturally ascribes to the posterity, as being related together, and united in the imagination. The present *king* of *France* makes *Hugh Capet* a more lawful prince than *Cromwell;* as the establish'd liberty of the *Dutch* is no inconsiderable apology for their obstinate resistance to *Philip* the second.

SECTION XI.

Of the laws of nations.

WHEN civil government has been establish'd over the greatest part of mankind, and different societies have been form'd contiguous to each other, there arises a new set of duties among the neighbouring states, suitable to the nature of that commerce, which they carry on with each other. Political writers tell us, that in every kind of intercourse, a body politic is to be consider'd as one person; and indeed this assertion is so far just, that different nations, as well as private persons, require mutual assistance; at the same time that their selfishness and ambition are perpetual sources of war and discord.   But tho' nations in this particular resemble individuals, yet as they are very different in other respects, no wonder they regulate themselves by different maxims, and give rise to a new set of rules, which we call *the laws of nations*.   Under this head we may comprize the sacredness of the persons of ambassadors, the declaration of war, the abstaining from poison'd arms, with other duties of that kind, which are evidently calculated for the commerce, that is peculiar to different societies.

But tho' these rules be super-added to the laws of nature, the former do not entirely abolish the latter; and one may safely affirm, that the three fundamental rules of justice, the stability of possession, its transference by consent, and the performance of promises, are duties of princes, as well as of subjects.   The same interest produces the same effect in both cases.   Where possession has no stability, there must be perpetual war.   Where property is not transferr'd by consent, there can be no commerce.   Where promises are not observ'd there can be no leagues nor alliances.   The advantages, therefore, of peace, commerce, and mutual succour, make us extend to different kingdoms the same notions of justice which take place among individuals.

There is a maxim very current in the world, which few politicians are willing to avow, but which has been authoriz'd by the practice of all ages, *that there is a system of morals calculated for princes, much more free than that which ought to govern private persons*.   'Tis evident this is not to be understood of the lesser *extent* of public duties and obligations; nor will any one be so extravagant as to assert, that the most solemn treaties ought to have no force among princes.   For princes do actually form treaties among themselves, they must propose some advantage from the execution of them; and the prospect of such advantage for the future must engage them to perform their part, and must establish that law of nature.   The meaning, therefore, of this political maxim is, that tho' the morality of princes has the same *extent*, yet it has not the same *force* as that of private persons, and may lawfully be trangress'd from a more trivial motive. However shocking such a proposition may appear to certain philosophers, 'twill be easy to defend it upon those principles, by which we have accounted for the origin of justice and equity.

When men have found by experience, that 'tis impossible to subsist without society, and that 'tis impossible to maintain society, while they give free course to their appetites; so urgent an interest quickly restrains their actions, and imposes an obligation to observe those rules, which we call *the laws of justice.* This obligation of interest rests not here; but by the necessary course of the passions and sentiments, gives rise to the moral obligation of duty; while we approve of such actions as tend to the peace of society, and disapprove of such as tend to its disturbance. The same *natural* obligation of interest takes place among independent kingdoms, and gives rise to the same *morality;* so that no one of ever so corrupt morals will approve of a prince, who voluntarily, and of his own accord, breaks his word, or violates any treaty. But here we may observe, that tho' the intercourse of different states be advantageous, and even sometimes necessary, yet it is not so necessary nor advantageous as that among individuals, without which 'tis utterly impossible for human nature ever to subsist. Since, therefore, the *natural* obligation to justice, among different states, is not so strong as among individuals, the *moral* obligation, which arises from it, must partake of its weakness ; and we must necessarily give a greater indulgence to a prince or minister, who deceives another ; than to a private gentleman, who breaks his word of honour.

Shou'd it be ask'd, *what proportion these two species of morality bear to each other?* I wou'd answer, that this is a question, to which we can never give any precise answer ;

nor is it possible to reduce to numbers the proportion, which we ought to fix betwixt them. One may safely affirm, that this proportion finds itself, without any art or study of men ; as we may observe on many other occasions. The practice of the world goes farther in teaching us the degrees of our duty, than the most subtile philosophy, which was ever yet invented. And this may serve as a convincing proof, that all men have an implicit notion of the foundation of those moral rules concerning natural and civil justice, and are sensible, that they arise merely from human conventions, and from the interest, which we have in the preservation of peace and order. For otherwise the diminution of the interest wou'd never produce a relaxation of the morality, and reconcile us more easily to any transgression of justice among princes and republics, than in the private commerce of one subject with another.

SECTION XII.

Of chastity and modesty.

IF any difficulty attend this system concerning the laws of nature and nations, 'twill be with regard to the universal approbation or blame, which follows their observance or transgression, and which some may not think sufficiently explain'd from the general interests of society. To remove, as far as possible, all scruples of this kind, I shall here consider another set of duties, *viz.* the *modesty* and *chastity* which belong to the fair sex : And I doubt not but these virtues will be found to be still more conspicuous instances of the operation of those principles, which I have insisted on.

There are some philosophers, who attack the female virtues with great vehemence, and fancy they have gone very far in detecting popular errors, when they can show, that there is no foundation in nature for all that exterior modesty, which we require in the expressions, and dress, and behaviour of the fair sex. I believe I may spare myself the trouble of insisting on so obvious a subject, and may proceed, without farther preparation, to examine after what manner such notions arise from education, from the voluntary conventions of men, and from the interest of society.

Whoever considers the length and feebleness of human infancy, with the concern which both sexes naturally have for their offspring, will easily perceive, that there must be an union of male and female for the education of the young, and that this union must be of considerable duration. But in order to induce the men to impose on themselves this restraint, and undergo chearfully all the fatigues and expences, to which it subjects them, they must believe, that the children are their own, and that their natural instinct is not directed to a wrong object, when they give a loose to love and tenderness. Now if we examine the structure of the human body, we shall find, that this security is very difficult to be attain'd on our part ; and that since, in the copulation of the sexes, the principle of generation goes from the man to the woman, an error may easily take place on the side of the former, tho' it be utterly impossible with regard to the latter. From this trivial and anatomical observation is deriv'd that vast difference betwixt the education and duties of the two sexes.

Were a philosopher to examine the matter *a priori*, he wou'd reason after the following manner. Men are induc'd to labour for the maintenance and education of their children, by the persuasion that they are really their own ; and therefore 'tis reasonable, and even necessary, to give them some security in this particular. This security cannot consist entirely in the imposing of severe punishments on any transgressions of conjugal fidelity on the part of the wife ; since these public punishments cannot be inflicted without legal proof, which 'tis difficult to meet with in this subject. What restraint, therefore, shall we impose on women, in order to counter-balance so strong a temptation as they have to infidelity? There seems to be no restraint possible, but in the punishment of bad fame or reputation; a punishment, which has a mighty influence on the human mind, and at the same time is inflicted by the world upon surmizes, and conjectures, and proofs, that wou'd never be receiv'd in any court of judicature. In order, therefore, to impose a due restraint on the female sex, we must attach a peculiar degree of shame to their infidelity, above what arises merely from its injustice, and must bestow proportionable praises on their chastity.

But tho' this be a very strong motive to fidelity, our philosopher wou'd quickly discover, that it wou'd not alone be sufficient to that purpose. All human creatures, especially of the female sex, are apt to over-look remote motives in favour of any present temptation : The temptation is here the strongest imaginable : Its approaches are insensible and seducing : And a woman easily finds, or flatters herself she shall find, certain means of securing her reputation, and preventing all the pernicious consequences of her pleasures. 'Tis necessary, therefore, that, beside the infamy attending such licences, there shou'd be some preceding backwardness or dread, which may prevent their first approaches, and may give the female sex a repugnance to all expressions, and postures, and liberties, that have an immediate relation to that enjoyment.

Such wou'd be the reasonings of our speculative philosopher : But I am persuaded, that if he had not a perfect knowledge of human nature, he would be apt to regard them as mere chimerical speculations, and wou'd consider the infamy attending infidelity, and backwardness to all its approaches, as principles that were rather to be wish'd than hop'd for in the world. For what means, wou'd he say, of persuading mankind, that the transgressions of conjugal duty are more infamous than any other kind of injustice, when 'tis evident they are more excusable, upon account of the greatness of the temptation. And what possibility of giving a backwardness to the approaches of a pleasure, to which nature has inspir'd so strong a propensity; and a propensity that 'tis absolutely necessary in the end to comply with, for the support of the species?

But speculative reasonings, which cost so much pains to philosophers, are often formed by the world naturally, and without reflection : As difficulties, which seem unsurmountable in theory, are easily got over in practice. Those, who have an interest in the fidelity of women, naturally disapprove of their infidelity, and all the approaches to it. Those, who have no interest, are carried along with the stream. Education takes possession of the ductile minds of the fair sex in their infancy. And when a general rule of this kind is once establish'd, men are apt to extend it beyond those principles, from which it first arose. Thus batchelors, however debauch'd, cannot chuse but be shock'd with any instance of lewdness or impudence in women. And tho' all these maxims have a plain reference to generation, yet women past child-bearing have no more privilege in this respect, than those who are in the flower of their youth and beauty. Men have undoubtedly an implicit notion, that all those ideas of modesty and decency have a regard to generation; since they impose not the same laws, *with the same force*, on the male sex, where that reason takes not place. The exception is there obvious and extensive, and founded on a remarkable difference, which produces a clear separation and disjunction of ideas. But as the case is not the same with regard to the different ages of women, for this reason, tho' men know that these notions are founded on the public interest, yet the general rule carries us beyond the original principle, and makes us extend the notions of modesty over the whole sex, from their earliest infancy to their extremest old-age and infirmity.

Courage, which is the point of honour among men, derives its merit, in a great measure, from artifice, as well as the chastity of women ; tho' it has also some foundation in nature, as we shall see afterwards.

As to the obligations which the male sex lie under, with regard to chastity, we may observe, that according to the general notions of the world, they bear nearly the same proportion to the obligations of women, as the obligations of the law of nations do to those of the law of nature. 'Tis contrary to the interest of civil society, that men shou'd have an *entire* liberty of indulging their appetites in venereal enjoyment: But as this interest is weaker than in the case of the female sex, the moral obligation arising from it, must be proportionably weaker. And to prove this we need only appeal to the practice and sentiments of all nations and ages.

PART III.

OF THE OTHER VIRTUES AND VICES.

SECTION I.

Of the origin of the natural virtues and vices.

WE come now to the examination of such virtues and vices as are entirely natural, and have no dependance on the artifice and contrivance of men. The examination of these will conclude this system of morals.

The chief spring or actuating principle of the human mind is pleasure or pain; and when these sensations are remov'd, both from our thought and feeling, we are, in a great measure, incapable of passion or action, of desire or volition. The most immediate effects of pleasure and pain are the propense and averse motions of the mind; which are diversified into volition, into desire and aversion, grief and joy, hope and fear, according as the pleasure or pain changes its situation, and becomes probable or improbable, certain or uncertain, or is consider'd as out of our power for the present moment. But when along with this, the objects, that cause pleasure or pain, acquire a relation to ourselves or others; they still continue to excite desire and aversion, grief and joy: But cause, at the same time, the indirect passions of pride or humility, love or hatred, which in this case have a double relation of impressions and ideas to the pain or pleasure.

We have already observ'd, that moral distinctions depend entirely on certain peculiar sentiments of pain and pleasure, and that whatever mental quality in ourselves or others gives us a satisfaction, by the survey or reflection, is of course virtuous ; as every thing of this nature, that gives uneasiness, is vicious. Now since every quality in ourselves or others, which gives pleasure, always causes pride or love ; as every one, that produces uneasiness, excites humility or hatred: It follows, that these two particulars are to be consider'd as equivalent, with regard to our mental qualities, *virtue* and the power of producing love or pride, *vice* and the power of producing humility or hatred. In every case, therefore, we must judge of the one by the other ; and may pronounce any *quality* of the mind virtuous, which causes love or pride; and any one vicious, which causes hatred or humility.

If any *action* be either virtuous or vicious, 'tis only as a sign of some quality or character. It must depend upon durable principles of the mind, which extend over the whole conduct, and enter into the personal character. Actions themselves, not proceeding from any constant principle, have no influence on love or hatred, pride or humility ; and consequently are never consider'd in morality.

This reflection is self-evident, and deserves to be attended to, as being of the utmost importance in the present subject.

We are never to consider any single action in our enquiries concerning the origin of morals; but only the quality or character from which the action proceeded. These alone are *durable* enough to affect our sentiments concerning the person. Actions are, indeed, better indications of a character than words, or even wishes and sentiments; but 'tis only so far as they are such indications, that they are attended with love or hatred, praise or blame.

To discover the true origin of morals, and of that love or hatred, which arises from mental qualities, we must take the matter pretty deep, and compare some principles, which have been already examin'd and explain'd.

We may begin with considering a-new the nature and force of *sympathy*. The minds of all men are similar in their feelings and operations; nor can any one be actuated by any affection, of which all others are not, in some degree, susceptible. As in strings equally wound up, the motion of one communicates itself to the rest; so all the affections readily pass from one person to another, and beget correspondent movements in every human creature. When I see the *effects* of passion in the voice and gesture of any person, my mind immediately passes from these effects to their causes, and forms such a lively idea of the passion, as is presently converted into the passion itself. In like manner, when I perceive the *causes* of any emotion, my mind is convey'd to the effects, and is actuated with a like emotion. Were I present at any of the more terrible operations of surgery, 'tis certain, that even before it begun, the preparation of the instruments, the laying of the bandages in order, the heating of the irons, with all the signs of anxiety and concern in the patient and assistants, wou'd have a great effect upon my mind, and excite the strongest sentiments of pity and terror. No passion of another discovers itself immediately to the mind. We are only sensible of its causes or effects. From *these* we infer the passion: And consequently *these* give rise to our sympathy.

Our sense of beauty depends very much on this principle; and where any object has a tendency to produce pleasure in its possessor, it is always regarded as beautiful; as every object, that has a tendency to produce pain, is disagreeable and deform'd. Thus the conveniency of a house, the fertility of a field, the strength of a horse, the capacity, security, and swift-sailing of a vessel, form the principal beauty of these several objects. Here the object, which is denominated beautiful, pleases only by its tendency to produce a certain effect. That effect is the pleasure or advantage of some other person. Now the pleasure of a stranger, for whom we have no friendship, pleases us only by sympathy. To this principle, therefore, is owing the beauty, which we find in every thing that is useful. How considerable a part this is of beauty will easily appear upon reflection. Wherever an object has a tendency to produce pleasure in the possessor, or in other words, is the proper *cause* of pleasure, it is sure to please the spectator, by a delicate sympathy with the possessor. Most of the works of art are esteem'd beautiful, in proportion to their fitness for the use of man, and even many of the productions of nature derive their beauty from that source. Handsome and beautiful, on most occasions, is not an absolute but a relative quality, and pleases us by nothing but its tendency to produce an end that is agreeable.[1]

The same principle produces, in many instances, our sentiments of morals, as well as those of beauty. No virtue is more esteem'd than justice, and no vice more detested than injustice; nor are there any qualities, which go farther to the fixing the character, either as amiable or odious. Now justice is a moral virtue, merely because it has that tendency

---

[1] Decentior equus cujus astricta sunt ilia; sed idem velocior. Pulcher aspectu sit athleta, cujus lacertos exercitatio expressit; idem certamini paratior. Nunquam vero *species* ab *utilitate* dividitur. Sed hoc quidem discernere, modici judicii est. *Quinct.* lib. 8.

to the good of mankind; and indeed, is nothing but an artificial invention to that purpose. The same may be said of allegiance, of the laws of nations, of modesty, and of good-manners. All these are mere human contrivances for the interest of society. And since there is a very strong sentiment of morals, which in all nations, and all ages, has attended them, we must allow, that the reflecting on the tendency of characters and mental qualities, is sufficient to give us the sentiments of approbation and blame. Now as the means to an end can only be agreeable, where the end is agreeable ; and as the good of society, where our own interest is not concern'd, or that of our friends, pleases only by sympathy : It follows, that sympathy is the source of the esteem, which we pay to all the artificial virtues.

Thus it appears *that* sympathy is a very powerful principle in human nature, *that* it has a great influence on our taste of beauty, and *that* it produces our sentiment of morals in all the artificial virtues. From thence we may presume, that it also gives rise to many of the other virtues ; and that qualities acquire our approbation, because of their tendency to the good of mankind. This presumption must become a certainty, when we find that most of those qualities which we *naturally* approve of, have actually that tendency, and render a man a proper member of society : While the qualities, which we *naturally* disapprove of, have a contrary tendency, and render any intercourse with the person dangerous or disagreeable. For having found, that such tendencies have force enough to produce the strongest sentiment of morals, we can never reasonably, in these cases, look for any other cause of approbation or blame ; it being an inviolable maxim in philosophy, that where any particular cause is sufficient for an effect, we ought to rest satisfied with it, and ought not to multiply causes without necessity. We have happily attain'd experiments in the artificial virtues, where the tendency of qualities to the good of society, is the *sole* cause of our approbation, without any suspicion of the concurrence of another principle. From thence we learn the force of that principle. And where that principle may take place, and the quality approv'd of is really beneficial to society, a true philosopher will never require any other principle to account for the strongest approbation and esteem.

That many of the natural virtues have this tendency to the good of society, no one can doubt of. Meekness, benefi-cence, charity, generosity, clemency, moderation, equity, bear the greatest figure among the moral qualities, and are commonly denominated the *social* virtues, to mark their tendency to the good of society. This goes so far, that some philosophers have represented all moral distinctions as the effect of artifice and education, when skilful politi-cians endeavour'd to restrain the turbulent passions of men, and make them operate to the public good, by the notions of honour and shame. This system, however, is not con-sistent with experience. For, *first*, there are other virtues and vices besides those which have this tendency to the public advantage and loss. *Secondly*, had not men a natural sentiment of approbation and blame, it cou'd never be excited by politicians ; nor wou'd the words *laudable* and *praise-worthy*, *blameable* and *odious*, be any more intelligible, than if they were a language perfectly unknown to us, as we have already observ'd. But tho' this system be erroneous, it may teach us, that moral distinctions arise, in a great measure, from the tendency of qualities and characters to the interests of society, and that 'tis our concern for that interest, which makes us approve or disapprove of them. Now we have no such extensive concern for society but from sympathy ; and consequently 'tis that principle, which takes us so far out of ourselves, as to give us the same pleasure or uneasiness in the characters of others, as if they had a tendency to our own advantage or loss.

The only difference betwixt the natural virtues and justice lies in this, that the good, which results from the former, arises from every single act, and is the object of some natural passion : Whereas a single act of justice, consider'd in itself, may often be contrary to the public good; and 'tis only the concurrence of mankind, in a general scheme or system of action, which is advantageous. When I relieve persons in distress, my natural humanity is my motive ; and so far as my succour extends, so far have I promoted the happiness of my fellow-creatures. But if we examine all the questions, that come before any tribunal of justice, we shall find, that, considering each case apart, it wou'd as often be an instance of humanity to decide contrary to the laws of justice as conformable to them. Judges take from a poor man to give to a rich; they bestow on the dissolute the labour of the industrious; and put into the hands of the vicious the means of harming both themselves and others. The whole scheme, however, of law and justice is advantageous to the society; and 'twas with a view to this advantage, that men, by their voluntary conventions, establish'd it. After it is once establish'd by these conventions, it is *naturally* attended with a strong sentiment of morals; which can proceed from nothing but our sympathy with the interests of society. We need no other explication of that esteem, which attends such of the natural virtues, as have a tendency to the public good.

I must farther add, that there are several circumstances, which render this hypothesis much more probable with regard to the natural than the artificial virtues. 'Tis certain, that the imagination is more affected by what is particular, than by what is general; and that the sentiments are always mov'd with difficulty, where their objects are, in any degree, loose and undetermin'd: Now every particular act of justice is not beneficial to society, but the whole scheme or system : And it may not, perhaps, be any individual person, for whom we are concern'd, who receives benefit from justice, but the whole society alike. On the contrary, every particular act of generosity, or relief of the industrious and indigent, is beneficial ; and is beneficial to a particular person, who is not undeserving of it. 'Tis more natural, therefore, to think, that the tendencies of the latter virtue will affect our sentiments, and command our approbation, than those of the former; and therefore, since we find, that the approbation of the former arises from their tendencies, we may ascribe, with better reason, the same cause to the approbation of the latter. In any number of similar effects, if a cause can be discover'd for one, we ought to extend that cause to all the other effects, which can be accounted for by it : But much more, if these other effects be attended with peculiar circumstances, which facilitate the operation of that cause.

Before I proceed farther, I must observe two remarkable circumstances in this affair, which may seem objections to the present system. The first may be thus explain'd. When any quality, or character, has a tendency to the good of mankind, we are pleas'd with it, and approve of it; because it presents the lively idea of pleasure; which idea affects us by sympathy, and is itself a kind of pleasure. But as this sympathy is very variable, it may be thought, that our sentiments of morals must admit of all the same variations. We sympathize more with persons contiguous to us, than with persons remote from us : With our acquaintance, than with strangers : With our countrymen, than with foreigners. But notwithstanding this variation of our sympathy, we give the same approbation to the same moral qualities in *China* as in *England.* They appear equally virtuous, and recommend themselves equally to the esteem of a judicious spectator. The sympathy varies without a variation in our esteem. Our esteem, therefore, proceeds not from sympathy.

To this I answer: The approbation of moral qualities most certainly is not deriv'd from reason, or any comparison of ideas; but proceeds entirely from a moral taste, and from certain sentiments of pleasure or disgust, which arise upon the contemplation and view of particular qualities or characters. Now 'tis evident, that those sentiments, whence-ever they are deriv'd, must vary according to the distance or contiguity of the objects; nor can I feel the same lively pleasure from the virtues of a person, who liv'd in *Greece* two thousand years ago, that I feel from the virtues of a familiar friend and acquaintance. Yet I do not say, that I esteem the one more than the other: And therefore, if the variation of the sentiment, without a variation of the esteem, be an objection, it must have equal force against every other system, as against that of sympathy. But to consider the matter a-right, it has no force at all; and 'tis the easiest matter in the world to account for it. Our situation, with regard both to persons and things, is in con-tinual fluctuation; and a man, that lies at a distance from us, may, in a little time, become a familiar acquaintance. Besides, every particular man has a peculiar position with regard to others; and 'tis impossible we cou'd ever converse together on any reasonable terms, were each of us to con-sider characters and persons, only as they appear from his peculiar point of view. In order, therefore, to prevent those continual *contradictions*, and arrive at a more *stable* judgment of things, we fix on some *steady* and *general* points of view; and always, in our thoughts, place ourselves in them, what-ever may be our present situation. In like manner, exter-nal beauty is determin'd merely by pleasure; and 'tis evident, a beautiful countenance cannot give so much pleas-ure, when seen at the distance of twenty paces, as when it is brought nearer us. We say not, however, that it appears to us less beautiful: Because we know what effect it will have in such a position, and by that reflection we correct its momentary appearance.

In general, all sentiments of blame or praise are variable, according to our situation of nearness or remoteness, with regard to the person blam'd or prais'd, and according to the present disposition of our mind. But these variations we regard not in our general decisions, but still apply the terms expressive of our liking or dislike, in the same manner, as if we remain'd in one point of view. Experience soon teaches us this method of correcting our sentiments, or at least, of correcting our language, where the sentiments are more stubborn and inalterable. Our servant, if diligent and faithful, may excite stronger sentiments of love and kindness than *Marcus Brutus*, as represented in history; but we say not on that account, that the former character is more laudable than the latter. We know, that were we to approach equally near to that renown'd patriot, he wou'd command a much higher degree of affection and admiration. Such corrections are common with regard to all the senses; and indeed 'twere impossible we cou'd ever make use of language, or communicate our sentiments to one another, did we not correct the momentary appearances of things, and overlook our present situation.

'Tis therefore from the influence of characters and qualities, upon those who have an intercourse with any person, that we blame or praise him. We consider not whether the persons, affected by the qualities, be our acquaintance or strangers, countrymen or foreigners. Nay, we over-look our own interest in those general judgments; and blame not a man for opposing us in any of our pretensions, when his own interest is particularly concern'd. We make allowance for a certain degree of selfishness in men; because we know it to be inseparable from human nature, and inherent in our frame and constitution. By this reflection we correct those sentiments of blame, which so naturally arise upon any opposition.

But however the general principle of our blame or praise may be corrected by those other principles, 'tis certain, they are not altogether efficatious, nor do our passions often correspond entirely to the present theory. 'Tis seldom men heartily love what lies at a distance from them, and what no way redounds to their particular benefit ; as 'tis no less rare to meet with persons, who can pardon another any opposition he makes to their interest, however justifiable that opposition may be by the general rules of morality. Here we are contented with saying, that reason requires such an impartial conduct, but that 'tis seldom we can bring ourselves to it, and that our passions do not readily follow the determination of our judgment. This language will be easily understood, if we consider what we formerly said concerning that *reason*, which is able to oppose our passion ; and which we have found to be nothing but a general calm determination of the passions, founded on some distant view or reflection. When we form our judgments of persons, merely from the tendency of their characters to our own benefit, or to that of our friends, we find so many contradictions to our sentiments in society and conversation, and such an uncertainty from the incessant changes of our situation, that we seek some other standard of merit and demerit, which may not admit of so great variation. Being thus loosen'd from our first station, we cannot afterwards fix ourselves so commodiously by any means as by a sympathy with those, who have any commerce with the person we consider. This is far from being as lively as when our own interest is concern'd, or that of our particular friends ; nor has it such an influence on our love and hatred : But being equally conformable to our calm and general principles, 'tis said to have an equal authority over our reason, and to command our judgment and opinion. We blame equally a bad action, which we read of in history, with one perform'd in our neighbourhood t'other day : The meaning of which is, that we know from reflection, that the former action wou'd excite as strong sentiments of disapprobation as the latter, were it plac'd in the same position.

I now proceed to the *second* remarkable circumstance, which I propos'd to take notice of. Where a person is possess'd of a character, that in its natural tendency is beneficial to society, we esteem him virtuous, and are delighted with the view of his character, even tho' particular accidents prevent its operation, and incapacitate him from being serviceable to his friends and country. Virtue in rags is still virtue ; and the love which it procures, attends a man into a dungeon or desart, where the virtue can no longer be exerted in action, and is lost to all the world. Now this may be esteem'd an objection to the present system. Sympathy interests us in the good of mankind ; and if sympathy were the source of our esteem for virtue, that sentiment of approbation cou'd only take place, where the virtue actually attain'd its end, and was beneficial to mankind. Where it fails of its end, 'tis only an imperfect means ; and therefore can never acquire any merit from that end. The goodness of an end can bestow a merit on such means alone as are compleat, and actually produce the end.

To this we may reply, that where any object, in all its parts, is fitted to attain any agreeable end, it naturally gives us pleasure, and is esteem'd beautiful, even tho' some external circumstances be wanting to render it altogether effectual. 'Tis sufficient if every thing be compleat in the object itself. A house, that is contriv'd with great judgment for all the commodities of life, pleases us upon that account ; tho' perhaps we are sensible, that no-one will ever dwell in it. A fertile soil, and a happy climate, delight us by a reflection on the happiness which they wou'd afford the inhabitants, tho' at present the country be desart and uninhabited. A man, whose limbs and shape promise strength and activity, is esteem'd handsome, tho' condemn'd to perpetual imprisonment. The imagination has a set of passions belonging to it, upon which our sentiments of beauty much depend. These passions are mov'd by degrees of liveliness and strength, which are inferior to *belief*, and independent of the real existence of their objects. Where a character is, in every respect, fitted to be beneficial to society, the imagination passes easily from the cause to the effect, without considering that there are still some circumstances wanting to render the cause a compleat one. *General rules* create a species of probability, which sometimes influences the judgment, and always the imagination.

'Tis true, when the cause is compleat, and a good disposition is attended with good fortune, which renders it really beneficial to society, it gives a stronger pleasure to the spectator, and is attended with a more lively sympathy. We are more affected by it; and yet we do not say that it is more virtuous, or that we esteem it more. We know, that an alteration of fortune may render the benevolent disposition entirely impotent; and therefore we separate, as much as possible, the fortune from the disposition. The case is the same, as when we correct the different sentiments of virtue, which proceed from its different distances from ourselves. The passions do not always follow our corrections; but these corrections serve sufficiently to regulate our abstract notions, and are alone regarded, when we pronounce in general concerning the degrees of vice and virtue.

'Tis observ'd by critics, that all words or sentences, which are difficult to the pronunciation, are disagreeable to the ear. There is no difference, whether a man hear them pronounc'd, or read them silently to himself. When I run over a book with my eye, I imagine I hear it all; and also, by the force of imagination, enter into the uneasiness, which the delivery of it wou'd give the speaker. The uneasiness is not real; but as such a composition of words has a natural tendency to produce it, this is sufficient to affect the mind with a painful sentiment, and render the discourse harsh and disagreeable. 'Tis a similar case, where any real quality is, by accidental circumstances, render'd impotent, and is depriv'd of its natural influence on society.

Upon these principles we may easily remove any contradiction, which may appear to be betwixt the *extensive sympathy*, on which our sentiments of virtue depend, and that *limited generosity* which I have frequently observ'd to be natural to men, and which justice and property suppose, according to the precedent reasoning. My sympathy with another may give me the sentiment of pain and disapprobation, when any object is presented, that has a tendency to give him uneasiness ; tho' I may not be willing to sacrifice any thing of my own interest, or cross any of my passions, for his satisfaction. A house may displease me by being ill-contriv'd for the convenience of the owner; and yet I may refuse to give a shilling towards the rebuilding of it. Sentiments must touch the heart, to make them controul our passions: But they need not extend beyond the imagination, to make them influence our taste. When a building seems clumsy and tottering to the eye, it is ugly and disagreeable ; tho' we be fully assur'd of the solidity of the workmanship. 'Tis a kind of fear, which causes this sentiment of disapprobation ; but the passion is not the same with that which we feel, when oblig'd to stand under a wall, that we really think tottering and insecure. The *seeming tendencies* of objects affect the mind: And the emotions they excite are of a like species with those, which proceed from the *real consequences* of objects, but their feeling is different. Nay, these emotions are so different in their feeling, that they may often be contrary, without destroying each other; as when the fortifications of a city belonging to an enemy are esteem'd beautiful upon account of their strength, tho' we cou'd wish that they were entirely destroy'd. The imagination adheres to the *general* views of things, and distinguishes the feelings they produce, from those which arise from our particular and momentary situation.

If we examine the panegyrics that are commonly made of great men, we shall find, that most of the qualities, which are attributed to them, may be divided into two kinds, *viz.* such as make them perform their part in society; and such as render them serviceable to themselves, and enable them to promote their own interest. Their *prudence, temperance, frugality, industry, assiduity, enterprise, dexterity,* are celebrated, as well as their *generosity* and *humanity.* If we ever give an indulgence to any quality, that disables a man from making a figure in life, 'tis to that of *indolence,* which is not suppos'd to deprive one of his parts and capacity, but only suspends their exercise ; and that without any inconvenience to the person himself, since 'tis, in some measure, from his own choice. Yet indolence is always allow'd to be a fault, and a very great one, if extreme: Nor do a man's friends ever acknowledge him to be subject to it, but in order to save his character in more material articles. He cou'd make a figure, say they, if he pleas'd to give application: His understanding is sound, his conception quick, and his memory tenacious ; but he hates business, and is indifferent about his fortune. And this a man sometimes may make even a subject of vanity ; tho' with the air of confessing a fault: Because he may think, that this incapacity for business implies much more noble qualities ; such as a philosophical spirit, a fine taste, a delicate wit, or a relish for pleasure and society. But take any other case: Suppose a quality, that without being an indication of any other good qualities, incapacitates a man *always* for business, and is destructive to his interest ; such as a blundering understanding, and a wrong judgment of every thing in life ; inconstancy and irresolution ; or a want of address in the management of men and business: These are all allow'd to be imperfections in a character; and many men wou'd rather acknowledge the greatest crimes, than have it suspected, that they are, in any degree, subject to them.

'Tis very happy, in our philosophical researches, when we find the same phænomenon diversified by a variety of circumstances ; and by discovering what is common among them, can the better assure ourselves of the truth of any hypothesis we may make use of to explain it. Were nothing esteem'd virtue but what were beneficial to society, I am persuaded, that the foregoing explication of the moral sense ought still to be receiv'd, and that upon sufficient evidence : But this evidence must grow upon us, when we find other kinds of virtue, which will not admit of any explication except from that hypothesis. Here is a man, who is not remarkably defective in his social qualities; but what principally recommends him is his dexterity in business, by which he has extricated himself from the greatest difficulties, and conducted the most delicate affairs with a singular address and prudence. I find an esteem for him immediately to arise in me: His company is a satisfaction to me ; and before I have any farther acquaintance with him, I wou'd rather do him a service than another, whose character is in every other respect equal, but is deficient in that particular. In this case, the qualities that please me are all consider'd as useful to the person, and as having a tendency to promote his interest and satisfaction. They are only regarded as means to an end, and please me in proportion to their fitness for that end. The end, therefore, must be agreeable to me. But what makes the end agreeable? The person is a stranger: I am no way interested in him, nor lie under any obligation to him: His happiness concerns not me, farther than the happiness of every human, and indeed of every sensible creature: That is, it affects me only by sympathy. From that principle, whenever I discover his happiness and good whether in its causes or effects, I enter so deeply into it, that it gives me a sensible emotion. The appearance of qualities that have a *tendency* to promote it, have an agreeable effect upon my imagination, and command my love and esteem.

This theory may serve to explain, why the same qualities, in all cases, produce both pride and love, humility and hatred ; and the same man is always virtuous or vicious, accomplish'd or despicable to others, who is so to himself. A person, in whom we discover any passion or habit, which originally is only incommodious to himself, becomes always disagreeable to us, merely on its account ; as on the other hand, one whose character is only dangerous and disagreeable to others, can never be satisfied with himself, as long as he is sensible of that disadvantage. Nor is this observable only with regard to characters and manners, but may be remark'd even in the most minute circumstances. A violent cough in another gives us uneasiness ; tho' in itself it does not in the least affect us. A man will be mortified, if you tell him he has a stinking breath ; tho' 'tis evidently no annoyance to himself. Our fancy easily changes its situation ; and either surveying ourselves as we appear to others, or considering others as they feel themselves, we enter, by that means, into sentiments, which no way belong to us, and in which nothing but sympathy is able to interest us. And this sympathy we sometimes carry so far, as even to be displeas'd with a quality commodious to us, merely because it displeases others, and makes us disagreeable in their eyes ; tho' perhaps we never can have any interest in rendering ourselves agreeable to them.

There have been many systems of morality advanc'd by philosophers in all ages ; but if they are strictly examin'd, they may be reduc'd to two, which alone merit our attention. Moral good and evil are certainly distinguish'd by our *sentiments*, not by *reason :* But these sentiments may arise either from the mere species or appearance of characters and passions, or from reflections on their tendency to the happiness of mankind, and of particular persons. My opinion is, that both these causes are intermix'd in our judgments of morals ; after the same manner as they are in our decisions concerning most kinds of external beauty : Tho' I am also of opinion, that reflections on the tendencies of actions have by far the greatest influence, and determine all the great lines of our duty. There are, however, instances, in cases of less moment, wherein this immediate taste or sentiment produces our approbation. Wit, and a certain easy and disengag'd behaviour, are qualities *immediately agreeable* to others, and command their love and esteem. Some of these qualities produce satisfaction in others by particular *original* principles of human nature, which cannot be accounted for: Others may be resolv'd into principles, which are more general. This will best appear upon a particular enquiry.

As some qualities acquire their merit from their being *immediately agreeable* to others, without any tendency to public interest ; so some are denominated virtuous from their being *immediately agreeable* to the person himself, who possesses them. Each of the passions and operations of the mind has a particular feeling, which must be either agreeable or disagreeable. The first is virtuous, the second vicious. This particular feeling constitutes the very nature of the passion ; and therefore needs not be accounted for.

But however directly the distinction of vice and virtue may seem to flow from the immediate pleasure or uneasiness, which particular qualities cause to ourselves or others ; 'tis easy to observe, that it has also a considerable dependence on the principle of *sympathy* so often insisted on. We approve of a person, who is possess'd of qualities *immediately agreeable* to those, with whom he has any commerce ; tho' perhaps we ourselves never reap'd any pleasure from them. We also approve of one, who is possess'd of qualities, that are *immediately agreeable* to himself ; tho' they be of no service to any mortal. To account for this we must have recourse to the foregoing principles.

Thus, to take a general review of the present hypothesis: Every quality of the mind is denominated virtuous, which gives pleasure by the mere survey; as every quality, which produces pain, is call'd vicious. This pleasure and this pain may arise from four different sources. For we reap a pleasure from the view of a character, which is naturally fitted to be useful to others, or to the person himself, or which is agreeable to others, or to the person himself. One may, perhaps, be surpriz'd, that amidst all these interests and pleasures, we shou'd forget our own, which touch us so nearly on every other occasion. But we shall easily satisfy ourselves on this head, when we consider, that every particular person's pleasure and interest being different, 'tis impossible men cou'd ever agree in their sentiments and judgments, unless they chose some common point of view, from which they might survey their object, and which might cause it to appear the same to all of them. Now, in judging of characters, the only interest or pleasure, which appears the same to every spectator, is that of the person himself, whose character is examin'd ; or that of persons who have a connexion with him. And tho' such interests and pleasures touch us more faintly than our own, yet being more constant and universal, they counter-ballance the latter even in practice, and are alone admitted in speculation as the standard of virtue and morality. They alone produce that particular feeling or sentiment, on which moral distinctions depend.

As to the good or ill desert of virtue or vice, 'tis an evident consequence of the sentiments of pleasure or uneasiness. These sentiments produce love or hatred ; and love or hatred, by the original constitution of human passion, is attended with benevolence or anger ; that is, with a desire of making happy the person we love, and miserable the person we hate. We have treated of this more fully on another occasion.

SECTION II.

Of greatness of mind.

IT may now be proper to illustrate this general system of morals, by applying it to particular instances of virtue and vice, and shewing how their merit or demerit arises from the four sources here explain'd. We shall begin with examining the passions of *pride* and *humility*, and shall consider the vice or virtue that lies in their excesses or just proportion. An excessive pride or over-weaning conceit of ourselves is always esteem'd vicious, and is universally hated; as modesty, or a just sense of our weakness, is esteem'd ·virtuous, and procures the good-will of every-one. Of the four sources of moral distinctions, this is to be ascrib'd to the *third;* viz. the immediate agreeableness and disagreeableness of a quality to others, without any reflections on the tendency of that quality.

In order to prove this, we must have recourse to two principles, which are very conspicuous in human nature. The *first* of these is the *sympathy*, and communication of sentiments and passions above-mention'd. So close and intimate is the correspondence of human souls, that no sooner any person approaches me, than he diffuses on me all his opinions, and draws along my judgment in a greater or lesser degree. And tho', on many occasions, my sympathy with him goes not so far as entirely to change my sentiments, and way of thinking ; yet it seldom is so weak as not to disturb the easy course of my thought, and give an authority to that opinion, which is recommended to me by his assent and approbation. Nor is it any way material upon what subject he and I employ our thoughts. Whether we judge of an indifferent person, or of my own character, my sympathy gives equal force to his decision : And even his sentiments of his own merit make me consider him in the same light, in which he regards himself.

This principle of sympathy is of so powerful and insinuating a nature, that it enters into most of our sentiments and passions, and often takes place under the appearance of its contrary. For 'tis remarkable, that when a person opposes me in any thing, which I am strongly bent upon, and rouzes up my passion by contradiction, I have always a degree of sympathy with him, nor does my commotion proceed from any other origin. We may here observe an evident conflict or rencounter of opposite principles and passions. On the one side there is that passion or sentiment, which is natural to me ; and 'tis observable, that the stronger this passion is, the greater is the commotion. There must also be some passion or sentiment on the other side ; and this passion can proceed from nothing but sympathy. The sentiments of others can never affect us, but by becoming, in some measure, our own ; in which case they operate upon us, by opposing and encreasing our passions, in the very same manner, as if they had been originally deriv'd from our own temper and disposition. While they remain conceal'd in the minds of others, they can never have any influence upon us : And even when they are known, if they went no farther than the imagination, or conception ; that faculty is so accustom'd to objects of every different kind, that a mere idea, tho' contrary to our sentiments and inclinations, wou'd never alone be able to affect us.

The *second* principle I shall take notice of is that of *comparison*, or the variation of our judgments concerning objects, according to the proportion they bear to those with which we compare them, We judge more of objects by comparison, than by their intrinsic worth and value ; and regard every thing as mean, when set in opposition to what is superior of the same kind. But no comparison is more obvious than that with ourselves ; and hence it is that on all occasions it takes place, and mixes with most of our passions. This kind of comparison is directly contrary to sympathy in its operation, as we have observ'd in treating of *compassion* and *malice. In all kinds of comparison an object makes us always receive from another, to which it is compar'd, a sensation contrary to what arises from itself in its direct and immediate survey. The direct survey of another's pleasure naturally gives us pleasure; and therefore produces pain, when compar'd with our own. His pain, consider'd in itself, is painful; but augments the idea of our own happiness, and gives us pleasure.*[1]

Since then those principles of sympathy, and a comparison with ourselves, are directly contrary, it may be worth while to consider, what general rules can be form'd, beside the particular temper of the person, for the prevalence of the one or the other. Suppose I am now in safety at land, and wou'd willingly reap some pleasure from this consideration : I must think on the miserable condition of those who are at sea in a storm, and must endeavour to render this idea as strong and lively as possible, in order to make me more sensible of my own happiness. But whatever pains I may take, the comparison will never have an equal efficacy, as if I were really on the shore,[2] and saw a ship at a distance, tost by a tempest, and in danger every moment of perishing on a rock or sand-bank. But suppose this idea to become still more lively. Suppose the ship to be driven so near me, that I can perceive distinctly the horror, painted on the countenance of the seamen and passengers, hear their lamentable cries, see the dearest friends give their last adieu, or embrace with a resolution to perish in each others arms : No man has so savage a heart as to reap any pleasure from such a spectacle, or withstand the motions of the tenderest compassion and sympathy. 'Tis evident, therefore, there is

---

[1] Book II. Part II. sect. 8.
[2] Suave mari magno turbantibus æquora ventis
  E terra magnum alterius spectare laborem;
  Non quia vexari quenquam est jucunda voluptas,
  Sed quibus ipse malis careas quia cernere suav' est.
  Lucret.

a medium in this case ; and that if the idea be too feint, it has no influence by comparison ; and on the other hand, if it be too strong, it operates on us entirely by sympathy, which is the contrary to comparison. Sympathy being the conversion of an idea into an impression, demands a greater force and vivacity in the idea than is requisite to comparison.

All this is easily applied to the present subject. We sink very much in our own eyes, when in the presence of a great man, or one of a superior genius ; and this humility makes a considerable ingredient in that *respect*, which we pay our superiors, according to our foregoing[1] reasonings on that passion. Sometimes even envy and hatred arise from the comparison ; but in the greatest part of men, it rests at respect and esteem. As sympathy has such a powerful influence on the human mind, it causes pride to have, in some measure, the same effect as merit; and by making us enter into those elevated sentiments, which the proud man entertains of himself, presents that comparison, which is so mortifying and disagreeable. Our judgment does not entirely accompany him in the flattering conceit, in which he pleases himself ; but still is so shaken as to receive the idea it presents, and to give it an influence above the loose conceptions of the imagination. A man, who, in an idle humour, wou'd form a notion of a person of a merit very much superior to his own, wou'd not be mortified by that fiction : But when a man, whom we are really persuaded to be of inferior merit, is presented to us ; if we observe in him any extraordinary degree of pride and self-conceit ; the firm persuasion he has of his own merit, takes hold of the imagination, and diminishes us in our own eyes, in the same manner, as if he were really possess'd of all the good qualities which he so liberally attributes to himself. Our idea is here precisely in that medium, which is requisite to make

---

[1] Book II. Part II. sect. 10.

it operate on us by comparison. Were it accompanied with belief, and did the person appear to have the same merit, which he assumes to himself, it wou'd have a contrary effect, and wou'd operate on us by sympathy. The influence of that principle wou'd then be superior to that of comparison, contrary to what happens where the person's merit seems below his pretensions.

The necessary consequence of these principles is, that pride, or an over-weaning conceit of ourselves, must be vicious; since it causes uneasiness in all men, and presents them every moment with a disagreeable comparison. 'Tis a trite observation in philosophy, and even in common life and conversation, that 'tis our own pride, which makes us so much displeas'd with the pride of other people ; and that vanity becomes insupportable to us merely because we are vain. The gay naturally associate themselves with the gay, and the amorous with the amorous : But the proud never can endure the proud, and rather seek the company of those who are of an opposite disposition. As we are, all of us, proud in some degree, pride is universally blam'd and con-demn'd by all mankind ; as having a natural tendency to cause uneasiness in others by means of comparison. And this effect must follow the more naturally, that those, who have an ill-grounded conceit of themselves, are for ever making those comparisons, nor have they any other method of supporting their vanity. A man of sense and merit is pleas'd with himself, independent of all foreign considera-tions: But a fool must always find some person, that is more foolish, in order to keep himself in good humour with his own parts and understanding.

But tho' an over-weaning conceit of our own merit be vicious and disagreeable, nothing can be more laudable, than to have a value for ourselves, where we really have qualities that are valuable. The utility and advantage of any quality to ourselves is a source of virtue, as well as its agreeableness to others; and 'tis certain, that nothing is more useful to us in the conduct of life, than a due degree of pride, which makes us sensible of our own merit, and gives us a confidence and assurance in all our projects and enterprizes. Whatever capacity any one may be endow'd with, 'tis entirely useless to him, if he be not acquainted with it, and form not designs suitable to it. 'Tis requisite on all occasions to know our own force; and were it allowable to err on either side, 'twou'd be more advantageous to overrate our merit, than to form ideas of it, below its just standard. Fortune commonly favours the bold and enterprizing ; and nothing inspires us with more boldness than a good opinion of ourselves.

Add to this, that tho' pride, or self-applause, be sometimes disagreeable to others, 'tis always agreeable to ourselves ; as on the other hand, modesty, tho' it give pleasure to every one, who observes it, produces often uneasiness in the person endow'd with it. Now it has been observ'd, that our own sensations determine the vice and virtue of any quality, as well as those sensations, which it may excite in others.

Thus self-satisfaction and vanity may not only be allowable, but requisite in a character. 'Tis, however, certain, that good-breeding and decency require that we shou'd avoid all signs and expressions, which tend directly to show that passion. We have, all of us, a wonderful partiality for ourselves, and were we always to give vent to our sentiments in this particular, we shou'd mutually cause the greatest indignation in each other, not only by the immediate presence of so disagreeable a subject of comparison, but also by the contrariety of our judgments. In like manner, therefore, as we establish the *laws of nature*, in order to secure property in society, and prevent the opposition of self-interest ; we establish the *rules of good breeding*, in order to prevent the opposition of men's pride, and render conversation agreeable and inoffensive. Nothing is more disagreeable than a man's over-weaning conceit of himself : Every one almost has a strong propensity to this vice : No one can well distinguish *in himself* betwixt the vice and virtue, or be certain, that his esteem of his own merit is well-founded : For these reasons, all direct expressions of this passion are condemn'd ; nor do we make any exception to this rule in favour of men of sense and merit. They are not allow'd to do themselves justice openly, in words, no more than other people ; and even if they show a reserve and secret doubt in doing themselves justice in their own thoughts, they will be more applauded. That impertinent, and almost universal propensity of men, to over-value themselves, has given us such a *prejudice* against self-applause, that we are apt to condemn it, by a *general rule*, wherever we meet with it ; and 'tis with some difficulty we give a privilege to men of sense, even in their most secret thoughts. At least, it must be own'd, that some disguise in this particular is absolutely requisite ; and that if we harbour pride in our breasts, we must carry a fair outside, and have the appearance of modesty and mutual deference in all our conduct and behaviour. We must, on every occasion, be ready to prefer others to ourselves ; to treat them with a kind of deference, even tho' they be our equals ; to seem always the lowest and least in the company, where we are not very much distinguish'd above them : And if we observe these rules in our conduct, men will have more indulgence for our secret sentiments, when we discover them in an oblique manner.

I believe no one, who has any practice of the world, and can penetrate into the inward sentiments of men, will assert, that the humility, which good-breeding and decency require of us, goes beyond the outside, or that a thorough sincerity in this particular is esteem'd a real part of our duty. On the contrary, we may observe, that a genuine and hearty pride, or self-esteem, if well conceal'd and well founded, is essential to the character of a man of honour, and that there is no quality of the mind, which is more indispensibly requisite to procure the esteem and approbation of mankind. There are certain deferences and mutual submissions, which custom requires of the different ranks of men towards each other ; and whoever exceeds in this particular, if thro' interest, is accus'd of meanness ; if thro' ignorance, of simplicity. 'Tis necessary, therefore, to know our rank and station in the world, whether it be fix'd by our birth, fortune, employments, talents or reputation. 'Tis necessary to feel the sentiment and passion of pride in conformity to it, and to regulate our actions accordingly. And shou'd it be said, that prudence may suffice to regulate our actions in this particular, without any real pride, I wou'd observe, that here the object of prudence is to conform our actions to the general usage and custom ; and that 'tis impossible those tacit airs of superiority shou'd ever have been establish'd and authoriz'd by custom, unless men were generally proud, and unless that passion were generally approv'd, when well-grounded.

If we pass from common life and conversation to history, this reasoning acquires new force, when we observe, that all those great actions and sentiments, which have become the admiration of mankind, are founded on nothing but pride and self-esteem. *Go*, says *Alexander* the Great to his soldiers, when they refus'd to follow him to the *Indies*, *go tell your countrymen, that you left Alexander compleating the conquest of the world*. This passage was always particularly admir'd by the prince of *Conde*, as we learn from *St. Evremond*. '*Alexander*,' said that prince, 'abandon'd by his soldiers, among barbarians, not yet fully subdu'd, felt in himself such a dignity and right of empire, that he cou'd not believe it possible any one cou'd refuse to obey him. Whether in *Europe* or in *Asia*, among *Greeks* or *Persians*, all was indifferent to him : Wherever he found men, he fancied he had found subjects.'

In general we may observe, that whatever we call *heroic virtue*, and admire under the character of greatness and elevation of mind, is either nothing but a steady and well-establish'd pride and self-esteem, or partakes largely of that passion. Courage, intrepidity, ambition, love of glory, magnanimity, and all the other shining virtues of that kind, have plainly a strong mixture of self-esteem in them, and derive a great part of their merit from that origin. Accordingly we find, that many religious declaimers decry those virtues as purely pagan and natural, and represent to us the excellency of the *Christian* religion, which places humility in the rank of virtues, and corrects the judgment of the world, and even of philosophers, who so generally admire all the efforts of pride and ambition. Whether this virtue of humility has been rightly understood, I shall not pretend to determine. I am content with the concession, that the world naturally esteems a well-regulated pride, which secretly animates our conduct, without breaking out into such indecent expressions of vanity, as may offend the vanity of others.

The merit of pride or self-esteem is deriv'd from two circumstances, *viz.* its utility and its agreeableness to ourselves ; by which it capacitates us for business, and, at the same time, gives us an immediate satisfaction. When it goes beyond its just bounds, it loses the first advantage, and even becomes prejudicial ; which is the reason why we condemn an extravagant pride and ambition, however regulated by the decorums of good-breeding and politeness. But as such a passion is still agreeable, and conveys an elevated and sublime sensation to the person, who is actuated by it, the sympathy with that satisfaction diminishes considerably the blame, which naturally attends its dangerous influence on his conduct and behaviour. Accordingly we may observe, that an excessive courage and magnanimity, especially when it displays itself under the frowns of fortune, contributes, in a great measure, to the character of a hero, and will render a person the admiration of posterity ; at the same time, that it ruins his affairs, and leads him into dangers and difficulties, with which otherwise he wou'd never have been acquainted.

Heroism, or military glory, is much admir'd by the generality of mankind. They consider it as the most sublime kind of merit. Men of cool reflection are not so sanguine in their praises of it. The infinite confusions and disorder, which it has caus'd in the world, diminish much of its merit in their eyes. When they wou'd oppose the popular notions on this head, they always paint out the evils, which this suppos'd virtue has produc'd in human society ; the subversion of empires, the devastation of provinces, the sack of cities. As long as these are present to us, we are more inclin'd to hate than admire the ambition of heroes. But when we fix our view on the person himself, who is the author of all this mischief, there is something so dazling in his character, the mere contemplation of it so elevates the mind, that we cannot refuse it our admiration. The pain, which we receive from its tendency to the prejudice of society, is over-power'd by a stronger and more immediate sympathy.

Thus our explication of the merit or demerit, which attends the degrees of pride or self-esteem, may serve as a strong argument for the preceding hypothesis, by shewing the effects of those principles above explain'd in all the variations of our judgments concerning that passion. Nor will this reasoning be advantageous to us only by shewing, that the distinction of vice and virtue arises from the *four* principles of the *advantage* and of the *pleasure* of the *person himself*, and of *others :* But may also afford us a strong proof of some underparts of that hypothesis.

No one, who duly considers of this matter, will make any scruple of allowing, that any piece of ill-breeding, or any expression of pride and haughtiness, is displeasing to us, merely because it shocks our own pride, and leads us by sympathy into a comparison, which causes the disagreeable passion of humility. Now as an insolence of this kind is blam'd even in a person who has always been civil to ourselves in particular; nay, in one, whose name is only known to us in history; it follows, that our disapprobation proceeds from a sympathy with others, and from the reflection, that such a character is highly displeasing and odious to every one, who converses or has any intercourse with the person possest of it. We sympathize with those people in their uneasiness; and as their uneasiness proceeds in part from a sympathy with the person who insults them, we may here observe a double rebound of the sympathy; which is a principle very similar to what we have observ'd on another occasion.[1]

SECTION III.

Of goodness and benevolence.

HAVING thus explain'd the origin of that praise and approbation, which attends every thing we call *great* in human affections; we now proceed to give an account of their *goodness*, and shew whence its merit is deriv'd.

When experience has once given us a competent knowledge of human affairs, and has taught us the proportion they bear to human passion, we perceive, that the generosity of men is very limited, and that it seldom extends beyond their friends and family, or, at most, beyond their native country.   Being thus acquainted with the nature of man, we expect not any impossibilities from him ; but confine our view to that narrow circle, in which any person moves, in order to form a judgment of his moral character.   When the natural tendency of his passions leads him to be serviceable and useful within his sphere, we approve of his character,

---

[1] Book II. Part II. sect. 5.

and love his person, by a sympathy with the sentiments of those, who have a more particular connexion with him. We are quickly oblig'd to forget our own interest in our judgments of this kind, by reason of the perpetual contradictions, we meet with in society and conversation, from persons that are not plac'd in the same situation, and have not the same interest with ourselves. The only point of view, in which our sentiments concur with those of others, is, when we consider the tendency of any passion to the advantage or harm of those, who have any immediate connexion or intercourse with the person possess'd of it. And tho' this advantage or harm be often very remote from ourselves, yet sometimes 'tis very near us, and interests us strongly by sympathy. This concern we readily extend to other cases, that are resembling ; and when these are very remote, our sympathy is proportionably weaker, and our praise or blame fainter and more doubtful. The case is here the same as in our judgments concerning external bodies. All objects seem to diminish by their distance : But tho' the appearance of objects to our senses be the original standard, by which we judge of them, yet we do not say, that they actually diminish by the distance; but correcting the appearance by reflection, arrive at a more constant and establish'd judgment concerning them. In like manner, tho' sympathy be much fainter than our concern for ourselves, and a sympathy with persons remote from us much fainter than that with persons near and contiguous; yet we neglect all these differences in our calm judgments concerning the characters of men. Besides, that we ourselves often change our situation in this particular, we every day meet with persons, who are in a different situation from ourselves, and who cou'd never converse with us on any reasonable terms, were we to remain constantly in that situation and point of view, which is peculiar to us. The intercourse of sentiments, therefore, in society and conversation, makes us form some general inalterable standard, by which we may approve or disapprove of characters and manners. And tho' the *heart* does not always take part with those general notions, or regulate its love and hatred by them, yet are they sufficient for discourse, and serve all our purposes in company, in the pulpit, on the theatre, and in the schools.

From these principles we may easily account for that merit, which is commonly ascrib'd to *generosity, humanity, compassion, gratitude, friendship, fidelity, zeal, disinterestedness, liberality,* and all those other qualities, which form the character of good and benevolent. A propensity to the tender passions makes a man agreeable and useful in all the parts of life ; and gives a just direction to all his other qualities, which otherwise may become prejudicial to society. Courage and ambition, when not regulated by benevolence, are fit only to make a tyrant and public robber. 'Tis the same case with judgment and capacity, and all the qualities of that kind. They are indifferent in themselves to the interests of society, and have a tendency to the good or ill of mankind, according as they are directed by these other passions.

As love is *immediately agreeable* to the person, who is actuated by it, and hatred *immediately disagreeable* ; this may also be a considerable reason, why we praise all the passions that partake of the former, and blame all those that have any considerable share of the latter. 'Tis certain we are infinitely touch'd with a tender sentiment, as well as with a great one. The tears naturally start in our eyes at the conception of it ; nor can we forbear giving a loose to the same tenderness towards the person who exerts it. All this seems to me a proof, that our approbation has, in those cases, an origin different from the prospect of utility and advantage, either to ourselves or others.' To which we may add, that men naturally, without reflection, approve of that character, which is most like their own. The man of a mild disposition and tender affections, in forming a notion of the most perfect virtue, mixes in it more of benevolence and humanity, than the man of courage and enterprize, who naturally looks upon a certain elevation of mind as the most accomplish'd character. This must evidently proceed from an *immediate* sympathy, which men have with characters similar to their own. They enter with more warmth into such sentiments, and feel more sensibly the pleasure, which arises from them.

'Tis remarkable, that nothing touches a man of humanity more than any instance of extraordinary delicacy in love or friendship, where a person is attentive to the smallest concerns of his friend, and is willing to sacrifice to them the most considerable interest of his own. Such delicacies have little influence on society; because they make us regard the greatest trifles : But they are the more engaging, the more minute the concern is, and are a proof of the highest merit in any one, who is capable of them. The passions are so contagious, that they pass with the greatest facility from one person to another, and produce correspondent movements in all human breasts. Where friendship appears in very signal instances, my heart catches the same passion, and is warm'd by those warm sentiments, that display themselves before me. Such agreeable movements must give me an affection to every one that excites them. This is the case with every thing that is agreeable in any person. The transition from pleasure to love is easy : But the transition must here be still more easy ; since the agreeable sentiment, which is excited by sympathy, is love itself ; and there is nothing requir'd but to change the object.

Hence the peculiar merit of benevolence in all its shapes and appearances. Hence even its weaknesses are virtuous and amiable ; and a person, whose grief upon the loss of a friend were excessive, wou'd be esteem'd upon that account. His tenderness bestows a merit, as it does a pleasure, on his melancholy.

We are not, however, to imagine, that all the angry passions are vicious, tho' they are disagreeable. There is a certain indulgence due to human nature in this respect. Anger and hatred are passions inherent in our very frame and constitution. The want of them, on some occasions, may even be a proof of weakness and imbecillity. And where they appear only in a low degree, we not only excuse them because they are natural; but even bestow our applauses on them, because they are inferior to what appears in the greatest part of mankind.

Where these angry passions rise up to cruelty, they form the most detested of all vices. All the pity and concern which we have for the miserable sufferers by this vice, turns against the person guilty of it, and produces a stronger hatred than we are sensible of on any other occasion.

Even when the vice of inhumanity rises not to this extreme degree, our sentiments concerning it are very much influenc'd by reflections on the harm that results from it. And we may observe in general, that if we can find any quality in a person, which renders him incommodious to those, who live and converse with him, we always allow it to be a fault or blemish, without any farther examination. On the other hand, when we enumerate the good qualities of any person, we always mention those parts of his character, which render him a safe companion, an easy friend, a gentle master, an agreeable husband, or an indulgent father. We consider him with all his relations in society; and love or hate him, according as he affects those, who have any immediate intercourse with him. And 'tis a most certain rule, that if there be no relation in life, in which I cou'd not wish to stand to a particular person, his character must so far be allow'd to be perfect. If he be as little wanting to himself as to others, his character is entirely perfect. This is the ultimate test of merit and virtue.

SECTION IV.

Of natural abilities.

No distinction is more usual in all systems of ethics, than that betwixt *natural abilities* and *moral virtues;* where the former are plac'd on the same footing with bodily endowments, and are suppos'd to have no merit or moral worth annex'd to them. Whoever considers the matter accurately, will find, that a dispute upon this head wou'd be merely a dispute of words, and that tho' these qualities are not altogether of the same kind, yet they agree in the most material circumstances. They are both of them equally mental qualities : And both of them equally produce pleasure ; and have of course an equal tendency to procure the love and esteem of mankind. There are few, who are not as jealous of their character, with regard to sense and knowledge, as to honour and courage ; and much more than with regard to temperance and sobriety. Men are even afraid of passing for good-natur'd ; lest *that* shou'd be taken for want of understanding : And often boast of more debauches than they have been really engag'd in, to give themselves airs of fire and spirit. In short, the figure a man makes in the world, the reception he meets with in company, the esteem paid him by his acquaintances ; all these advantages depend almost as much upon his good sense and judgment, as upon any other part of his character. Let a man have the best intentions in the world, and be the farthest from all injustice and violence, he will never be able to make himself be much regarded, without a moderate share, at least, of parts and understanding. Since then natural abilities, tho', perhaps, inferior, yet are on the same footing, both as to their causes and effects, with those qualities which we call moral virtues, why shou'd we make any distinction betwixt them?

Tho' we refuse to natural abilities the title of virtues, we must allow, that they procure the love and esteem of mankind ; that they give a new lustre to the other virtues ; and that a man possess'd of them is much more entitled to our good-will and services, than one entirely void of them. It may, indeed, be pretended, that the sentiment of approbation, which those qualities produce, besides its being *inferior*, is also somewhat *different* from that, which attends the other virtues. But this, in my opinion, is not a sufficient reason for excluding them from the catalogue of virtues. Each of the virtues, even benevolence, justice, gratitude, integrity, excites a different sentiment or feeling in the spectator. The characters of *Cæsar* and *Cato*, as drawn by *Sallust*, are both of them virtuous, in the strictest sense of the word ; but in a different way : Nor are the sentiments entirely the same, which arise from them. The one produces love ; the other esteem : The one is amiable ; the other awful : We cou'd wish to meet with the one character in a friend ; the other character we wou'd be ambitious of in ourselves. In like manner, the approbation, which attends natural abilities, may be somewhat different to the feeling from that, which arises from the other virtues, without making them entirely of a different species. And indeed we may observe, that the natural abilities, no more than the other virtues, produce not, all of them, the same kind of approbation. Good sense and genius beget esteem : Wit and humour excite love.[1]

Those, who represent the distinction betwixt natural abilities and moral virtues as very material, may say, that the former are entirely involuntary, and have therefore no merit

---

[1] Love and esteem are at the bottom the same passions, and arise from like causes. The qualities, that produce both, are agreeable and give pleasure. But where this pleasure is severe and serious; or where its object is great, and makes a strong impression; or where it produces any degree of humility and awe: In all these cases, the passion, which arises from the pleasure, is more properly denominated esteem than love. Benevolence attends both: But it is connected with love in a more eminent degree.

attending them, as having no dependance on liberty and free-will. But to this I answer, *first*, that many of those qualities, which all moralists, especially the antients, comprehend under the title of moral virtues, are equally involuntary and necessary, with the qualities of the judgment and imagination. Of this nature are constancy, fortitude, magnanimity ; and, in short, all the qualities which form the *great* man. I might say the same, in some degree, of the others ; it being almost impossible for the mind to change its character in any considerable article, or cure itself of a passionate or splenetic temper, when they are natural to it. The greater degree there is of these blameable qualities, the more vicious they become, and yet they are the less voluntary. *Secondly*, I wou'd have any one give me a reason, why virtue and vice may not be involuntary, as well as beauty and deformity. These moral distinctions arise from the natural distinctions of pain and pleasure ; and when we receive those feelings from the general consideration of any quality or character, we denominate it vicious or virtuous. Now I believe no one will assert, that a quality can never produce pleasure or pain to the person who considers it, unless it be perfectly voluntary in the person who possesses it. *Thirdly*, As to free-will, we have shewn that it has no place with regard to the actions, no more that the qualities of men. It is not a just consequence, that what is voluntary is free. Our actions are more voluntary than our judgments ; but we have not more liberty in the one than in the other.

But tho' this distinction betwixt voluntary and involuntary be not sufficient to justify the distinction betwixt natural abilities and moral virtues, yet the former distinction will afford us a plausible reason, why moralists have invented the latter. Men have observ'd, that tho' natural abilities and moral qualities be in the main on the same footing, there is, however, this difference betwixt them, that the former are almost invariable by any art or industry ; while the latter, or at least, the actions, that proceed from them, may be chang'd by the motives of rewards and punishments, praise and blame. Hence legislators, and divines, and moralists, have principally applied themselves to the regulating these voluntary actions, and have endeavour'd to produce additional motives for being virtuous in that particular. They knew, that to punish a man for folly, or exhort him to be prudent and sagacious, wou'd have but little effect; tho' the same punishments and exhortations, with regard to justice and injustice, might have a considerable influence. But as men, in common life and conversation, do not carry those ends in view, but naturally praise or blame whatever pleases or displeases them, they do not seem much to regard this distinction, but consider prudence under the character of virtue as well as benevolence, and penetration as well as justice. Nay, we find, that all moralists, whose judgment is not perverted by a strict adherence to a system, enter into the same way of thinking; and that the antient moralists in particular made no scruple of placing prudence at the head of the cardinal virtues. There is a sentiment of esteem and approbation, which may be excited, in some degree, by any faculty of the mind, in its perfect state and condition; and to account for this sentiment is the business of *Philosophers.* It belongs to *Grammarians* to examine what qualities are entitled to the denomination of *virtue;* nor will they find, upon trial, that this is so easy a task, as at first sight they may be apt to imagine.

The principal reason why natural abilities are esteem'd, is because of their tendency to be useful to the person, who is possess'd of them. 'Tis impossible to execute any design with success, where it is not conducted with prudence and discretion; nor will the goodness of our intentions alone suffice to procure us a happy issue to our enterprizes. Men are superior to beasts principally by the superiority of their reason; and they are the degrees of the same faculty, which set such an infinite difference betwixt one man and another. All the advantages of art are owing to human reason ; and where fortune is not very capricious, the most considerable part of these advantages must fall to the share of the prudent and sagacious.

When it is ask'd, whether a quick or a slow apprehension be most valuable? whether one, that at first view penetrates into a subject, but can perform nothing upon study ; or a contrary character, which must work out everything by dint of application? whether a clear head, or a copious invention? whether a profound genius, or a sure judgment? in short, what character, or peculiar understanding, is more excellent than another? 'Tis evident we can answer none of these questions, without considering which of those qualities capacitates a man best for the world, and carries him farthest in any of his undertakings.

There are many other qualities of the mind, whose merit is deriv'd from the same origin. *Industry, perseverance, patience, activity, vigilance, application, constancy,* with other virtues of that kind, which 'twill be easy to recollect, are esteem'd valuable upon no other account, than their advantage in the conduct of life. 'Tis the same case with *temperance, frugality, oeconomy, resolution:* As on the other hand, *prodigality, luxury, irresolution, uncertainty,* are vicious, merely because they draw ruin upon us, and incapacitate us for business and action.

As wisdom and good-sense are valued, because they are *useful* to the person possess'd of them ; so *wit* and *eloquence* are valued, because they are *immediately agreeable* to others. On the other hand, *good humour* is lov'd and esteem'd, because it is *immediately agreeable* to the person himself. 'Tis evident, that the conversation of a man of wit is very satisfactory; as a chearful good-humour'd companion diffuses a joy over the whole company, from a sympathy with his gaiety. These qualities, therefore, being agreeable, they naturally beget love and esteem, and answer to all the characters of virtue.

'Tis difficult to tell, on many occasions, what it is that renders one man's conversation so agreeable and entertaining, and another's so insipid and distasteful. As conversation is a transcript of the mind as well as books, the same qualities, which render the one valuable, must give us an esteem for the other. This we shall consider afterwards. In the mean time it may be affirm'd in general, that all the merit a man may derive from his conversation (which, no doubt, may be very considerable) arises from nothing but the pleasure it conveys to those who are present.

In this view, *cleanliness* is also to be regarded as a virtue ; since it naturally renders us agreeable to others, and is a very considerable source of love and affection. No one will deny, that a negligence in this particular is a fault ; and as faults are nothing but smaller vices, and this fault can have no other origin than the uneasy sensation, which it excites in others, we may in this instance, seemingly so trivial, clearly discover the origin of the moral distinction of vice and virtue in other instances.

Besides all those qualities, which render a person lovely or valuable, there is also a certain *je-ne-sçai-quoi* of agreeable and handsome, that concurs to the same effect. In this case, as well as in that of wit and eloquence, we must have recourse to a certain sense, which acts without reflection, and regards not the tendencies of qualities and characters. Some moralists account for all the sentiments of virtue by this sense. Their hypothesis is very plausible. Nothing but a particular enquiry can give the preference to any other hypothesis. When we find, that almost all the virtues have such particular tendencies : and also find, that these tendencies are sufficient alone to give a strong sentiment of approbation : We cannot doubt, after this, that qualities are approv'd of, in proportion to the advantage, which results from them.

The *decorum* or *indecorum* of a quality, with regard to the age, or character, or station, contributes also to its praise or blame. This decorum depends, in a great measure, upon experience. 'Tis usual to see men lose their levity, as they advance in years. Such a degree of gravity, therefore, and such years, are connected together in our thoughts. When we observe them separated in any person's character, this imposes a kind of violence on our imagination, and is disagreeable.

That faculty of the soul, which, of all others, is of the least consequence to the character, and has the least virtue or vice in its several degrees, at the same time, that it admits of a great variety of degrees, is the *memory*. Unless it rise up to that stupendous height as to surprize us, or sink so low as, in some measure, to affect the judgment, we commonly take no notice of its variations, nor ever mention them to the praise or dispraise of any person. 'Tis so far from being a virtue to have a good memory, that men generally affect to complain of a bad one; and endeavouring to persuade the world, that what they say is entirely of their own invention, sacrifice it to the praise of genius and judgment. Yet to consider the matter abstractedly, 'twou'd be difficult to give a reason, why the faculty of recalling past ideas with truth and clearness, shou'd not have as much merit in it, as the faculty of placing our present ideas in such an order, as to form true propositions and opinions. The reason of the difference certainly must be, that the memory is exerted without any sensation of pleasure or pain ; and in all its middling degrees serves almost equally well in business and affairs. But the least variations in the judgment are sensibly felt in their consequences ; while at the same time that faculty is never exerted in any eminent degree, without an extraordinary delight and satisfaction. The sympathy with this utility and pleasure bestows a merit on the understanding ; and the absence of it makes us consider the memory as a faculty very indifferent to blame or praise.

Before I leave this subject of *natural abilities*, I must observe, that, perhaps, one source of the esteem and affection, which attends them, is deriv'd from the *importance* and *weight*, which they bestow on the person possess'd of them. He becomes of greater consequence in life. His resolutions and actions affect a greater number of his fellow-creatures. Both his friendship and enmity are of moment. And 'tis easy to observe, that whoever is elevated, after this manner, above the rest of mankind, must excite in us the sentiments of esteem and approbation. Whatever is important engages our attention, fixes our thought, and is contemplated with satisfaction. The histories of kingdoms are more interesting than domestic stories : The histories of great empires more than those of small cities and principalities : And the histories of wars and revolutions more than those of peace and order. We sympathize with the persons that suffer, in all the various sentiments which belong to their fortunes. The mind is occupied by the multitude of the objects, and by the strong passions, that display themselves. And this occupation or agitation of the mind is commonly agreeable and amusing. The same theory accounts for the esteem and regard we pay to men of extraordinary parts and abilities. The good and ill of multitudes are connected with their actions. Whatever they undertake is important, and challenges our attention. Nothing is to be over-look'd and despis'd, that regards them. And where any person can excite these sentiments, he soon acquires our esteem; unless other circumstances of his character render him odious and disagreeable.

SECTION V.

Some farther reflections concerning the natural virtues.

It has been observ'd, in treating of the passions, that pride and humility, love and hatred, are excited by any advantages or disadvantages of the *mind, body,* or *fortune;* and that these advantages or disadvantages have that effect, by producing a separate impression of pain or pleasure. The pain or pleasure, which arises from the general survey or view of any action or quality of the *mind,* constitutes its vice or virtue, and gives rise to our approbation or blame, which is nothing but a fainter and more imperceptible love or hatred. We have assign'd four different sources of this pain and pleasure; and in order to justify more fully that hypothesis, it may here be proper to observe, that the advantages or disadvantages of the *body* and of *fortune,* produce a pain or pleasure from the very same principles. The tendency of any object to be *useful* to the person possess'd of it, or to others; to convey *pleasure* to him or to others; all these circumstances convey an immediate pleasure to the person, who considers the object, and command his love and approbation.

To begin with the advantages of the *body;* we may observe a phænomenon, which might appear somewhat trivial and ludicrous, if any thing cou'd be trivial, which fortified a conclusion of such importance, or ludicrous, which was employ'd in a philosophical reasoning. 'Tis a general remark, that those we call good *women's men,* who have either signaliz'd themselves by their amorous exploits, or whose make of body promises any extraordinay vigour of that kind, are well received by the fair sex, and naturally engage the affections even of those, whose virtue prevents any design of ever giving employment to those talents. Here 'tis evident, that the ability of such a person to give enjoyment, is the real source of that love and esteem he meets with among the females ; at the same time that the women, who love and esteem him, have no prospect of receiving that enjoyment themselves, and can only be affected by means of their sympathy with one, that has a commerce of love with him. This instance is singular, and merits our attention.

Another source of the pleasure we receive from considering boldily advantages, is their utility to the person himself, who is possess'd of them. 'Tis certain, that a considerable part of the beauty of men, as well as of other animals, consists in such a conformation of members, as we find by experience to be attended with strength and agility, and to capacitate the creature for any action or exercise. Broad shoulders, a lank belly, firm joints, taper legs ; all these are beautiful in our species, because they are signs of force and vigour, which being advantages we naturally sympathize with, they convey to the beholder a share of that satisfaction they produce in the possessor.

So far as to the *utility,* which may attend any quality of the body. As to the immediate *pleasure,* 'tis certain, that an air of health, as well as of strength and agility, makes a considerable part of beauty; and that a sickly air in another is always disagreeable, upon account of that idea of pain and uneasiness, which it conveys to us. On the other hand, we are pleas'd with the regularity of our own features, tho' it be neither useful to ourselves nor others; and 'tis necessary for us, in some measure, to set ourselves at a distance, to make it convey to us any satisfaction. We commonly consider ourselves as we appear in the eyes of others, and sympathize with the advantageous sentiments they entertain with regard to us.

How far the advantages of *fortune* produce esteem and approbation from the same principles, we may satisfy ourselves by reflecting on our precedent reasoning on that subject. We have observ'd, that our approbation of those, who are possess'd of the advantages of fortune, may be ascrib'd to three different causes. *First,* To that immediate pleasure, which a rich man gives us, by the view of the beautiful cloaths, equipage, gardens, or houses, which he possesses. *Secondly,* To the advantage, which we hope to reap from him by his generosity and liberality. *Thirdly,* To the pleasure and advantage, which he himself reaps from his possessions, and which produce an agreeable sympathy in us. Whether we ascribe our esteem of the rich and great to one or all of these causes, we may clearly see the traces of those principles, which give rise to the sense of vice and virtue. I believe most people, at first sight, will be inclin'd to ascribe our esteem of the rich to self-interest, and the prospect of advantage. But as 'tis certain, that our esteem or deference extends beyond any prospect of advantage to ourselves, 'tis evident, that that sentiment must proceed from a sympathy with those, who are dependent on the person we esteem and respect, and who have an immediate connexion with him. We consider him as a person capable of contributing to the happiness or enjoyment of his fellow-creatures, whose sentiments, with regard to him, we naturally embrace. And this consideration will serve to justify my hypothesis in preferring the *third* principle to the other two, and ascribing our esteem to the rich to a sympathy with the pleasure and advantage, which they themselves receive from their possessions. For as even the other two principles cannot operate to a due extent, or account for all the phænomena, without having recourse to a sympathy of one kind or other; 'tis much more natural to chuse that sympathy, which is immediate and direct, than that which is remote and indirect. To which we may add, that where the riches or power are very great, and render the person considerable and important in the world, the esteem attending them, may, in part, be ascrib'd to another source, distinct from these three, *viz.*, their interesting the mind by a prospect of the multitude, and importance of their consequences : Tho', in order to account for the operation of this principle, we must also have recourse to *sympathy;* as we have observ'd in the preceding section.

It may not be amiss, on this occasion, to remark the flexibility of our sentiments, and the several changes they so readily receive from the objects, with which they are conjoin'd. All the sentiments of approbation, which attend any particular species of objects, have a great resemblance to each other, tho' deriv'd from different sources ; and, on the other hand, those sentiments, when directed to different objects, are different to the feeling, tho' deriv'd from the same source. Thus the beauty of all visible objects causes a pleasure pretty much the same, tho' it be sometimes deriv'd from the mere *species* and appearance of the objects ; sometimes from sympathy, and an idea of their utility. In like manner, whenever we survey the actions and characters of men, without any particular interest in them, the pleasure, or pain, which arises from the survey (with some minute differences) is, in the main, of the same kind, tho' perhaps there be a great diversity in the causes, from which it is deriv'd. On the other hand, a convenient house, and a virtuous character, cause not the same feeling of approbation ; even tho' the source of our approbation be the same, and flow from sympathy and an idea of their utility. There is something very inexplicable in this variation of our feelings ; but 'tis what we have experience of with regard to all our passions and sentiments.

SECTION VI.

Conclusion of this book.

THUS upon the whole I am hopeful, that nothing is wanting to an accurate proof of this system of ethics. We are certain, that sympathy is a very powerful principle in . human nature. We are also certain, that it has a great influence on our sense of beauty, when we regard external objects, as well as when we judge of morals. We find, that it has force sufficient to give us the strongest sentiments of approbation, when it operates alone, without the concurrence of any other principle ; as in the cases of justice, allegiance, chastity, and good-manners. We may observe, that all the circumstances requisite for its operation are found in most of the virtues ; which have, for the most part, a tendency to the good of society, or to that of the person possess'd of them. If we compare all these circumstances, we shall not doubt, that sympathy is the chief source of moral distinctions ; especially when we reflect, that no objection can be rais'd against this hypothesis in one case, which will not extend to all cases. Justice is certainly approv'd of for no other reason, than because it has a tendency to the public good : And the public good is indifferent to us, except so far as sympathy interests us in it. We may presume the like with regard to all the other virtues, which have a like tendency to the public good. They must derive all their merit from our sympathy with those, who reap any advantage from them ; As the virtues, which have a tendency to the good of the person possess'd of them, derive their merit from our sympathy with him.

Most people will readily allow, that the useful qualities of the mind are virtuous, because of their utility. This way of thinking is so natural, and occurs on so many occasions, that few will make any scruple of admitting it. Now this being once admitted, the force of sympathy must necessarily be acknowledg'd. Virtue is consider'd as means to an end. Means to an end are only valued so far as the end is valued. But the happiness of strangers affects us by sympathy alone. To that principle, therefore, we are to ascribe the sentiment of approbation, which arises from the survey of all those virtues, that are useful to society, or to the person possess'd of them. These form the most considerable part of morality.

Were it proper in such a subject to bribe the reader's assent, or employ any thing but solid argument, we are here abundantly supplied with topics to engage the affections. All lovers of virtue (and such we all are in speculation, however we may degenerate in practice) must certainly be pleas'd to see moral distinctions deriv'd from so noble a source, which gives us a just notion both of the *generosity* and *capacity* of human nature. It requires but very little knowledge of human affairs to perceive, that a sense of morals is a principle inherent in the soul, and one of the most powerful that enters into the composition. But this sense must certainly acquire new force, when reflecting on itself, it approves of those principles, from whence it is deriv'd, and finds nothing but what is great and good in its rise and origin. Those who resolve the sense of morals into original instincts of the human mind, may defend the cause of virtue with sufficient authority; but want the advantage, which those possess, who account for that sense by an extensive sympathy with mankind. According to their system, not only virtue must be approved of, but also the sense of virtue : And not only that sense, but also the principles, from whence it is deriv'd. So that nothing is presented on any side, but what is laudable and good.

This observation may be extended to justice, and the other virtues of that kind. Tho' justice be artificial, the sense of its morality is natural. 'Tis the combination of men, in a system of conduct, which renders any act of justice beneficial to society. But when once it has that tendency, we *naturally* approve of it ; and if we did not so, 'tis impossible any combination or convention cou'd ever produce that sentiment.

Most of the inventions of men are subject to change. They depend upon humour and caprice. They have a vogue for a time, and then sink into oblivion. It may, perhaps, be apprehended, that if justice were allow'd to be a human invention, it must be plac'd on the same footing. But the cases are widely different. The interest, on which justice is founded, is the greatest imaginable, and extends to all times and places. It cannot possibly be serv'd by any other invention. It is obvious, and discovers itself on the very first formation of society. All these causes render the rules of justice stedfast and immutable ; at least, immutable as human nature. And if they were founded on original instincts, cou'd they have any greater stability ?

The same system may help us to form a just notion of the *happiness*, as well as of the *dignity* of virtue, and may interest every principle of our nature in the embracing and cherishing that noble quality. Who indeed does not feel an accession of alacrity in his pursuits of knowledge and ability of every kind, when he considers, that besides the advantage, which immediately result from these acquisitions, they also give him a new lustre in the eyes of mankind, and are universally attended with esteem and approbation? And who can think any advantages of fortune a sufficient compensation for the least breach of the *social* virtues, when he considers, that not only his character with regard to others, but also his peace and inward satisfaction entirely depend upon his strict observance of them ; and that a mind will never be able to bear its own survey, that has been wanting in its part to mankind and society? But I forbear insisting on this subject. Such reflections require a work a-part, very different from the genius of the present. The anatomist ought never to emulate the painter ; nor in his accurate dissections and portraitures of the smaller parts of the human body, pretend to give his figures any graceful and engaging attitude or expression. There is even something hideous, or at least minute in the views of things, which he presents ; and 'tis necessary the objects shou'd be set more at a distance, and be more cover'd up from sight, to make them engaging to the eye and imagination. An anatomist, however, is admirably fitted to give advice to a painter ; and 'tis even impracticable to excel in the latter art, without the assistance of the former. We must have an exact knowledge of the parts, their situation and connexion, before we can design with any elegance or correctness. And thus the most abstract speculations concerning human nature, however cold and unentertaining, become subservient to *practical morality ;* and may render this latter science more correct in its precepts, and more persuasive in its exhortations.

INDEX.

Abilities, natural, 256, 258.
Accession, and property, 155.
Action, internal, 110, 121.
Actions, and truth, 103, 104.
—— and will, 73, 74, 84, 85, 258.
—— merit of, 85, 106, 118, 122–123, 124.
Agent, 81, 106.
Allegiance. *See Government.*
Measures of, 197 f. Objects of, 201 f.
Anger, 255.
Artifice, 134, 142, 146, 168, 180–181, 226–227.
Artificial, 61, 121, 128–129, 134, 142, 173, 176, 226, 269.
Association, of ideas, 79, 158.

Benevolence, 91, 126–127, 141, 251 f.
Bentham, 24.
Berkeley, 13, 19, 23.
Butler, 21 f.

Calm passions, 91, 93.
Cause, 79–80, 83, 104.
Chance, 81–82.
Character, 73 f., 85, 118, 223, 231, 257.
Chastity, 218 f.
Choice, 113.

Civil, opposed to natural, 120 n., 191.
Clarke, 24, 43, 48.
Collins, 30.
Conscience, 104.
Convention, 61, 134–135, 136, 163, 169, 190.
Courage, 222.
Cudworth, 24, 43, 57
Custom, 96 f., 149.

Decorum, 262.
Deliberate actions, 8.
Desire, 91.
Direct passions, 99.
Duty. *See Obligations, Moral.*

Education, 146.

Fact, matter of, 114 f.
Family, 131, 188.
Feeling (moral), 114, 116–118, 223.
Free, and Freedom. *See Necessity, Liberty, Will.* 26, 29.
Friendship, 168.

Good, 91 ; three species of, 133.
Goodness and Benevolence, 251 f.
Golden Age, 139.
Government, origin of, 181 f. ; allegiance to, 186 f. ; objects of allegiance, 201 f.

273

www.ingramcontent.com/pod-product-compliance
Lightning Source LLC
Chambersburg PA
CBHW030632030726
47497CB00006B/1744